Arabic-Speaking Immigrants
to the United States before 1940

Crossing the Waters

Arabic-Speaking Immigrants to
the United States Before 1940

CROSSING

THE WATERS

EDITED BY ERIC J. HOOGLUND

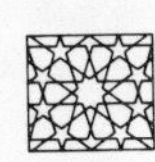

Smithsonian Institution Press
Washington, D.C.
London

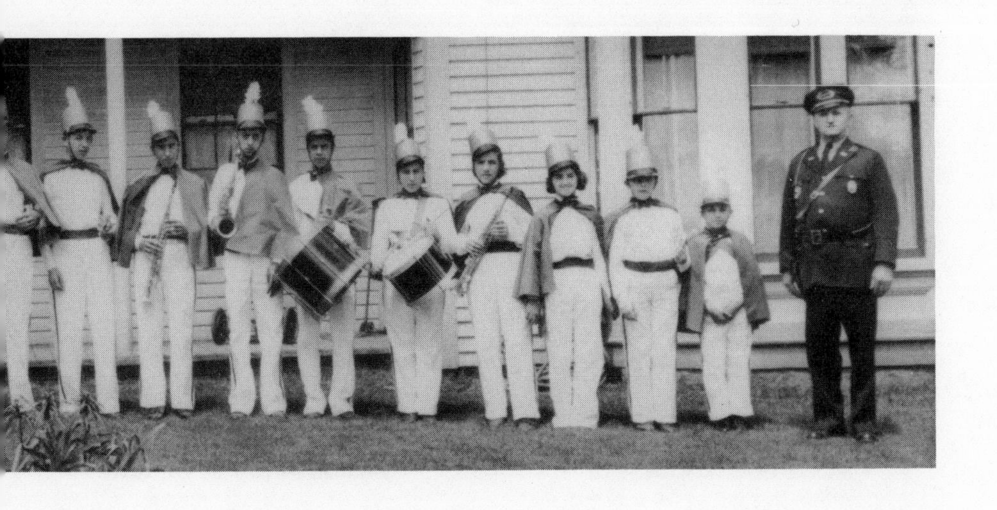

Cover: Members of the Syrian Ladies' Aid Society of Boston preparing to march in the Armistice Day Parade of 1925.
Photo courtesy of Evelyn Shakir.

Title page: The Saint Joseph's Maronite Church youth band in Waterville, Maine, in 1937 or 1938. All of the musicians are children of Arabic-speaking immigrants who settled in the textile town before the First World War.
Photo courtesy of Annie Shepherd and Janet George.

Library of Congress Catloging-in-Publication Data

Crossing the waters.

Bibliography: p.
1. Arab Americans—History. 2. Immigrants—United States—History. I. Hooglund, Eric J. (Eric James), 1944– .
E184.A65C76 1987 9731.04927 87-43031
ISBN 0-87474-548-9

British Library Cataloguing-in-Publication Data is available.

The paper used in this publication meets the minimum requirements of the American National Standard for Permanence of Paper for Printed Library Materials Z39.48–1984.

Designed by Linda McKnight.
Edited by Jane McAllister.

Contents

List of Tables

Contributors

Nancy Faires Conklin is senior research associate at the Northwest Regional Educational Laboratory's Literacy and Language Program in Portland, Oregon, where she continues her studies of cross-cultural communications as they affect non-English- and non-standard-speaking groups in the United States. She is coauthor of *A Host of Tongues: Language Communities in the United States,* coeditor of *A Pluralistic Nation: The Language Issue in the United States,* and has written essays on cultural and linguistic maintenance among Greek-Americans and Southern black women. Her current research includes studying literacy among street kids, the linguistic adjustment of corporate professionals to automated office communication technologies, and bilingual and bicultural educational development in American Micronesia.

Dina Dahbany-Miraglia, a linguistic anthropologist, is the author of several articles on Yemenite Jewish language and culture. She is currently working on a book, *Yemenite Jewish Ethnic Identity,* and is researching the traditional oral poetry of Yemenite Jewish women. She teaches English as a second language at the New York City Technical College in Brooklyn and lives in Boro Park with her mother and her three children.

Nora Faires has focused her primary interests on issues of ethnicity and religion in American history. She is currently an associate professor of history and the director of the Masters of Liberal Studies Program in American Culture at the University of Michigan in Flint. She is the author of several studies of German-Americans, including *Ethnicity in Evolution: Religion and Economy Among German Immigrants in Pittsburgh and Allegheny City, Pennsylvania, 1845–1875,* "Occupational Patterns Among German Americans in the Nineteenth Century", and "In the Country and in the City: Texas Germans in the Nineteenth Century." She has also written essays about urban and women's history during the nineteenth and twentieth centuries. Professor Faires has directed a variety of community and oral history projects in Michigan and in Pennsylvania, and has lectured on the use of archival documents for ethnic studies. Her research on ethnic acculturation in the United States is now directed toward a long-term study of the political economy of food consumption in the twentieth century.

Jean Gibran, a Boston teacher, has worked closely with her husband, Kahlil, on the biography of their cousin, *Kahlil Gibran: His Life and Work,* and on the new edition of Gibran's play, *Lazarus and his Beloved.* Jean Gibran believes that their search for the poet's earliest artistic roots has revealed an exciting sequence of social and literary events that link Gibran to important trends and personalities during the first decade of the twentieth century.

Kahlil Gibran, grew up in Boston amidst recollections of his famous cousin and namesake. Entrusted with a formidable collection of manuscripts, letters, drawings, and memorabilia left by the poet, he interrupted his own career as a sculptor to research and synthesize the accounts of the life of the poet Gibran, and to prepare a study that demonstrates how Gibran was a man of two worlds, one Western and one Middle Eastern.

Raouf Jamil Halaby is a native of Jerusalem, Palestine. He received his elementary and secondary education in Jerusalem and in Beirut, Lebanon. He came to the United States in 1965. He holds a doctorate in English, has written several articles for anthologies and professional journals, and is a regular contributor to national and international journals and magazines. Dr. Halaby lives in Arkadelphia, Arkansas, with his wife and their two sons and is an associate professor of English at Ouachita Baptist University.

Eric J. Hooglund is a senior analyst at the National Security Archive in Washington, D.C. He has taught Middle East history and politics for several years at various colleges and universities, including at Bowdoin College in Maine, Shiraz University in Iran, the Ohio State University, and the University of Tennessee at Knoxville. He is an editor of and contributor to the Middle East Information Project's (MERIP) bimonthly publication *Middle East Report,* and has written numerous articles for other scholarly journals, the *Encyclopaedia Iranica,* and the *Encyclopedia of Asian History.* His books include *Land and Revolution in Iran* (University of Texas Press, 1982); *Taking Root: Arab-American Community Studies* (ADC Research Institute, 1985); and *The Iranian Revolution and the Islamic Republic* (Syracuse University Press, 1986).

Sarah E. John received a B.A. degree in inter-American studies and an M.A. in history from the University of Texas at El Paso (UTEP), where she wrote her thesis entitled, " 'Trade Will Lead A Man Far': Syrian Immigration to the El Paso Area, 1900–1935." Ms. John worked at UTEP's Institute of Oral History, where she was acting director for two years. She now is an educational development specialist with the Curriculum and Instructional Development Services at El Paso Community College.

Samir Khalaf was born and educated in Lebanon. He received his Ph.D. in sociology from Princeton University in 1964, and since then has been engaged in teaching and research at the American University of Beirut. His publications include *Prostitution in a Changing Society* (Khayats, 1965); *Hamra of Beirut* (E. J. Brill, 1973); *Persistence and Change in Nineteenth Century Lebanon* (Syracuse University Press, 1979);

Lebanon's Predicament (Columbia University Press, 1986); and numerous articles and essays. He has held teaching and research appointments at Harvard and Princeton universities and currently is a Visiting Professor of Near Eastern sociology, jointly at New York University and Princeton. He is working on a study of civil violence and social change in Lebanon.

Gregory Orfalea is the author of *Before the Flames: A Quest for the History of Arab-Americans* (University of Texas Press, 1988). He has also written two volumes of fiction and three collections of poetry, including *The Capital of Solitude* (Ithaca House, forthcoming). He is the coeditor of *Grapeleaves,* an anthology of nineteen Arab-American writers (University of Utah Press, forthcoming). Mr. Orfalea works as an editor in Washington, D.C., where he lives with his wife and their two sons.

Evelyn Shakir, the daughter of Lebanese immigrants, has published several articles on Arab-American women and on Arab-American literature. She has also produced a one-hour documentary on the Syrian-Lebanese community of Boston for the public radio station WGBH. Ms. Shakir currently teaches English at Bentley College in Waltham, Massachusetts, and is preparing an anthology on Arab women in America as well as a television documentary on the same subject.

Michael W. Suleiman has written widely on Arab politics, Arab-Americans, and American attitudes toward the Middle East. His publications include *Political Parties in Lebanon* (Cornell University Press, 1967), and *American Images of Middle East Peoples: Impact of the High School* (Middle East Studies Association, 1977). He currently is engaged in the preparation of a comprehensive bibliography of Arab-Americans and a major study on Arabs in the United States. Dr. Suleiman is a professor of political science at Kansas State University.

Bayly Winder is a professor of Near East languages and literature and of history at New York University. He taught at Princeton University for eighteen years before becoming the founding director of the Hagop Kevorkian Center for Near Eastern Studies and founding chairman of the Department of Near Eastern Languages and Literatures at New York University. Dr. Winder also was one of the Founding Fellows who set up the Middle East Studies Association, the major professional organization of Middle East scholars in the United States. He is the author, translator, and editor of several books and numerous scholarly articles.

Foreword

Vital to any field of scholarship is dialogue among colleagues. Creative work in the humanities and social sciences does not flourish in isolation. We need the stimulus, challenges, and encouragement of testing and confirming our ideas by trying them out on our peers. The first Philip K. Hitti International Symposium on Near Eastern American Studies served this purpose. When the idea for such a conference was first suggested, skepticism was expressed about whether sufficient research had been done on the subject for a substantial program on the Arabic-speaking immigration to North America up to World War II. We were gratified by the response to the conference call. Thirty-seven persons participated in the ten sessions; more than a hundred registered for the conference. They came from all over the United States as well as from Lebanon and the United Arab Emirates. Most gratifying was the lively and wide-ranging discussion that followed the presentations, spilling over into the coffee breaks and social events. As one participant commented, "It was wonderful to see such a diverse group of people so excited about sharing ideas." Another observed that the conference created a sense of community among scholars who had previously not known of each other's existence.

Crossing the Waters is a unique collection of eleven original essays and case studies on Arabic-speaking communities in cities as diverse as Birmingham and Boston, El Paso and Waterville. This volume should stimulate studies of the experience of immigrants from the Near East to communities throughout this country.

Some may wonder why the Philip K. Hitti International Symposium was sponsored by the University of Minnesota and held in St. Paul. Since its founding in 1965, the Immigration History Research Center (IHRC) has been building research collections documenting the history of American ethnic groups originating from eastern, central, and southern Europe *and* from the Near East. Among these groups are the immigrants and their descendants from Syria and Lebanon. The center has gathered numerous Arabic-language books, periodicals, and newspapers as well as manuscripts.

While a visiting professor at the University of Minnesota in 1967, Hitti learned of the center and expressed enthusiasm for the project. He, himself an immigrant from Lebanon, had long been involved in the affairs of his ethnic community and had written some of the early studies of the Arabic-speaking group.

The suggestion that Professor Hitti deposit his papers at the IHRC was first broached to him by his friend and fellow Arabist the late Professor Anwar G. Chejne of the University of Minnesota. In response to this invitation Hitti responded, with customary modesty, "I never thought my 'papers' would be of value to anyone and have therefore kept only a few." However, he applauded the idea of such a collection and made a number of suggestions regarding materials to be gathered. Subsequently, in a letter of March 21, 1972, Hitti agreed to give his manuscripts to the center. "There is no doubt in my mind that your archives will be the best place for the preservation of such papers."

In August 1973, I visited Professor and Mrs. Hitti in their home in Princeton. I have a pleasant memory of their warm hospitality. Professor Hitti reiterated his intention to send his papers to Minnesota. Shortly after his death in December 1978, his son-in-law, Professor Bayly Winder, informed me that Viola Hitti Winder and he, in accord with Professor Hitti's wishes, were shipping the papers to the center. Professor Hitti had in fact kept substantial files of personal and professional correspondence, research materials, and organizational records. The Hitti Papers immediately became the crown jewel of the IHRC's Near Eastern American Collection.

Shortly after the acquisition of the papers, the idea surfaced of establishing the Philip K. Hitti Memorial Fund to help develop the Near Eastern American Collection, promote research in the collection, and sponsor lectures and publications. With the endorsement and active support of Viola Hitti Winder and Bayly Winder, the fund soon reached sizable proportions. It seemed altogether fitting and proper that the Philip K. Hitti International Symposium should be the first activity under the aegis of the Hitti Memorial Fund. It was our intention to commemorate this outstanding scholar, ethnic leader, and human being and to make an original contribution to Near Eastern American studies. Professor Hitti wrote: "I have felt over the years that American historians and social scientists are afflicted with a blind spot for the contributions of new Americans from the eastern Mediterranean basin to American culture." We hope that the symposium and now this volume will help to correct that blind spot.

RUDOLPH VECOLI
Director, Immigration History
Research Center, University of
Minnesota, St. Paul

This book is dedicated to Sitto
(Saada Harb George)

Saada Harb, about age twenty, working at a loom in a Waterville, Maine, woolen mill in 1917 or 1918. She had immigrated to Maine from a village in southern Lebanon in 1912. Photo courtesy of Annie Shepherd and Janet George.

Introduction

ERIC J. HOOGLUND

This book is a unique collection of original research on an aspect of American immigration history that hitherto has received scant scholarly attention: the migration of more than 125,000 native speakers of Arabic to the United States before 1940. The ethnic Arabs were a barely perceptible current in the great wave of immigrants—more than twenty-seven million persons—who crested into the country during the high (1881–1914) and ebb (1915–25) tides of immigration. During the high tide, roughly composed of the generation leading up to the outbreak of World War I, some twenty-one million immigrants arrived in the United States. They came primarily from the villages of eastern and southern Europe and settled predominantly in the fast-growing cities of the northern and central states. Those immigrants, the majority of whom were peasants, provided the human power that was crucial in transforming the United States from a semiagricultural economy to one of the world's preeminent industrial powers by 1914.

The mass migration to the United States was severely disrupted by the First World War. As the major European powers squared off against one another, most of the Continent and the Mediterranean Sea basin became inhospitable to normal civilian travel, especially by ship, which was the only way of reaching America at the time. It was not until the end of 1919 that immigration began to assume its prewar dimensions. The United States, however, was no longer eager to receive millions of immigrants. A wave of antiforeign prejudice swept over the "nonalien" population and led to the enactment of the country's first restrictive immigration law in 1921. That law was followed in 1924 by the Immigration Quota Act, which limited the total number of persons who could be admitted annually as immigrants. An important provision of the law was the establishment of immigration quotas on the basis of nationality. The number of immigrants from any one ethnic or nationality group was restricted each year to 2 percent of the number from that group residing in the United States at the time of the 1890 census. The 1890 date was significant because, before that time, the majority of immigrants had come from the countries of northern Europe; after 1890 the majority of the immigrants—and the total number of immigrants was also high—came from eastern and southern Europe. The practical effect of the Immigration Quota Act between 1925 and 1965 was to end the relatively open immigration policies that had distinguished the United States for more than one hundred years.

During the 1881–1925 immigration wave, seven nationality and/or ethnic groups accounted for two-thirds of the twenty-seven million immigrants. These were the British, Germans, Irish, Italians, Poles, Polish and Russian Jews (Yiddish), and the Scandanavians. A variety of literature details and documents the process of their adaptation to and assimilation within American society. Much less has been written, however, about the score of other ethnic groups who collectively accounted for more than 7.5 million of the immigrants. In particular, our knowledge about the Arabic-speaking immigrants has been virtually nonexistent. Thus, a number of essential questions have, up to now, not been systematically examined: What were the origins of the Arab immigrants? Why did they join the immigration wave to the United States? What kinds of problems did they confront? How did they adjust in their adopted country? The paucity of information has denied students of ethnic and immigration history valuable data about the assimilation experience of ethnic Arabs, and concealed their participation in the evolution of American culture up to 1940.

The dearth of information about Arabic-speaking immigrants stimulated curious individuals to initiate independent research beginning in the 1970s. Their efforts involved their recording oral histories of immigrants who were still living, collecting relevant documents, studying early newspapers and organizational records, and researching archives in local and national libraries. The efforts were largely uncoordinated until 1983, when those involved in Arab-immigration research had their first opportunity, literally, to discover one another. The occasion was the Philip K. Hitti International Symposium on the subject of the Arabic-speaking immigration to North America up to World War II. The two-day conference organized by the Immigration History Research Center brought together more than thirty scholars and other interested persons to share the results of their research.

It was obvious to all participants that the Hitti Symposium had significantly advanced knowledge and discourse about Arabic-speaking immigrant communities in the United States. For the first time, empirical evidence was provided for the basic questions: Where did the immigrants come from? What factors motivated their immigration? Where did they settle? What did they do? How did they assimilate? At the end of the conference the participants were enthusiastic about sharing with students of ethnic and immigration history and other interested people the wealth of information presented at the conference. Thus, the organizers of the conference decided that several of the papers should be published in a collection that would provide insightful documentation of the history and assimilation of Arabic-speaking immigrants in America. This book is the result of that effort.

While the essays in this collection provide important data about the Arabic-speaking immigration, some gaps in our knowledge still exist. Significantly, we do not know, and probably never will know, precisely how many Arabic-speaking immigrants came to the United States up to 1940. That is because before 1899, immigration officials did not employ a standard term for identifying the immigrants. Between 1899 and 1920 they were classified as "Syrians"; earlier they were variously listed as Syrians, Turks, Ottomans, Armenians, Greeks, or Arabs. Even with the incomplete statistics, we do know, nevertheless, that as many as 110,000 Arabic-speaking immigrants arrived in the United States between 1881 and 1914. These statistics permit us to examine how the pattern of Arab immigration corresponded to the pattern of overall immigration.

The 110,000 immigrants who had arrived in the United States by the end of 1914 represent about 85 percent of the total Arabic-speaking immigration up to 1940. During and immediately after the First World War, less than four thousand Arab immigrants reached America. Once relative security had returned to the eastern Mediterranean area and before immigration restrictions had been fully implemented, that is from 1920 to 1924, total immigration of ethnic Arabs approximated twelve thousand. However, during the next fifteen years, when national origins quotas were in effect, less than twenty-five hundred Arabic-speaking immigrants were admitted to the United States.

Up until 1918 the Arabic-speaking immigrants came almost exclusively from the province of Syria in the Ottoman Empire. Since nearly 90 percent of the pre–World War II immigrants were already in the United States by the end of 1918, it is appropriate to discuss briefly the country they left to resettle in America. Popularly known as Turkey, the tricontinental, multiethnic Ottoman Empire originated with a Turkish dynastic family in Anatolia during the late thirteenth and early fourteenth centuries. By 1517, when the Ottomans took Syria from Egypt, its territorial extent reached across North Africa, into the Balkans of southeastern Europe, and up to Asia's Caucasus Mountains. In the late nineteenth century, however, the Ottoman Empire's de facto power had been restricted to Anatolia, historic Syria, Mesopotamia, and the restive Slavic territories in the Balkans. The province of Syria was more extensive than the country that now bears its name. Historic Syria included the Alexandretta District in present-day Turkey, all of present-day Syria, all of present-day Lebanon, all of Palestine (present-day Israel, the West Bank, and the Gaza Strip), and part of Jordan.

Ottoman Syria was divided into three main districts: Mount Lebanon, Syria, and Palestine. Several linguistic minorities, including Armenians, Circassians, Greeks, Kurds, and Turks, lived in Syria, but most of the population were Arabs. Nevertheless, it was not common to identify oneself as an Arab. The Ottomans grouped their subjects according to their religious beliefs. In Syria this was not a simple matter of being Christian or Muslim, for both the Christians and Muslims were divided into numerous sects. Among the Arab population the most important Christian groups included the Maronites, the Greek Orthodox, and the Melchites. The Maronites predominated in the district known as Mount Lebanon, but their communities were also found in Syria and in Palestine. The Maronites accepted the primacy of the Roman Catholic pope but retained their own liturgy, which had been developed before the Crusades and was based upon the ancient Syriac language rather than Latin.

The Greek Orthodox lived in most of the principal cities, as well as in villages in Mount Lebanon, Syria proper, and Palestine. They were part of the international Greek Orthodox church, which, before World War I, was under the general spiritual guidance of the Orthodox clergy in Tsarist Russia. The Orthodox patriarch of Antioch was the recognized head of the Arabic-speaking Greek Orthodox communicants, and sometimes they were/are referred to as Antiochian Orthodox to distinguish them from Greek-speaking Orthodox. During the eighteenth century the Arab followers of the Orthodox Church split, with a minority deciding to accept the authority of the Roman Catholic pope. The new converts were permitted to keep their Greek liturgy, and thus they were/are sometimes referred to as Greek Catholics; before World War I, however, they were commonly called Melchites.

The most important Muslim sect was the Sunni. Since Arabic-speaking Sunnis were coreligionists of the Ottoman Turks, many of them were incorporated into the political elite of Syria, especially in the major administrative centers. Sunnis were found in all towns, and in the villages of Palestine and of Syria proper. The other Muslim sects included the Druze, the Matawilah (Twelve-Imam Shi'is), the Alawis, and the Ismailis. The Druze were significant in Mount Lebanon, where intense rivalry prevailed between them and the Maronites for control of resources and political power. In the past their competition had led to violence. Indeed, the creation of the special district of Mount Lebanon had come about as a result of serious conflict in 1860 that had escalated into civil war.

In addition to the various Christian and Muslim sects, communities of Arabic-speaking Jews were scattered in Syria. An ancient and sizable Jewish community was in Damascus, but Jews were also found in other cities, such as Beirut and Jerusalem. Arab Jewish communities tended to be larger and more prominent in other Ottoman areas, such as Baghdad in Mesopotamia (Iraq), Yemen, and Egypt, which was a de jure part of the empire until 1914, although it had been under British occupation since 1882.

For all of Syria the total number of Muslims of all sects comprised a small majority of the population. In Mount Lebanon, however, the Christians constituted the majority. Indeed, the boundaries of the district had been drawn to assure that majority. Mount Lebanon had been created in 1861 following a series of sectarian massacres in several cities of Syria and the outbreak of communal hostilities in Lebanon. Its area was approximately two thousand square miles, about half the size of the modern country of Lebanon, and included the port cities of Beirut and Sidon together with their agricultural hinterlands. Mount Lebanon was established according to the terms of a *règlement organique* signed by Turkey and five European governments. The *règlement* provided for a Christian governor of Mount Lebanon, who was to be appointed by the Ottoman government in consultation with the European signatories. While Mount Lebanon certainly could not be called autonomous, its administration was carefully observed by interested European powers, especially France and Great Britain, who were establishing their own colonial empires at the expense of the Ottomans. Turkey abrogated the special status for Mount Lebanon when it entered the First World War on the side of Germany and the Austro-Hungarian Empire against France, Great Britain, and Tsarist Russia.

A description of Mount Lebanon during the period of the *règlement* is provided by Samir Khalaf in the first article of this book, "The Background and Causes of Lebanese/Syrian Immigration to the United States before World War I." Mount Lebanon under the *règlement* apparently enjoyed a relatively prosperous commercial economy, and during the last half of the nineteenth century, Beirut developed as a major Mediterranean port. The security and economic growth were probably factors that stimulated a population increase. By 1900 the population of Mout Lebanon is estimated to have reached 400,000, or an average density of two hundred per square mile. Most of the population lived in villages and worked in agriculture. While the majority of rural families owned the land they cultivated, the actual size of the typical holding was less than twenty acres.

Khalaf suggests that the overpopulation and resultant pressures on land were important causes of the rural emigration from Mount Lebanon. The division of a family farm among several children through inheritance—by 1900 the average family could expect up to five children to survive to adulthood—would have the effect of reducing holdings to mere subsistence plots. To avoid such certain impoverishment of their children, many families began to encourage younger offspring, especially "surplus sons" who had not yet acquired extensive farming experience, to seek their fortunes outside of the villages, in Beirut or the urban centers of the new world. This was during the same time that stories of the opportunities in America were reaching the villages and stimulating dreams of earning unheard-of riches. Thus, several young men began to leave, then several hundred young men and a few women, then several thousand men and women. By 1914 an estimated one hundred thousand persons had left Mount Lebanon; about 60 percent of them migrated to the United States, and the rest to other countries such as Brazil, Argentina, Canada, Chile, Columbia, Mexico, Venezuela, and even to Australia.

Mount Lebanon was not isolated from the rest of Syria, which also experienced some of the same changes. Agriculture in other parts of Syria was characterized, however, by greater peasant poverty and indebtedness than existed in Mount Lebanon. Thus, both the incentives to immigrate and the economic pressures impeding migration were stronger. Nevertheless, an estimated one hundred thousand persons left greater Syria, exclusive of Mount Lebanon, in the twenty-five years up to 1914. In some districts the "out" migration was particularly heavy, such as from the mountainous hinterlands of the Mediterranean port towns of Latakia and Tripoli and from the plains near Aleppo, Damascus, and Homs. Farther south in the Palestine district, limited numbers of persons also began to join the migratory movement. Finally, it can be mentioned that stories about the wealth of America were not confined to Syria, but reached other areas where Arabic-speaking communities lived. Thus, by 1914 a few enterprising immigrants had made their way to the United States from Iraq, Yemen, Egypt, and North Africa. Of this total migration, about half went to the United States and half to other parts of the Americas; a few settled in Africa.

Up to 1914, then, migration out of Ottoman Syria to both North and South America was relatively heavy. The migration reached its peak in the years immediately preceding World War I. The outbreak of that war drastically curtailed immigration. The Ottoman Empire's entry into the war had unanticipated consequences that changed the political history of Syria. The empire was dissolved after 1918, and the victorious war allies, Great Britain and France, seized Syria and proceeded to divide it among themselves. France expanded Mount Lebanon into the mandate of Lebanon by adding to it the Tripoli district in the north, the Tyre district in the south and the Biqa' Valley. Britain occupied south Syria, out of which it created two mandates, Palestine and Transjordan, the latter by adding an extensive stretch of desert to the populated strip paralleling the river on the east bank of the Jordan. This left about half of the former province, which France controlled and eventually set up as the mandate of Syria. The mandates were supposed to become independent countries after an unspecified time during which the French and British would tutor the people about how to manage a government.

The extended discussion about Syria is important not only because that is the province from which at least 90 percent of the Arabic-speaking immigration originated right up to 1940, but also because Syria was used as a means of identity, especially up to 1918. The immigrants did not refer to themselves as Arabs, but rather as Syrians. During the last years of the Ottoman Empire the term "Arab" connoted a Muslim, and in particular an Arabic-speaking Bedouin. Non-Bedouin, let alone non-Muslims, were not considered to be Arabs. The term "Syrian" may have been initiated by American and European Christian missionaries who had begun to come to Syria before 1860. By the end of the nineteenth century it was widely used outside of Syria, and since Syria was the homeland of the immigrants, the immigrants readily accepted being identified as Syrians.

Interestingly, the development of the idea of Arab nationalism was initiated by Arabic-speaking Christian intellectuals in Syria. The concept of a common national identity that transcended religious differences gathered support only gradually during the last half of the nineteeth century. It is likely that the overwhelming majority of pre–World War I immigrants were unaware of the nascent Arab nationalist thought. The creation of several dependent Arab states in the aftermath of that conflict greatly intensified Arab nationalism as a movement enjoying broad support. At the same time, however, the development of local identities such as Lebanese, Syrian, and Palestinian was encouraged by the postwar political conditions. The immigrants, who generally accepted that they were becoming Americans, now questioned their origins. Were the Syrians who had immigrated from villages in Lebanon and Palestine still Syrian? Or, were they Arabs, as some of the intellectual and political leaders in the "new" old countries contended? Or, were they Lebanese and Palestinians? The tendency was to identify according to the new lines of nationality, that is, as Lebanese, Syrians, and Palestinians. By 1940 even this tendency had not won universal acceptance, however, and many immigrants still considered themselves Syrians even though their ancestoral villages were not within the international borders of the new state of Syria.

Whatever terms were eventually used by the immigrants, it is important to point out that the question of identity was not so much concerned about resolving the origins of the immigrants, but rather was concerned with how they should situate themselves within the "melting pot" of American society. In other words, could the Arabic-speaking Syrians from Asia fit into a country that favored its European roots and practiced varying degrees of prejudice against those perceived as "non-whites"? The process of adjustment in this sense is explained in this book by Michael Suleiman in "Early Arab-Americans: The Search for Identity." Suleiman has found that most of the early Arab immigrants arrived in the United States with a idealized, almost fairy-tale-like, view of what life would be like. While the reality of living in America rarely accorded with the preimmigration dreams, most Arabs had relatively positive experiences in terms of securing acceptable employment; they soon established roots and opted to become Americans. This choice meant that the immigrants had to prove that they were equal to other Americans, especially those of European ancestry who controlled and defined culture. On the intellectual level, they advanced theories attesting to the Caucasian racial origins of Syrians specifically, and of Arabs generally. On the more practical level they worked hard and generally avoided any political activities that might draw undue attention to Syrians as a community.

The assimilation of Arabic-speaking immigrants was a process that involved sometimes painful choices about values: What customs and beliefs should they try to preserve? How should their American-born children be raised? How should they confront instances of antiforeign bigotry, social ostracism, and injustice? In the 1920s, when the second generation was coming of age, these questions acquired greater significance as "Americanized" immigrants began to wonder whether their adult children, who were generally ignorant of Arab society and culture, would be fully accepted in an American society and culture that was then characterized by different forms of discrimination against ethnic and racial minorities. Indeed, Raouf Halaby demonstrates in this book that the contradictory experiences and feelings of assimilation caused the Arabic-speaking community to become divided, at least from an intellectual perspective, into two opposing camps: the "nativists" who wanted to maintain Arab traditions intact, or even return to the Middle East; and the "Americanists," who advocated wholesale adoption of American ways. In his article titled "Dr. Michael Shadid and the Debate over Identity in *The Syrian World*," Halaby focuses upon the views of these two groups as expressed in publications circulated widely within the community in the late 1920s. Generally, the nativists included those immigrants and second-generation Arab-Americans who had become embittered on account of the many instances of prejudice they had encountered and believed that persons of Arab origins would never be fully accepted by American white society. The Americanists, in contrast, dismissed anti-Arab prejudice as the bigotry of a minority and insisted that complete assimilation was the best means of assuring Arab-American participation in the wider society.

The debate between the Americanists and the nativists had relevance for most immigrants and their children because the experience of discrimination was a fairly universal one before 1940. Syrians were not, of course, the only immigrants to encounter forms of discrimination. In addition, the actual intensitity of discrimination varied considerably from city to city, and especially from region to region. For example, in the industrial cities of the northeast and midwest that grew rapidly after 1880 as a result of immigration and also had attracted a multiplicity of ethnic groups, overt antiforeign prejudice tended to be subtle and usually was ignored by the immigrants. In those parts of the country where immigrants did not constitute a significant element of the population, discriminatory practices, especially against those who did not fit the white-Anglo-Saxon-Protestant stereotype, were more blatant.

In some of the cities and towns of the deep south where the white ruling class was creating a strictly segregated society, the dark-complexioned Syrians and other Mediterranean peoples occupied an ambiguous status in terms of the institutionalized racism that prevailed. In their essay, " 'Colored' and Catholic: The Lebanese in Birmingham, Alabama," Nancy Faires Conklin and Nora Faires describe the experiences with prejudice faced by the Arabic-speaking immigrants who were perceived as nonwhite and as adherents of suspect religions. Interestingly, the very pervasiveness of discrimination served to be important in solidifying a Lebanese identity. This identity manifested itself through the creation of institutions for the preservation of a distinct culture. Conklin and Faires demonstrate that the churches and clubs were, respectively, religious and secular organizations where the Lebanese could congregate regularly to reaffirm the legitimacy of their own roots. These community settings provided in essence the emotional strength not just to survive but, more important, to prosper in Birmingham's racially segregated society.

When the Lebanese immigrants initially began to settle in Birmingham in the 1890s, most of the adult males, as well as some of the adult females, had engaged in peddling both within the rapidly growing city itself and in the Alabama countryside. Gradually, they became established in more permanent retail trade. By the 1920s most of the families operated stores in the city. A similar form of entrepreneurial mobility occurred among the Syrian immigrants who began settling in El Paso, Texas, at the turn of the century. Sarah John in her essay "Arabic-Speaking Immigration to the El Paso Area, 1900–1935," finds that the ethnic Arabs, initially as peddlers and later as wholesale and retail merchants, served as commerical intermediaries for trade between the United States and Mexico in this border city. Peddling also was adopted by ethnic Arabs in other areas as a means of earning livelihoods upon first arriving in America. Not all of those who engaged in peddling found it a congenial occupation, and most of the novices probably did not advance to being managers and proprietors of their own shops. Some communities, however, most notably the one in Vicksburg, Mississippi, and part of the community in Providence, Rhode Island, did follow the patterns of Birmingham and El Paso.[1]

A 1908 survey found 3,077 Syrian businesses dispersed throughout the continental United States, with the exception of the states of Delaware, Utah, and Wyoming.[2] The overwhelming majority of these businesses were established retail shops, although some itinerant salesmen are also listed. Nevertheless, probably as many as seventy-five thousand Syrian immigrants lived in the country by 1908. Even if we multiply the number of enterprises by a factor of four to account for spouses and immigrant—but not American born—minor children, the number of immigrants involved in business would be only 12,500. This figure represents less than 20 percent of the total number of immigrants estimated to be in the country at that time. Thus, it is reasonable to inquire about what occupations engaged the time of and provided the income for the majority of Arabic-speaking immigrants.

Dina Dahbany-Miraglia's essay "Yemenite Jewish Immigration and Adaptation to the United States, 1905–41" provides insight into the diverse ways Arabic-speaking immigrants earned a living. Between 1890 and 1940, New York City was the home of the single largest community of ethnic Arabs in the country. The Yemeni Jews represented but one small component of this community, that originally settled along and near Water Street in lower Manhattan. In terms of occupation, the Jews from Yemen apparently were typical of the Christian, Muslim, and Jewish Syrians: some engaged in peddling; others were in retail trade; some worked as painters; some worked in garment factories; and others worked in construction. The majority of Yemeni Jews in New York, and a majority of other Arab immigrants in the city, were employed essentially as unskilled laborers.

The demand for unskilled laborers, not just in New York City but throughout the United States, was high at the turn of the century. The generation leading up to World War One was a period of rapid industrialization, and the thousands of factories and construction sites hired millions of immigrants as workers. Although the overwhelming majority of the immigrants had few or no industrial skills, most were willing to work long hours at low wages and without job security or benefits. This was an era when labor unions were weak, their leaders harrassed, and their goals set at trying to obtain maximum work hours per day and minimum hourly wages. Employers considered unions—where workers' organizations were legal—as nuisances, and preferred hiring immigrants whose inadequate language skills, ignorance of labor laws, and fear of authority combined to make them generally docile workers.

The high tide of Arabic-speaking immigration occurred between 1900 and 1915. The immigrants settled not just in large cities such as Boston, Cleveland, and New York, but also in scores of medium-sized cities and towns primarily in the East and the Great Lakes region. In 1910 more than half of all Arab immigrants were living in just four states: Massachusetts, New York, Pennsylvania, and Ohio. Major industrial centers in those states had sizable ethnic Arab communities, including Fall River, Lawrence, and Worcester in Massachusetts; Niagara Falls, Syracuse, and Utica in New

York; Johnstown, New Castle, Pittsburgh, and Scranton in Pennsylvania; and Cincinnati, Toledo, and Youngstown in Ohio. In addition, there were notable ethnic Arab communities in industrial cities and towns in several other states including Connecticut, Illinois, Indiana, Michigan, New Jersey, Rhode Island, and West Virginia. In all of these areas, a majority of the adult male immigrants (ranging from 60 to 90 percent of the total) were employed as unskilled laborers, mostly in factories but also in a variety of other occupations.

The town of Waterville, Maine, is fairly representative of the type of factory town in which Arabic-speaking immigrants settled before 1915. At the turn of the century, Waterville was a classic New England textile manufacturing center whose mills attracted immigrant workers. As demonstrated in my essay "From the Near East to Down East: Ethnic Arabs in Waterville, Maine," fully 86 percent of the employed adult immigrants worked as laborers in 1910. As in other New England textile towns—such as Dover and Manchester in New Hampshire, and Central Falls, Pawtucket, and Woonsocket in Rhode Island—the availability of jobs in the mills had lured the Arabic-speaking immigrants to Waterville. A similar pattern is observable from the historical data for the factory towns of upstate New York, northern New Jersey, western Pennsylvania, and the Great Lakes states. In Waterville, as in so many comparable industrial centers, the initial Arab immigrants before 1900 had come as peddlers, then eventually established businesses. This contact facilitated information about job opportunities for family, friends, and acquaintances in villages in Mount Lebanon, Palestine, and Syria. When immigration intensified after 1900, it was because the immigrants were coming to seek jobs. Those who were successful sent for siblings, cousins, and friends. In this way the ethnic Arab community gradually took root in Waterville, and did so similiarly in dozens of other towns and cities.

By the time the First World War began, at least 90 percent of the estimated 110,000 Arabic-speaking immigrants then in the country lived in essentially urban, industrialized environments, even though the overwhelming majority of them had come from villages. The majority of the immigrants either worked as laborers or derived their primary support from others, usually adult males, who were laborers. A minority, perhaps as many as 15 percent of the total, were involved directly or indirectly via spouses, parents, and the like in entrepreneurial activities such as barbering; running a bakery, grocery store, or restaurant; engaging in carpentry or transportation; manufacturing, wholesaling, peddling, or retailing dry goods; or painting. A tiny percent were professionals such as clergymen, dentists, doctors, lawyers, pharmacists, and teachers. Most of the small numbers of Arab immigrants living in rural America worked as farm hands or owned their own farms. A community of homesteaders was established in western North

Dakota, and Arab families owned farms in such states as California, Maine, Michigan, Minnesota, Nebraska, and Utah. A few immigrants also worked as miners in such states as Montana, Pennsylvania, and West Virginia.

By 1915 more than fifty cities and towns across the United States had Arabic-speaking immigrant communities of at least fifty families, with the largest communities including several hundred households. Like other immigrants, the Arabs tended to congregate in neighborhoods, or ghettoes. It was in these neighborhoods, often referred to as "Little Syrias" by other groups, that the ethnic Arab communities took root to become part of the American cultural mosaic. The three essays by Conklin and Faires, Dahbany-Miraglia, and Hooglund mentioned above contain considerable information on the establishment of institutions that had the objective of maintaining certain Old World traditions within the adopted New World. These institutions not only helped to preserve heritage but also facilitated adjustment to American customs. A good example of this process is described by Evelyn Shakir in her essay "Good Works, Good Times: The Syrian Ladies' Aid Society of Boston, 1917–32." This detailed case study demonstrates how the immigrant women and later some of their American-born children adapted an American tradition, the voluntary association, to benefit their own community. As a charitable organization, the Syrian Ladies' Aid Society became adept at raising funds by using methods long established in New England: suppers, back sales, raffles, and door-to-door solicitations.

The activities of the women who were members of the Syrian Ladies' Aid Society remind us that the ethnic Arab communities that developed and flourished in the years between the two world wars did so because of the hard work and commitment of thousands of immigrants. For that reason it is appropiate to conclude this collection of essays with case studies of three individuals who in very different ways contributed to weaving ethnic Arabs into the fabric of American society. The first essay, by Bayly Winder, "Philip Hitti (1886–1978): An Homage," is about an immigrant from Mount Lebanon who became one of America's most preeminent scholars of Middle East history. Hitti was deeply concerned about his compatriots in the United States and devoted much of his life to documenting their immigration history. In many respects, he is the father of studies about the Arabic-speaking immigration.

Hitti was exceptional among the immigrants in that he was highly educated when he arrived in this country. More typical of Arab immigrants was Kahlil Gibran (1883–1933). Gibran emigrated from a village in Mount Lebanon while still a boy and lived in poverty in Boston. Despite his humble origins, he was unusually talented and struggled to become an artist and poet. Jean and Kahlil Gibran trace the various intellectual and artistic influences upon this extraordinary figure in their essay "The Symbolic Quest of Kahlil Gibran: The Arab as Artist in America." Gibran wrote original poetry in both Arabic and English and eventually became acclaimed both in the United States and in the Arab world.

Few of the Arabic-speaking immigrants achieved the fame of Hitti or Gibran. Nevertheless, their contributions in the daily evolution of the immigrants into ethnic communities were no less significant. Among the countless unsung heroes and heroines was Nazera Orfalea, a woman who immigrated to America as a youth, worked at many jobs, including peddling for several years, to raise a family. Her grandson, Gregory Orfalea, has written a poetically moving account of this remarkable woman by adapting Nazera's own diary and recollections of stories she told him. Nazera Orfalea exemplies in many respects the many thousands of Arabic-speaking immigrants who settled in this country up to 1940. For that reason it is most appropriate that that essay, "There's a Wire Brush at My Bones," concludes this book.

I would like to end this introductory essay by acknowledging my gratitude to all those who have helped to make this book a reality. The literal godfather of the book is Prof. Rudolph Vecoli, the director of the the University of Minnesota's Immigration History Research Center in Saint Paul. Rudi Vecoli recognized the significance of the papers presented at the 1983 Philip Hitti International Symposium and enthusiastically supported the publication of a collection of the best papers. Most important, he made available valuable time of the staff of the Immigration History Research Center to assist in the project of turning conference papers into a thematically integrated book. In particular, the center's associate director, Stephanie Cain Van D'Elden, assumed the uneviable task of coordinating the circulation of copies of papers between editors, readers, and contributors and also handled the contacts with prospective publishers. She provided sage advice on manuscripts and proved to be exceptionally skillful in dealing with any number of seemingly inevitable complications.

Among those who read the entire manuscript before publication is Dr. Evelyn Hansen, dean of the General College of the University of Minnesota, to whom I extend a special thanks. Evelyn Hansen helped me to select the papers that comprise this volume. She is a superb editor and her suggestions inspired many of the revisions that various of the contributors undertook. Her advice, including her apt suggestion of the title for the book, has been valuable throughout the various phases of this project. Professor Laurence Michalak, acting director of the Center for Middle East Studies of the University of California at Berkeley served as a reader of the manuscript and provided valuable suggestions for revisions, many of which were incorporated by the contributors. A second anonymous reader likewise offered helpful suggestions.

The list of persons who read one or more essays and offered suggestions is numerous. Those whom I would like to single out for a special thanks include Amelia Azar, Marie Deeb, Alan Dehmer, Eleanor Dumato, Robert Hazo, Philip Kayal, Joseph Schechla, and Anthony Toth. On behalf of each of the contributors I would like also to extend a collective thanks to all those who helped with editorial, intellectual, typing and other assistance. Daniel Goodwin and others among the staff of the Smithsonian Institution Press, including Jane McAllister, Ruth Spiegel, and Linda McKnight, faithfully saw this project through to the end. Last, I want to thank my family in Maine for unknowingly providing me with so many ideas, and my wife Martha Ramage and my daughter Karima for their constant enthusiasm and encouragement for this project.

Notes

1. For more information about the Arabic-speaking entrepreneurs in Vicksburg and Providence see Joseph Schechla, "Dabkeh in the Delta," pp. 25–57, and Eleanor Dumato, "Celebrating Tradition in Rhode Island," pp. 101–8, in *Taking Root: Arab-American Community Studies, Volume II*, ed. Eric Hooglund (Washington, D.C.: ADC Research Institute, 1985).

2. The information about Syrian businesses in 1908 has been taken from S. A. Mokarzel and H. F. Otash, *The Syrian Business Directory: First Edition, 1908–1909* (New York, 1908).

PART ONE

OVERVIEW OF ARAB IMMIGRATION

The Background and Causes of Lebanese/Syrian Immigration to the United States before World War I

SAMIR KHALAF

In accounting for the nature and causes of emigration from Lebanon and Syria, one encounters two general perspectives in the voluminous literature on the subject. One group, predominantly philosophers, humanists, and literary figures, perceives migration as a reflection of the innate predisposition of the Lebanese to be on the move. This predisposition, they argue, is rooted in the Phoenician heritage and the maritime and seafaring tradition, and accounts for much of the roving and itinerant national character. Others have been more inclined to focus on the particular socioeconomic, political, and historical circumstances that either "pushed" or "pulled" the Lebanese out of their familiar surroundings and prompted them to uproot themselves and seek fortunes in the distant corners of the globe.

Both agree, however, that in terms of its magnitude, scale, and implications, Lebanese emigration is a unique historic phenomenon and hence deserves fuller study and analysis than it has received thus far. This paper will focus briefly on three dimensions of this complex phenomenon to: (1) provide some concrete evidence regarding the changing pattern and magnitude of emigration to North America between 1880 and 1914; (2) identify the socioeconomic profile of the emigrants and how and why it changed over the years; and (3) elucidate and account for some of the major causes of such exodus. Because the scope of the paper is limited, I am naturally more concerned with the "push" than the "pull" factors, although it is admittedly difficult to maintain at all times a clear distinction between the two.

PATTERN AND MAGNITUDE

Despite some of the inevitable ambiguities in the early recorded evidence, one can discern some general and meaningful patterns of emigration from Lebanon and Syria. Almost all the historic sources begin with the almost epiclike story of Antonius al-Bishalany, the young man from Salima who landed in Boston in 1854. Perhaps because his life was dramatic and tragic, he is often singled out as the first emigrant to the New World.[1] Evidence exists, however, of earlier visitors. Two of the earliest immigrants were, in fact, church officials: Father Ilyas al-Musali, the son of a Chaldean priest from Aleppo who came to North America in 1740, and two Melkite priests—Flavinous Khuri and Nassif Shedoudi—who arrived in New York in 1849 to raise funds for the convent at Shwayr destroyed during the civil disturbances of 1841.[2]

Initially, the numbers were small and the emigrants were identified as coming from "Turkey in Asia," since Syria at the time was not an independent nation. Many of the early emigrants were, in fact, labeled as "Turkos," Arabs, Asisatic Turks, and sometimes as Armenians and Greeks in U.S. immigration records. It was only in 1899 that the Immigration Service began to classify such immigrants as Syrians.[3] Even then, no attempt was made to distinguish between the emigrants coming from the interior of the country and those from the coastal regions of Lebanon and Palestine.[4]

As shown in table 1, only two Syrian immigrants entered the United States in 1869. In the following decade, between 1871 and 1880, another sixty-seven persons—that is, a trickle of about six to seven per year—were recorded. In the early 1880s, however, the first sizable outflow (around two hundred persons per year) took place, mostly from the town of Zahleh. By the late 1880s the figure leaped to nearly six hundred.

Incidentally, the source of the early waves of migrants is open to conjecture. While some writers claim that migration began in the Biqa',[5] others state with equal conviction that many of the first immigrants came from the north, especially from the town of Bisharri.[6]

Irrespective of where immigration began, there is virtual consensus that by the early 1890s the movement began to assume large proportions. As shown in table 1, close to twenty-five hundred immigrants had entered the United States by 1891. By that time, every village in Lebanon could claim at least one immigrant son. By the late 1890s the exodus almost doubled, reaching an estimated forty-seven hundred in 1897. Despite its widespread character, the outflow was not even. Some villages lost more than others. The town of Zahleh, for example, had lost "within eighteen months about one ninth of its population, one in every twenty being a Protestant. . . .

The emigrants were the best and most industrious, and their departure created an economic crisis."[7]

One factor that accounts for the sharp and sudden increase, as we shall see later, was the impact of the returing emigrants. As early as 1890 some of the early emigrants returned home with stories and evidence of their stunning and swift success. Such episodes were usually followed by waves of renewed exodus. During the first decade of the twentieth century, the exodus sustained a persistent annual increase until it peaked at nine thousand on the eve of World War I. The outflow grew to such an extent that entire regions were left underpopulated.[8] Naturally, the U.S. was not the only recipient country. By then, even larger numbers were already settled in South America, Australia, Canada, and West Africa. Of an estimated population of 442,000 in 1913, Mount Lebanon by 1914 had lost to emigration more than one hundred thousand—more than one-fourth of its population.[9]

The figures fell sharply during and after the First World War, then rose again, albeit briefly, to a level of about five thousand in 1921. From then on, the incidence started to fall gradually, until it tapered off to an annual rate of about one hundred entries during the 1930s.

The sharp decline in the postwar years should not be interpreted as a growing disinterest on the part of the Lebanese to immigrate to America. The decline reflects, in part, the war years' conditions and the difficulty in securing safe exit. But more important, it reflects the change in the U.S. immigration laws. Soon after World War I, a law was passed limiting the total annual immigration from any one country of the world to 3 percent of its population already in the U.S.[10] For Syria, this meant that 103 immigrants could enter each year. Following the establishment of separate political states in 1920, Lebanon and Syria were each assigned a quota of one hundred immigrants per year. Furthermore, visas were granted on the basis of kinship ties to American citizens, priority being given to individuals with education and skills. Subsequent legislation, particularly the immigration acts of 1921, 1924, and 1929, restricted further, and almost stopped, immigration. For example, while the 1921 act fixed the annual quota at 3 percent of the number of immigrants in 1910, the act of 1924 restricted it to only 2 percent of the number of immigrants in 1890, when, as shown in table 1, the numbers were substantially lower. The act of 1929, on the other hand, arbitrarily fixed the total number of immigrants to 150,000 people annually, and allocated to Lebanon and Syria, jointly, a yearly quota of 123 immigrants.[11]

Judging then by the entries listed in table 1, around 123,000 had entered the U.S. by 1924. Since entries were insignificant in subsequent years, the 1924 figures should give us a fairly realistic impression of the magnitude of immigration for the period under consideration. Incidentally,

Table 1.
Emigration from Lebanon/Syria to the United States, 1869–1938

Year	*Number*	*Year*	*Number*
1869	2	1911	5,444
		1912	5,525
1871–1880	67	1913	9,210
		1914	9,023
1887	208	1915	1,767
1888	273	1916	676
1889	593	1917	976
1890	1,126	1918	210
		1919	231
1891	2,483	1920	3,045
1892			
1893		1921	5,105
1894		1922	1,334
1895	2,767	1923	1,207
1896	4,139	1924	1,595
1897	4,732	1925	
1898	4,275	1926	227
1899	3,708	1927	
1900	2,920	1928	341
		1929	442
1901	4,064	1930	332
1902	4,982		
1903	5,551	1931	180
1904	3,653	1932	149
1905	4,882	1933	135
1906	5,624	1934	100
1907	5,880	1935	103
1908	5,520	1936	99
1909	3,668	1937	162
1910	6,317	1938	61

Sources: For the years 1869–80, Elie Safa, *L'émigration libanise* (Beirut: Université Saint-Joseph, 1960), pp. 188, 196; for the years 1887–1924, National Bureau of Economic Research, *Statistics,* vol. 1 of *International Migrations,* ed. W. F. Willcox (New York: National Bureau of Economic Research, 1929), pp. 384–88, 432–43.

the estimates vary widely. For example, while the 1920 census showed 49,114 "Syrians" living in the United States, Philip Hitti estimates the number of "Syrians" and their descendants for that period to be about two hundred thousand.[12]

By 1940, U.S. official statistics indicated that about 350,000 immigrants were of "Arab-speaking" origin.[13] About 80 percent of those immigrants are estimated to have come from what is today Lebanon; 15 percent from Syria and Palestine; and the rest from Iraq and Yemen. Egypt's quota is negligible.[14]

SOCIOECONOMIC PROFILE

Although we do not know exactly how many actually came into the United States, we are better informed as to who came and why. The sources reveal a rather striking feature: that during the first big wave around the turn of the century, immigration was an overwhelmingly Christian phenomenon. Writing in 1924, Hitti estimated that more than 95 percent of all Syrian immigrants to the U.S. by then belonged to Christian sects. As shown in table 2, about 45 percent were Maronite, 43 percent Greek Orthodox, 5 percent Catholic, 2.5 percent Protestant, and only the remaining 4.5 percent Muslim and Druze.

As we shall see, obvious sociopolitical and cultural influences predisposed Christian groups toward migration to the United States. In the wake of the communal conflict that Mount Lebanon experienced during the middle of the nineteenth century, particularly the sectarian hostilities of 1841, 1845, and 1860, Christians were beginning to feel some of the anxieties and apprehensions of a persecuted minority within the context of the Ottoman Empire. Although the bulk of the early emigrants belonged to denominations that are rare in America, and only 2.5 percent were Protestants, they were nonetheless, Christians and thereby more likely to feel at home and be integrated into the New World. On the other hand, their Muslim counterparts, as several historians have pointed out, faced psychological, religious, and cultural obstacles, and hence initially displayed considerable reluctance to immigrate to the West.[15] Another, possibly more plausible, explanation is that owing to his relatively lower socioeconomic status compared to his Christian compatriot, the Muslim peasant at the time had greater difficulty in securing the funds necessary to pay for his passage to America.[16] Whatever the cause, it is clear that Christians had a substantial head start over their Muslim counterparts.

Table 2.
Religious Affiliation of Syrians in the United States, 1924

Religion	*Number*	*Percentage*
Maronite	90,000	45 %
Greek Orthodox	85,000	43 %
Greek Catholic	10,000	5 %
Protestant	5,000	2.5%
Muslim	8,000	4 %
Druze	1,000	0.5%
Total	199,000	100.0%

Source: Philip K. Hitti, *The Syrians in America* (New York: Doran, 1924), pp. 58, 104.

Another composite feature stands out. Typical of other mobile and itinerant groups, the early emigrants were on the whole fairly young, unattached, and unmarried males, with relatively low levels of skills or formal schooling. Hitti asserts that in its early history the movement was entirely a male phenomenon, involving youths in their mid-twenties drawn from the lower strata of society.[17] With the possible exception of a small educated minority, the bulk were poor peasants without any formal schooling. Their socioeconomic level is apparent through, among other evidence, records of the financial arrangements they made to secure the cost of their sea voyage (*nawlun,* as it was called at the time). In virtually all instances, it involved mortgaging property, borrowing money from extended family or relatives, and pledging and conscripting the returns of one's labors to creditors and other such taxing hardships.

Judging by autobiographical accounts and other historical sources, many of the early immigrants perceived much of the early movement as a transient phenomenon. Their ideal or dream was to amass all the wealth possible, in the shortest time, and then to return home to flaunt the material evidence of their success. Their overall aim no doubt accounts for the fact that youthful and uncommitted males were the primary émigrés in the formative phase of emigration.

As one would expect, the drain of the youthful and vigorous portion of the population, despite the emigration's initial transient quality, had serious socioeconomic implications. Many villages lost their most resourceful members and were reduced to merely becoming shelters for the elderly. The village of Bayt Shabab, literally "home of youth," for example, became known as Bayt al-Ajazah, or the "home of the aged."[18]

But the exclusively male and transient style of the early immigrants gradually began to change. The enterprising Lebanese immigrants discovered very early the economic value of women and how they could be resourcefully employed to augment family income. Since many of the early settlers engaged in peddling notions, laces, and undergarments—activities that required free access to homes—women proved more suitable as peddlers. Thus, the immigrants sent for women to join them in the United States. And the women came in relatively large numbers. For example, as early as 1910, 32 percent of the total number of "Syrian" immigrants in the United States was female. The proportion was considerably higher than for other comparable ethnic groups. The proportion of Armenian females, for example, was 23 percent; Spanish, 17 percent; Bulgarian and Serbian, 4 percent; Greek, 5 percent; while the average female proportion of the total immigrants of all races was 30 percent.[19] The percentage of "Syrian" females would have been still higher, Hitti maintains, had it not been for the fact that the Muslim and Druze immigrants at the time included only an insignificant number of women. In fact, out of an estimated eight thousand Muslims and one thousand Druze, only two dozen women were counted among the former and one dozen among the latter.[20]

The inference that can be made from this data is that as the proportion of women increased—and by 1940 the percentage of females rose to 44 percent of the total "Syrian" population[21]—immigration became more family centered and consequently a more stable and permanent phenomenon.

The educational background and skill levels of the immigrants had also undergone a perceptible change. As suggested earlier, with the exception of a small educated minority, the bulk of the early immigrants were not highly literate. Indeed, studies of literacy levels of "Syrians" entering the United States at the turn of the century estimated their literacy at 45 percent compared to an average literacy for all immigrants of 73 percent—that is, a differential deficiency of nearly 30 percent.[22] A survey of the literacy of the "Syrian" community in New York City made in 1903 revealed that about 60 percent of the males and 27 percent of the females could read and write in their native language. The proportion of those who could speak, read, and write English, as shown in table 3, was considerably lower: 32 percent for males and 23 percent for females. By 1930, however, the literacy in English of "Syrians" born outside the United States rose to nearly 75 percent. Lest this be taken as a fairly high figure, "Syrian" immigrants were ranked forty out of forty-two classifications, while the average literacy of all categories was 90 percent.[23]

The proportion of professionals among the first generation of immigrants was also extremely low. A survey of the "Syrians" in New York in 1903 revealed that only 2 percent of the male population were listed as professionals.[24] In 1912 another survey showed that in the United States as a whole, less than 1 percent of the "Syrians" were professionals, whereas craftsmen accounted for one-quarter and laborers almost half of the total.[25]

Table 3.
Literacy Levels of "Syrians" in New York City, ca. 1900

	Speak English	*Speak, read, and write English*	*Read and write Arabic*
Males	59.9	32.2	60.9
Adults	47.1	20.1	78.2
Children	87.8	61.6	39.9
Females	41.2	23.6	27.8
Adults	25.8	10.6	28.4
Children	74.8	53.6	28.5

Source: Lucius Hopkins Miller, *Our Syrian Population: A Study of Syrian Communities of Greater New York* (n.p.: 1903), p. 35.

Although the bulk of the early immigrants were not highly literate, one still encounters evidence of educated "Syrians" who began coming to America long before emigration from "Syria" had become a mass movement. In 1864, a certain Sahli Sabranji arrived in New York to assist the American missionary Dr. Cornelius Van Dyck in correcting proofs of the Arabic translation of the Bible being carried out in Beirut at the time.[26] Before the 1880s several "Syrians" came to the United States for the purpose of studying medicine. Dr. Ibrahim Arbeely, for example, had already graduated in medicine from the Syrian Protestant College before he came to America in 1878. In fact, numerous graduates of that college immigrated to the United States upon completion of their studies. George Tumeh mentions five medical graduates from the Syrian Protestant College who immigrated to America during the 1890s: Rashid Baddur, Jamil Barbur, Nassib Birbari, William Zurayq, and Yusif Saqr.[27]

Autobiographical and other sensational accounts abound in "success stories" of penniless immigrants being transformed into millionaires. Although such stories are doubtlessly exaggerated, empirical evidence exists, nonetheless, to substantiate the fact that many "Syrians" did become fairly prosperous in a relatively short period.[28] Their success is not difficult to account for. First, it must be kept in mind that although the bulk of the early immigrants were drawn from villages and towns, a fairly large number were engaged in trade as small merchants and shopkeepers and were quite familiar with urban life and occupations. For example, of the ten thousand adult males with identifiable occupations who entered the United States between 1899 and 1907, nearly 15 percent indicated that they had been merchants in the old country.[29] More important, perhaps, they carried with them the frugal and austere lifestyles they were accustomed to in Lebanon. Since many of them were eager to return home, they were predisposed to subsist on relatively little and save the bulk of their earnings. Even when they were in the lower income brackets, the "Syrians" had, in fact, as Berger among others has argued, displayed many of the social characteristics of the middle classes in urban centers in America.[30] A score of studies of several "Syrian" communities, conducted in the mid-1930s and early 1940s, all revealed a common pattern: low incidence of deviance and crime, better health, higher IQs among the children, more regular school attendance, and few intermarriages and divorces.[31]

THE SPECIAL CASE OF THE SYRIAN PROVINCE OF MOUNT LEBANON

For a fuller understanding of the background to and causes of emigration, particularly since the bulk of it occurred during the last four decades of Ottoman rule and was drawn largely from Mount Lebanon, it is essential to view the massive outflow of population within the context of the socioeconomic and political transformations generated between 1861 and 1915, when Mount Lebanon was administered as a separate province with a governor appointed directly by Istanbul in consultation with the European powers. During that period a general change took place in Mount Lebanon's socioeconomic base. The gradual transformation of the economy from a subsistence to a market system was accompanied by marked shifts in the position of various groups within the social hierarchy. Peasants in Mount Lebanon, both Christian and Druze, acquired real estate and became landowners. In the large towns, prosperous communities of merchants and money lenders gained social prominence and political influence. In the coastal cities of Beirut and Tripoli, swift commercialization and the opening up of urban society to Western contacts and new economic opportunities provided favorable conditions for the emergence of a new "aristocracy."

Concomitant with these changes—possibly because of them—Lebanon witnessed an educational and intellectual awakening that began to transform the social and cultural life of the country. The extension of foreign and missionary education activity, initiated earlier in the century, encouraged further indigenous initiatives in the field of popular education. Benevolent, literary, scientific, and other voluntary associations participated more effectively in the intellectual and reform movements of the day. Literacy became more widespread. Presses published a variety of books, periodicals, and newspapers covering a broad range of topics and reaching an audience beyond the confines of Lebanon. It was then that Lebanon acquired—deservedly or not—the slightly arrogant and overbearing reputation of being a "center of illumination" (*balad al-isha*).[32] It was also then that the popular and catchy saying "Happy was he who had a goat's enclosure in Lebanon" became more widespread.

Such accomplishments notwithstanding, clearly a darker side surrounded developments in Mount Lebanon. Indeed, one could easily reappraise the nature and magnitude of socioeconomic and political changes during that period, as several writers have done, and emerge with a less flattering picture.[33] Coming in the wake of nearly four decades of civil unrest and communal hostility, the relative "peace, tranquility, and prosperity," often attributed to the 1861–1915 period, may be unduly exaggerated. It is clear that such subjective perceptions belie some of the stark socioeconomic and political realities of the time.

The first striking reality is a geographic and territorial shortcoming, which had serious demographic and socioeconomic implications. Mount Lebanon was a largely mountainous terrain with inhospitable soil unsuitable for agriculture. With pronatalist norms encouraging high fertility, a scarcity of mineral resources and virtually no industry, Mount Lebanon suffered all the classic symptoms associated with demographic pressures. These were occasionally accentuated because the mountain often served as a sanctuary and a refuge for persecuted minorities escaping oppression from other provinces of the Ottoman Empire.

The general laissez-faire economic policy that the Ottoman authorities followed actually contributed to a stagnation or decline of agriculture, handicraft industry, and commerce. The decline of the silk industry had a momentous impact on the economy of the mountain, particularly since entire families and village communities were dependent on silk reeling as a primary source of livelihood. For years, observers had warned about the downward trend in silk production and documented the decline in the number of looms and manpower involved. Factors such as high domestic taxation, the absence of protective tariffs in the face of competition by machine-made imported goods, and the eventual change in local tastes to European-made clothing were all associated with the decline. The final blow, however, was dealt by the opening in 1869 of the Suez Canal, which shortened the trade route from the Far East to Europe. Chinese and Japanese silk, which had previously not been competitive with silk from Syria, could now be brought to Europe more cheaply than silk from the eastern Mediterranean. In addition, the quality of the Far Eastern silk was generally higher since the producers there had introduced modern techniques that insured more uniform production than could be obtained through the comparatively primitive methods still used in Mount Lebanon.

The First World War and its aftermath were so devastating in their effect upon Lebanon that they wiped out the remaining evidence of stability, harmony, and prosperity frequently associated with the prewar era. Of all the Ottoman provinces, Lebanon suffered the most damaging hardships. Foreign remittances, tourism, and revenue from summer resorts, by then major sources of national income, came to a sudden halt. A tight blockade was imposed on food, medical supplies, and clothing. Staple items and basic commodities were scarce; prices rose, and shortages became more widespread. By the fall of 1916, famine, successive swarms of locusts, and epidemics (particularly typhoid, typhus, malaria, dysentery, and bubonic plague) hit an already enfeebled and demoralized population. Entire villages were deserted. Others were left in partial ruin, depleted of their manpower and other resources. Altogether, some 100,000 out of a population of 450,000 are estimated to have lost their lives. Many of the remaining were in a pitiful state of destitution.[34]

It is little wonder that as soon as the war stopped, and people could resume travel again, masses of immigrants fled their devastated country in desperation. Since entry to the United States was restricted by the new immigration acts, immigrants sought other countries, particularly Brazil, Argentina, Uruguay, British Africa, and Senegal. Between 1921 and 1939 a total of eighty thousand left Lebanon at approximately the rate of five thousand per annum.[35]

CONCLUSION

Given such a background, we can summarize some of the general causes of emigration. In highlighting these, one should not, of course, overlook the role of seemingly small private tragedies or fortuitous circumstances that could be the final trigger, or the proverbial straw, that ultimately drives a person to emigrate. Hitti, for example, notes that in many instances the cause of emigration was nothing more significant than the death of a farmer's horse or a quarrel between a single-minded son and a stubborn parent.[36]

1. The literature reveals the consensus that the bulk of immigrants, particularly peasants and members of lower socioeconomic groups, left primarily because of economic and demographic pressures. Hitti, as usual, succinctly and clearly describes that situation:

> *A country with inhospitable soil . . . with a scarcity of mineral wealth, and no industrial development is always threatened with over-population. This is particularly true if the methods of cultivation are primitive, and the people prolific. A temporary draught or occasional failure of crops is enough to force the surplus to seek elbow room in other than its land. . . . Syria has always been an inhospitable place to live in and a splendid place to leave.*[37]

One could, of course, single out more specific economic causes, such as the change in trade routes and the consequent decline of the silk industry. The literature also abundantly references the importance of the Chicago fair in 1893 and that of Saint Louis in 1906 for attracting and spreading immigrants all over the country. On the whole, however, "there is hardly any doubt that the general economic insecurity, ruinous taxation and, above all, the awareness of a better life elsewhere drove the Syrians to emigrate."[38]

2. While peasants and members of the poorer strata were inclined to justify their departure from Lebanon on economic grounds and on their inability to find a satisfactory means of life in their native country, intellectuals and more educated groups desired to be liberated from the repressive political atmosphere that subjected them to all forms of censure, oppression, and sometimes outright persecution.

As we have seen, Lebanon experienced during the second half of the nineteenth century an intellectual and literary awakening. Foreign and native schools and universities were established and education became more accessible. The popular media, through newspapers, periodicals, and books, aroused the consciousness of masses with regard to public issues such as social equality, freedom, liberty, and national and civic consciousness. Participation in voluntary associations, clubs, and literary societies also became more accessible. That awakening, as several writers have observed, was doubtlessly made possible and stimulated by the relative freedom of thought and expression that prevailed in Syria until 1880.

Immigrants who are known to look back on the political situation in their country have decried a system that bred personal ambition and corruption, incited factionalism and confessional rivalry, and denied individuals their rights and sense of justice. Some of the same themes naturally permeate the writings of emigrant poets.[39] Abraham Rihbany, in relating his own story, could not contain his disgust and outrage. He said bluntly that he and his friends "left our mother country with nothing but curses for her government on our lips."[40] In summarizing the causes of emigration, Hitti states that "hardly a Syrian writer in English or Arabic, in discussing emigration, fails to refer to this desire of the Syrian to live his life free and unhampered from political restraints as the chief motive for his coming to the U.S."[41]

Closely associated with the above-mentioned political considerations is the desire to escape military conscription. During the nineteenth century, it must be recalled, the Ottoman government initiated a number of reforms, albeit at the insistence of European powers, which were designed to improve the political position of minority groups in the Empire. Those efforts culminated in the Constitution of 1908, which decreed, among other mandates, that citizenship with equal rights and duties would be granted to all the sultan's subjects. For the Muslims, the Constitution meant the loss of their traditional superiority. For the Christians, it meant that they would be subject to military conscription, a requirement from which they had been exempted since the Muslim invasion of Syria more than twelve centuries earlier. The effect of the loss of that traditional privilege was that many Christians began to leave for Egypt and America to escape the impending draft.

Of all the measures associated with the Ottomans, conscription was by far the most widely feared. Since it involved permanent absence from a village or town, it imposed a serious drain on the economic resources or livelihood of Mount Lebanon. It meant a prolonged isolation from kinship and other primordial ties, which are the source of personal reinforcement and support in village society. Indeed, it was so despised that potential conscripts would do their utmost to avoid it. Beiruti Muslims—and their coreligionists in Sidon and Tripoli—were known to seek refuge in European consulates and foreign residences, hide in caverns and excavations, or take to the sea in a vain effort to flee from the pursuit of conscription officers. The Druze sought immunity in baptism or conversion, and reports of mutilation were widespread. Subjects suspected of concealing or aiding fugitives suffered severe punishment. Hitti quotes a correspondent of the *New York*

Sun reporting from Haifa in 1913 that "every steamer bound for North or South America has been crowded, mostly with Christians anxious to evade the military draft."[42] By 1913, it must be recalled, the inflow of immigrants into the United States had peaked to a level of 9,210 (see table 1).

Finally, people left for an equally compelling political motive: they wanted to gain genuine attachment or loyalty to any national political entity. Such sentiment, quite pervasive at the time, was expressed by a Christian Lebanese who followed his father to the Sudan:

> *No attachment to the soil of Syria, no idea that Syria was the natural home of the Syrians, ever developed in my mind. Rather it seemed that the best thing people who had been so unfortunate as to be born in Syria could do was to leave it as soon as they could, and adopt some other country.*[43]

3. In addition to economic and political insecurity, religious persecution—particularly after the massacres of 1860—has often been singled out as a major cause of emigration. The literature dealing with persecution is controversial, inconsistent, and often exaggerated. Said Himadeh and Charles Issawi, for example, maintain that emigration developed gradually from 1860 to 1900 at an average of about three thousand annually.[44] Henry Jessup speaks of a "thousand refugees" who immigrated to Alexandria on a Russian steamer shortly after the Damascus massacre of 1860.[45] Muhammad Kurd Ali, on the other hand, makes reference to "some" who escaped to Egypt, Istanbul, and other areas in the Mediterranean.[46] Not only do writers differ in their quantitative estimates of the magnitude or impact of confessional hostility, but they also diverge in their qualitative assessment of the significance of the persecution thesis. Hitti, for example, maintains that religious factors take precedence over economic motives as a cause of emigration, at least as perceived by the emigrants[47]; Najib Saliba, on the other hand, argues that "religious persecution was a supplementary rather than a primary factor in emigration."[48]

What is undisputed, however, is that only a few of those persecuted emigrants ended up in America. As shown in table 1, it was not until the 1890s that immigration to the U.S. began to assume a substantial magnitude. In other words, since Christians who felt persecuted waited nearly thirty years before they left Syria, it seems doubtful that fear of religious harrassment was a primary motive for emigration.

4. The role of the missionaries is equally controversial. American missionaries in Lebanon had realized as early as the 1830s the need for educational development and basic instruction at the village and the popular levels. The first American-type public schools were opened in 1834. By 1867, twenty-one such schools, with a total enrollment of about eight hundred pupils, were open in Beirut and nearby villages. The initial success of such efforts encouraged native groups, with foreign support, to establish

their own schools. This cooperation between foreign missionaries and local groups was fruitful. For the first time in Lebanon, a coordinated system of village schools was bringing primary instruction within the easy reach of ordinary laymen.[49]

American missionary groups did not confine their efforts to primary schooling. In 1834 they introduced presses into Lebanon and in no time started publishing, in addition to religious material, several secular works that found popular appeal among the growing number of readers. The success of the Americans encouraged the Catholics to establish in 1853 the Imprimerie Catholique. The foreign presses were instrumental in awakening the spirit of journalism in the Arab world as a whole and in creating a popular but critical audience with intensive interest in the arts and sciences and other related issues of everyday life. Though many of the early newspapers and magazines were actually published in Egypt, men educated at the Beirut universities wrote for them, and men trained at presses in Beirut printed them.[50]

More important, perhaps, were the accomplishments of the missionaries in university education. By establishing in 1866 the Syrian Protestant College (later renamed American University of Beirut), they were, to a considerable extent, responsible for creating a new "class" of a professional and intellectual elite eager to share their knowledge and newly acquired skills with the rest of their countrymen.

Having been exposed to Western ideas and culture, young Lebanese were often unwilling to return to a way of life that had become unnatural for them. A spirited and intelligent boy who attended school for even a few years could no longer readily return to his village to spend the rest of his life happily herding goats, picking olives, or praying in a remote and secluded monastery. Instead, he would realize that options were within reach for a richer and fuller life elsewhere.

Hitti quotes from an interview with a well-known "Syrian" immigrant in New York in 1903. Reflecting on his education at an American school in Mount Lebanon, the immigrant said:

> *The teacher in an American mission school had a great many pictures of American cities, streets and scenes, and I could see that life in that land was very different from ours. I heard about the telephone, telegraph and railroad, and as I already knew about ships on account of seeing them go by on the water, it began to dawn on me that there was a very great and active land outside of Mt. Lebanon and that it might be possible to find something better to do than be a monk.*[51]

Because the immigrants expressed such sentiments, the American missionaries have often been credited with, or accused of, initiating and encouraging immigration to the United States.[52] Hitti, however, points out that the missionaries were not directly interested in encouraging emigration, but rather in raising the levels of literacy and the socioeconomic standards of the village communities. By creating a desire for a better life, however, missionaries must have indirectly and unconsciously encouraged emigration as the shortest and most accessible means of obtaining it.

5. Another indirect but facilitating factor was the role played by steamship agents and money lenders. The sight of a well-groomed agent on horseback roaming from one village to another in search of potential clients was, apparently, a familiar sight in Mount Lebanon. Autobiographical accounts and other historical sources do provide evidence indicating that the agents often exaggerated opportunities in America to encourage prospective customers.[53]

While the coerciveness was undoubtedly real, evidence also indicates that the "hunt" for emigrants by steamship or other agents was not as intensive or binding as it was in other Mediterranean countries. For example, the contract labor system (that is, the padrone system), introduced by the Italians in connection with railroad labor and utilized by the Greeks in the shoe-shining industry, was unknown among the Syrians and Lebanese. The same is true of the peonage system in which the immigrant was virtually in a status of involuntary or compulsory labor based upon his indebtedness, as a peon, to the master who advanced the fare. That practice, too, was not known among the Lebanese emigrants.

The influence, however, of steamship agents cannot be entirely discounted. They did play a definite role in "smuggling" immigrants at a time when exit from Ottoman ports was strictly forbidden. They also provided tempting financial arrangements and often devious routes and means to guarantee eventual passage to America. For example, even if an adventurous young immigrant were to reach New York, he could not be certain of being admitted. The U.S. Immigration authorities were often strict about debarring individuals from entry on the pretect of minor medical ailments. One of the most common causes for a "Syrian" to be debarred was the presence of trachoma.[54] Many steamship lines, in an attempt to increase the volume of their traffic, guaranteed safe passage to America by routes that carried no U.S. Immigration or health officials.[55]

Such ploys did not always work. Consequently, many emigrants who sailed from Beirut were often not certain where they were going, or where they would ultimately disembark. The fact that they were heading for "America" and the opportunities that it promised was all that drove them forward.[56] The tales told by the emigrants of the hardships they had to endure before they reached their destination are often tragic and dramatic. George Tumeh tells the story of how five brothers left Beirut for New York,[57] paying for their passage by borrowing money in Beirut. When the ship stopped in Marseilles, they discovered that their tickets did not guarantee their passage any further, and they were compelled to purchase new tickets at exorbitant prices. When the brothers finally reached America, they discovered that they were not in New York, but in Mexico. With their money completely exhausted, four of the brothers remained in Texas while the fifth began his long trek across the continent. By working in restaurants and hotels along the way, he finally reached his destination in four months.

6. Finally, one should not overlook the impact the returning emigrants had, with tales and tangible evidence of their swift economic success, in creating a psychological disposition favorable to emigration. Though the accounts were often exaggerated, they did convince many determined villagers that it was possible in a relatively short time to amass a small fortune and return home. Those who did return—and many were able to do so within three or four years—almost always chose to display their wealth by building houses with red-tiled roofs to emulate the ostentatious suburban villas that the newly emerging upper classes were building in the cities. Those graceful houses became landmarks that further advertised the opportunities to be found in America. In addition to that mode of conspicuous consumption, the returning emigrants brought back capital, which helped improve the socioeconomic standards of their communities. "No longer were departing sons an economic loss to their families or the community at large, for they began to send, or bring back with them, money in considerable amount by Syrian standards. A medical missionary reported . . . that in certain places three-fourths of the new houses were built with money earned in America."[58]

One should not belittle the impact of such "success stories." The tales—often told with dramatic gesture around the flickering light of an oil lamp on a stormy night in a mountain village with all the relatives and friends packed into the one-room cottage—undoubtedly inspired the determination and adventurous spirit of a countless number of villagers to do likewise and to seek their fortunes in the New World.

The influence that relatives had on the future course of emigration is not only apparent in the autobiographical accounts of emigrants. It is also visible in the U.S. Immigration reports for the year ending June 1909. The figures show that of the Syrians who entered the United States in the preceding twelve months, 95 percent had stated that they intended to settle with relatives or friends.[59]

What, if any, general inference can be drawn from such an experience? The magnitude and scale of immigration, substantiated by the "success stories" of Lebanese immigrants abroad, have prompted some observers to perceive emigration and the decision to uproot oneself as a felicitous and positive phenomena. It is, after all, the daring and adventurous, the able-bodied and determined, those inspired by a passion for progress—as compared with those who remained behind and were incapable of undertaking this adventure—who willfully decide to break away from their familiar surroundings and seek the unknown. As John F. Kennedy—himself a descendant of a family of emigrants—once said: "There is nothing more extraordinary than the decision to emigrate, nothing more extraordinary than this accumulation of feelings and thoughts which finally makes a family decide to say goodbye to the community within which it has lived for centuries, to break old bonds, leave the familiar landscape and cross the threatening oceans in the direction of an unknown land."[60] In other words, more than poverty and oppression, it was the unknown land that was the cause of emigration, particularly as it provided the image of a promised land where prosperity and happiness were within the reach of all.[61]

Notes

1. As a young man, al-Bishalany was so impressed by the teachings of the Protestant missionaries that he felt impelled to disseminate them in his conservative Maronite village. As a result, he incurred the hostility of both his family and local clergy and came to the U.S. to pursue his training in theology. Hardly two years after his arrival, he died of tuberculosis without completing his studies. For further details, see Philip K. Hitti, *Muhajirah al-Suriyin wa Istimarihim bayn al-Ahd al-Finiqi wa al-Ahd al-Hadir* (Syrian emigration and colonization between the Phoenician era and present times) (New York: Al-Matbaah Al-Tijariyah al-Suriyah al-Amrikiyah, 1919).

2. For further details see Habib Ibrahim Katibah, *Arab-Speaking Americans* (New York: Institute of Arab American Affairs, 1946), p. 5; William Nimeh, *History of the Lebanon* (Mexico, D.F.: Editoria Nacional, 1954), pp. 395–96; and Adele L. Younis, "The Arabs Who Followed Columbus," *Arab World,* pt. I (March 1966): pp. 13–14; pt. II (August 1966): pp. 14–15.

3. Najib E. Saliba, "Emigration from Syria," *Arab Studies Quarterly* 3, no. 1 (1981): 61.

4. National Bureau of Economic Research, *Statistics,* vol. I of *International Migrations,* ed. W. F. Willcox (New York: National Bureau of Economic Research, 1929), p. 384.

5. Lucius Hopkins Miller, *Our Syrian Population: A Study of Syrian Communities of Greater New York* (N.p. 1903), p. 19.

6. Louise Seymour Houghton, "Syrians in the United States," *Survey,* 26 (1911), 484; Habib Ibrahim Katibah, "Syrian Americans," in *Our Racial and National Minorities,* ed. Francis J. Brown and Joseph S. Roucek (New York: Office of War Information, 1937), p. 431.

7. Abdul-Latif Tibawi, *American Interests in Syria 1800–1901* (Oxford: Clarendon Press, 1966), p. 238.

8. Leland James Gordon, *American Relations with Turkey 1830–1930: An Economic Interpretation* (Philadelphia: University of Pennsylvania Press, 1932), p. 315.

9. Saliba, "Emigration from Syria," p. 60; Philip K. Hitti, *A Short History of Lebanon* (New York: St. Martin's Press, 1965), p. 207.

10. Frank L. Auerbach, *Immigration Laws of the United States* (Indianapolis: Bobbs-Merrill Company, Inc., 1955).

11. For further details, see ibid., pp. 47, 51.

12. Philip K. Hitti, *The Syrians in America* (New York: Doran, 1924), p. 65.

13. Hitti, "The Emigrants," in *Al-Hoda, 1898–1968* (New York: Al-Hoda Press, 1968), p. 133.

14. Ibid., p. 132.

15. See, among others, Saliba, "Emigration from Syria," pp. 65–66.

16. See Helen Hatab, "Syrian-American Ethnicity: Structure and Ideology in Transition," M.A. thesis, American University of Beirut, 1975, p. 44.

17. Philip K. Hitti, "al-Suriyyun fi al-Wilayat al-Muttahidah" (The Syrians in the United States), *al-Mugtataf* 60, no. 1 (1922), 122; Hitti, *Syrians in America*, p. 57.

18. Saliba, "Emigration from Syria," p. 66.

19. Hitti, *Syrians in America*, p. 58.

20. Ibid.

21. See Edward Prince Hutchinson, *Immigrants and their Children, 1850–1950* (New York: John Wiley and Sons, 1956), p. 19.

22. For further details, see Jeremiah W. Jenks and W. Jett Lauck, *The Immigration Problem* (New York: Funk and Wagnalls, 1917), p. 35.

23. Maurice Davie, *World Immigration, with Special Reference to the United States* (New York: Macmillan, 1936), p. 265.

24. Miller, *Our Syrian Population*, p. 28.

25. Jenks and Lauck, *Immigration Problem*, p. 449.

26. Houghton, "Syrians in U.S.," p. 483.

27. George Tum̆eh, *Al-Mughtaribun al-Arab fi Amrika al-Shamaliyyah* (The Arab emigrants in North America) (Damascus: Wizarat al-Thaqafah wa al-Irshad al-Qawmi, 1965), pp. 54–61.

28. Morroe Berger, "Americans from the Arab World," in *The World of Islam: Studies in Honour of Philip K. Hitti*, ed. James Kritzeck and R. Bayly Winder (London: Macmillan, 1960), p. 355.

29. Houghton, "Syrians in U.S.," p. 658.

30. Berger, "Americans from the Arab World," p. 355.

31. Afif I. Tannous, "Acculturation of an Arab-Syrian Community in the Deep South," *American Sociological Review* 8, no. 3 (1943): 264–71; Berger, "Americans from the Arab World," 355.

32. For a critical assessment of this notion and its advocates, see Nabih Amin Faris, "Lebanon, 'Land of Light,' " in *The World of Islam: Studies in Honour of Philip K. Hitti*, ed. James Kritzeck and R. Bayly Winder (London: Macmillan, 1960), pp. 336–50.

33. See, for example, Asad Rustum, *Lubnan fi Ahd al-Mutesarrifiyah* (Lebanon during the Mutesarrifate) (Beirut: Al-Nar Publishing House, 1973); Lahd Khatir, *Ahd al-Mutessarifiyyin fi Lubnan* (Epoch of the Mutesarrifs in Lebanon) (Beirut: Lebanese University Publications, 1967); Samir Khalaf, *Persistence and Change in Nineteenth Century Lebanon* (Beirut: American University, 1979); and Saliba, "Emigration from Syria."

34. For further details, see Khatir, *Epoch of the Mutesarrifs*, pp. 197–201; and Philip K. Hitti, *Lebanon in History* (London: Macmillan 1957), pp. 483–86.

35. See Safa, *Lemigration libanise*, pp. 195–98.

36. See his "Preface" in Salloum Mokarzel, *Tarikh al-Tijarah al-Suriyah fi al-Mahajir al-Amrikiyah* (The history of Syrian trade in the Americas), vol. 1 (New York: Al-Matbaah al-Suriyah al-Amrikiyah, 1929), p. 8.

37. Hitti, *Syrians in America,* pp. 48–49.

38. Saliba, "Emigration from Syria," p. 63.

39. See Wadih Amin Deeb, *Al-Shir al-Arabi fi al-Mahjar al-Amriki* (Arab poetry in America) (Beirut: Dar Rihani li-l-Tabaah wa al-Nashr, 1955).

40. Abraham Rihbany, *A Far Journey* (Boston: Houghton Mifflin Company, 1914), p. 172.

41. Hitti, *Syrians in America,* p. 51.

42. Hitti, *Muhajirah al-Suriyin,* pp. 51–52.

43. Edward Atiyah, *An Arab Tells His Story* (London: John Murray, 1946), p. 27.

44. Said Himadeh, *Economic Organization of Syria* (Beirut: American University, 1936), p. 16; and Charles Issawi, *The Economic History of the Middle East, 1800–1914: A Book of Readings* (Chicago: University of Chicago Press, 1966), p. 269.

45. Henry Jessup, *Fifty-Three Years in Syria,* vol. 1 (New York: Fleming Revell Company, 1910), p. 204.

46. Muhammad Kurd Ali, *Khitat al-Sham,* vol. 3 (Damascus: Matbaat al-Mufid, 1925), p. 93.

47. Hitti, *Syrians in America,* p. 52.

48. Saliba, "Emigration from Syria," p. 64.

49. Kamal Salibi, *The Modern History of Lebanon* (London: Weidenfeld and Nicolson, 1965), p. 137.

50. Philip K. Hitti, "The Impact of the West on Syria and Lebanon in the Nineteenth Century," *Journal of World History* 2, no. 3 (1955): 616–17.

51. Hitti, *Syrians in America,* p. 55.

52. See, among others, Henry Pratt Fairchild, *Immigrant Backgrounds* (New York: John Wiley and Sons, 1927), p. 267; and John R. Commons, *Races and Immigrants in America* (New York: Macmillan, 1907), p. 100.

53. See Gordon, *American Relations with Turkey,* p. 302; and Mokarzal, *History of Syrian Trade,* p. 11.

54. Hitti, *Syrians in America,* pp. 65–66.

55. See Houghton, "Syrians in U.S.," p. 491, for further details.

56. Younis, "Arabs Who Followed Columbus," p. 14.

57. Tum̋eh, *Arabs Emigrants in North America,* p. 14.

58. Tibawi, *American Interests in Syria,* p. 279.

59. Michael Shibli, *Al-Muhajirah al-Lubnaniyah: Bahth Ilmi, Ijtimai, Iqtisadi* (Lebanese emigration: a scientific, social and economic survey) (Beirut: Catholic Press, 1927), p. 12; Mukarzel, *History of Syrian Trade,* p. 10; and Safa, *History of Syrian Trade,* p. 180.

60. John F. Kennedy, *A Nation of Immigrants* (New York: Harper and Row, 1964), p. 4.

61. Sélim Abou, "The Myth and Reality of Emigration," *Cultures* 7, no. 2 (1980): 77.

Early Arab-Americans

The Search for Identity

MICHAEL W. SULEIMAN

METHODOLOGY AND SOURCES

This study is of the views that Arabs held of themselves as well as of America and the Americans in the century preceding World War II. The study is based on three major sources: biographies and autobiographies of Arabs who came and settled in the U.S.; memoirs and travelogues written by Arab visitors to America; and articles appearing in *The Syrian World,* the main English-language journal of the Arab-American community in the 1920s. Many of the sources have not been adequately utilized, if utilized at all, in research and writing on Arab-Americans. The sources need to be used jointly, since they supplement each other, and as mentioned below, if used separately, they might provide misleading or inadequate information.

A word about the term "Arab" appearing in the title is in order. It refers to the Arabic-speaking groups and individuals who emigrated to the U.S. from the late nineteenth century to the beginning of World War II. They are often referred to as Syrian or Syrian-Lebanese, since most of them came from that geographic region. The interchangeability of those terms reflects an absence of a definite, precise, or enduring identity. Much of the paper is a discussion of that very point. As will soon become obvious, Arab views of America were shaped in part by American views of the Arabs, which, in turn, affected their identity, the view the Arabs held of themselves.

The paper focuses on three main areas, namely, the general view of America, its society, and its accomplishments; the Arabs' search for a niche in their new homeland; and the Arab views of American democracy and what role the Arabs play in the political system.

GENERAL VIEW OF AMERICA

People from the Arabic-speaking countries began to come to the United States in sizable numbers late in the nineteenth century, but their knowledge and views of, and attitudes toward, America were formed some thirty to forty years earlier. In particular, the population of geographic or greater Syria began to come in contact with Americans as early as the 1820s, when Protestant missionaries arrived and set up schools, medical facilities, and an Arabic printing press. When the missionaries failed miserably in their quest to convert Muslims to Christianity, they turned their attention to a task almost as important to them, namely, the salvation of souls captured by other Christian sects. Salvation was to be accomplished through the enticement of educational and medical facilities.[1] Regardless of the motivation, however, the "Syrian" population reacted positively to the American missionaries and, by extension, to Americans generally and to their homeland.

Among the first Arabic-language books about the Americans to be published was a French volume that was ordered translated by the Egyptian government in the 1840s.[2] Since most Arabs at the time were illiterate, however, their views of America were influenced primarily by two factors. One was the direct observation of Americans working or traveling in the region; the other was the reports, often embellished and exaggerated, that returning or visiting "Syrian" immigrants brought back. In both cases, the picture painted was somewhat unreal or at least incomplete in that it was highly positive, with hardly any mention of problems, hardships, or difficulties of any kind.[3] While almost all writers of, or about, that period record positive views, Salom Rizk captures that ethos better than any other writer when he reports his teacher's description of America:

> *[America] is really a country like heaven, and you cannot know what it is like until you have been there. . . . So many wonderful, unbelievable things my schoolmaster told me . . . the land of hope . . . the land of peace . . . the land of contentment . . . the land of liberty . . . the land of brotherhood . . . the land of plenty . . . where God has poured out wealth . . . where the dreams of men come true . . . where everything is bigger and grander . . . and more beautiful than it has ever been anywhere else in the world . . . where wheat grows waist high, shoulder high, sky high, and as thick as the hair on your head . . . where mountains press their snowy heads against the sky . . . where forests teem with trees as plentiful as the sands of the sea . . . where men do the deeds of giants and think the thoughts of God . . . where they harness rivers of water to turn great machines and drench the land with light . . . where merely the push of a button does the work of thousands of horses and donkeys and camels and men . . . and schools . . . schools everywhere, in cities, in towns, in villages, and even where there are no villages . . . where everybody has a chance to learn, even the humblest Syrian immigrant . . . where there are medals and honors and prizes waiting to be won . . . where every boy and girl can learn to be what he or she wants to be. . . .*[4]

As Rizk himself admits, the text "sound[s] like the fairylands my grandmother used to tell me about."[5] Yet, despite the fact that people knew fairylands and fairies did not exist, many of them, like Rizk, "wanted to believe all this, . . . had to believe it, and . . . did."[6] Though America was great, it was not exactly paradise on earth, and many Arabic-speaking immigrants found the hardships too much to bear and returned home. Others joined the ranks of the toiling masses, and some even became terrible failures. Committing suicide was a way out for some.[7] We have, however, only brief and sketchy accounts of the failures. The main sources of our research are the biographies, autobiographies, and memoirs of successful immigrants. Indeed, some wrote to record and perhaps magnify that success, and in the process not only heaped glory on themselves but also glorified the country that made such success possible. I add this cautionary note merely to illustrate that available sources do not provide a complete or, at times, even an accurate picture.

It should be pointed out that for most of the immigrants, the trip to the United States was a difficult, if not shattering, experience. Most of them were illiterate and could speak only Arabic, had little or no money, and fell prey to charlatans and thieves, often from among their own people—especially in the French ports where they normally embarked on their journey across the Atlantic.[8] Since they mainly traveled steerage, their accommodations were poor, and in case of rough seas the journey was a nightmare. The eager immigrants did not, however, associate the misery of their travel with America. Indeed, they saw America as the haven from such miseries. As soon as they spotted the Statue of Liberty, they forgot their troubles and began to imagine the life of freedom and the great wealth they would soon accumulate. One more hurdle however—and a major one at that—had to be overcome: the check and entry point at Ellis Island. Even by the accounts of the "successful" immigrants, the experience at Ellis Island was frightening. Everyone was apprehensive that something might go wrong or that a dreaded disease—usually trachoma—might prevent them from entering the new "promised land." For those who passed that hurdle, a new world with all its great opportunities and many challenges awaited them. But first they wanted to see and appreciate the great wonder they had heard and/or read about.

Even in our own day, visitors from the Arab world to America experience much excitement and delight at the great engineering and architectural feats of New York City. Obviously, the contrast between America and the Middle East was much greater a century ago. One can imagine, therefore, the awe that early Arab immigrants experienced upon arrival in America (usually landing in New York City first), an aspect barely mentioned in the few autobiographies that have been published. Apparently, by the time these Arabs wrote their memoirs, the wonders had become commonplace—at least to the potential readers of their books. To recapture that excitement and wonder, therefore, we have to turn to accounts by Arab travelers to America who returned and wrote for their countrymen, in Arabic, about the New World.

Every single visitor, it seems, marveled at the huge skyscrapers, the speed and precision of the elevators taking passengers up and down the many floors, the beautiful and huge bridges, the speed and congestion of traffic in New York City, and the overwhelming number of people of all nationalities and races going about their business in a peaceful, orderly fashion. All the writers also seemed to comment on the impressive plans of cities, where streets were designed to parallel each other and to cross almost at right angles—and often to be given numbers, rather than names. Thus, Muhammad al-Batanuni, writing in 1930, says that it is impossible for him to find a description fitting of the greatness of New York City, and he resorts, therefore, to using the term "great" and multiplying it thousands of times.[9] Amir Boktor, on the other hand, conveys his sense of wonder through a detailed description of the major structures of New York City, including the Woolworth building—at that time (1926) the tallest structure in the world. He then proceeds to write about the transportation system, including the subway, and the communication facilities, especially the telephone. Most of the electrical gadgets that are today taken for granted are described in minute detail, as if they were almost magical. To Boktor, however, the true industrial greatness of America is manifested in the home—where electricity is used for cooking, washing, drying, ironing, vacuuming, carpet cleaning, and water heating. All that is possible and available twenty-four hours a day, every day, and in every room in the house—even in the homes of lower middle-class people.[10] In other words, even the poorer sectors of the American population, thanks to the industrial revolution and the general wealth of the country, often had more of the daily comforts and luxuries of life than the rich people back in the Arab world!

New York City was not, of course, the only repository of greatness, and the travelers went on to describe the great buildings and bridges in the other big cities of the land, including Boston, Washington, D.C., Chicago, San Francisco, and Los Angeles.[11] The newcomer to America, having experienced that dazzling display of progress, greatness, and wonder, usually asked himself the "secret" behind those accomplishments. According to Boktor, "there is consensus that among the most important factors is the introduction of required courses in handicrafts and vocational training in elementary and secondary schools."[12] To Fuad Sarruf, however, the secret of America's greatness lies in the American character. Among the best and most important qualities in this regard are the love of, and respect for, work; the willingness to undertake major projects; the rush to adopt any and all profitable new techniques; and the freedom from any psychological or social inhibitions that normally bind the hands of the wealthy in Europe.[13]

The point is that wonder, excitement, and fascination with the greatness of America was very much a part of the view that Arabic-speaking immigrants had of their new world. They also communicated that extremely positive picture to their countrymen back home. While the immigrants suffered some heartaches and disappointments, they usually overcame such handicaps. Alternatively, they tried to compensate for, or alleviate, them by asking their relatives and close friends to join them in America. It was thus possible for many of them to truly have the advantages of both the old and the new countries combined, that is, the close family ties and the great material benefits.

IDENTITY

Bringing family members did not merely provide additional needed man- and womanpower. More important was the need to be with one's own people, especially since, as Hitti has noted, the "Syrian home-life is one of the best features of his entire life."[14] The early Arab immigrants, it must be remembered, were mainly Ottoman citizens or, more accurately, Ottoman subjects. Especially the Christians among them identified little, if at all, with their Turkish overlords. The concept of Arabism or Arab nationalism was then still rather nebulous and weak. Even attachment to a specific political entity (i.e., country) was to come later, after the dismemberment of the former Ottoman provinces. Thus, the early Arabic-speaking immigrants, coming mainly from the Asian part of the Middle East, thought of themselves primarily in terms of family and sect and gloried in their former homelands' wonderful physical environment. Again in the words of Hitti,

> *The Syrian is the man without a country* par excellence. *His patriotism takes the form of love for family and sect, and when expressed in inanimate terms, love for the unexcelled scenery of Syria with its glorious sunshine and invigorating air. Syrian patriotism has no political aspects.*[15]

What happened then to such individuals and groups when they came to the United States? Since most early arrivals came with the idea of staying only long enough to accumulate a fortune and return home, no identity questions arose at first. They were mere transients who sought and found social and psychological security within their family and church. The longer they stayed, however, the more obvious it became that America was not to be a mere temporary abode and that they had to make specific adjustments to accommodate the new environment and find the proper role for themselves within it. Unquestionably, the family and church continued to play a major role in the self-identity of "Arab" immigrants. In fact, among older Arab-Americans I have interviewed, a large majority have indicated that their greatest pride derives from their church activity over the years—especially the initial effort to raise and donate funds to build a church and recruit a priest from the old country. Also, in various memoirs, the association with the church or mosque is mentioned and, at times, emphasized.[16] Bashara Forzley, for instance, reports that he, his wife, and his children were involved in church activities and donated funds for two stained-glass windows in their church in Worcester, Massachusetts. Included in his book is a copy of the "Certificate of Service" given to him by the Syrian Antiochian Orthodox Archdiocese of New York and North America for almost fifty years of dedication and assistance. Furthermore, he records as "one of the most memorable episodes of my life" that he was asked to build a wing at the Saint Mary Convent in Saidinayia, Syria, in the name of his hometown, Karhoun. Forzley then saved money specifically for that purpose and had the wing built; it served as an inn for the Karhoun people whenever they made the pilgrimage to Saidinayia.[17]

While brief references to church activity are found in various Arab-American autobiographies, Philip and Joseph Kayal have provided us with useful documentation and a most worthwhile study showing the importance of the church as a source of identity for Melkites and Maronites in America.[18] The same was true of other Arabic-speaking Christian and Muslim denominations in the United States.

In their contacts with other American groups, Arabic-speaking immigrants and communities quickly felt the need to determine their own identity. Even before they made a conscious decision to stay permanently in the U.S., they discovered that ethnic or racial tolerance was not always practiced toward them. This is the one major area in which we detect a strong resentment against "Americans" and a negative view of America. The immigrants objected to being identified as "Turks" or "Other Asians," as the U.S. immigration and census records referred to them up to 1920. In fact, much of the time they left their native lands specifically to escape the tyranny, persecution, corruption, and military service of the Ottoman overlords. Besides, most early immigrants were Christian, whereas to Americans the term "Turk" was synonymous with Islam and Muslims—which were generally viewed negatively in the United States.[19] In the end, some identification had to be made, so they were called, and they called themselves, Syrians, that is, the people who came from geographic or greater Syria.

The Syrians' view of America was determined, in part at least, by how Americans viewed them. Here it is worthwhile to note that the available autobiographical accounts hardly mention, and then only in mild form, any discrimination or bias directed toward Syrian-Americans. Abraham Rihbany and George Haddad, for instance, do not write on the subject.[20] Rizk refers to a sense of insecurity and timidity, which stayed with him for a while after he was verbally assaulted for being a foreigner. That and other incidents made Rizk wonder at times, "Why did I have to be born in Syria, anyway, and fall heir to all this contempt, ridicule, and abuse?"[21] Ashad Hawie reports coming across Americans of a specific region who "seem to have a spirit of hatred towards all foreigners."[22] George Hamid relates how the girl he was courting, and whom he eventually married, did not like Arabs—this despite the fact that her sister was married to an Arab named Hassan Ben Ali, whom she described as the "finest person who ever lived."[23] Her mother also did not like Arabs, Syrians, Lebanese, and the like because she was "Jersey City aristocracy."[24] Among the early immigrants, Dr. Michael Shadid definitely related more incidents of bias and discrimination against him as a foreigner and a Syrian than did any other writer of memoirs. Still, he did not write much. He wrote, for instance, that he changed his name to Shade "to mitigate the prejudices against a foreigner that I have met with in many parts of the country."[25] However, he was easily persuaded by the dean of his medical school to return to his Syrian name because "many people prefer to go to a foreign doctor instead of a native."[26] Prejudice and discrimination against him apparently persisted, nevertheless—but the two accounts of his life do not dwell much on "racial" bias. We do know, however, that in the 1920s, Shadid raised a major controversy among his own people when he tried to show, in his words, that "Syrians, like the Jews, were socially ostracised in this country because of the prejudice that exists against our race."[27] He also attacked some of his own people for ignoring the issue, "those who, ostrich-like, bury their heads in the sand."[28]

The problem of social ostracism and discrimination against "Syrians" in America was discussed at length in many articles in *The Syrian World*, especially ones by the Rev. W. A. Mansur. Perhaps the strongest statement on the issue came in an article titled "Problems of Syrian Youth in America." The first problem discussed was that of "race" prejudice, and Mansur wrote:

> *I sympathize with Syrian-American youth because I know the meaning, suffering, and consequences of race prejudice. I have seen my crucifiers plan my crucifixion, prepare the cross, and with hammer and nails crucify me on that cross."*[29]

The issue of prejudice and discrimination was closely tied to the popularity and widespread acceptance at the time of racial, ethnic, and sociological theories claiming that distinct racial types or groups existed and that some races were superior and others inferior.[30] Because Americans believed that notion to be true, American legislators passed laws restricting the entry into the United States of members of inferior races so as to prevent any contamination and/or weakening of the "American" stock.[31] However, legislators were not unanimous as to the number and kinds of races and as to which peoples or nations belonged to which races. Often, in fact, the term "race" was used to designate a specific ethnic group or nation. Immigration officials and courts spent much time and effort trying to determine whether or not a particular group belonged to a specific race and whether that group was eligible for entry into the U.S. and/or for the acquisition of U.S. citizenship.[32] The problem of racial identification and citizenship traumatized the Arabic-speaking community for several years early in the century. Indeed, to resolve it the erstwhile "Syrian" community went searching for its roots and emerged to declare itself Arab and hence Caucasian, and therefore, eligible for U.S. citizenship!

In brief, the events took the following course. "Syrians" had come in large numbers and were admitted into the U.S. and granted U.S. citizenship since the 1880s. In 1914, however, a certain George Dow was denied petition to become a U.S. citizen by Judge Henry A. M. Smith, district judge in Charleston, South Carolina. The denial was based on the asumption that Dow, as a "Syrian of Asiatic birth," was not a free white person within the meaning of the statute approved on March 26, 1790.[33] In the words of Joseph W. Ferris, "this decision raised considerable discussion and controversy throughout the Syrian communities in the United States, resulting in an application for a rehearing."[34] The call for a rehearing spurred earlier efforts by the "Syrian" community to research its background and discover its roots. The major work on the issue was prepared by Kalil A. Bishara at the suggestion, and with the encouragement, of N. A. Mokarzel, the editor of *Al-Hoda* and the most "Syrian" or, especially later, most "Lebanese" member of the community. Bishara found, perhaps not surprisingly, that Syrians were really Arabs. As Bishara wrote in the English section of his *Origin of the Modern Syrian:*

> *Geographically speaking, Syria is naturally a part of Arabia. . . . At the present time, taking the country in general into consideration, about 75 percent of the Syrian people are Muslims, and consequently for the most part, pure Arabs. The Druzes of Syria are nearly all of Arab descent, originally migrating from Hira and Yemen, Arabia. Even the Christians of Syria have a liberal proportion of Arab blood in their veins—especially in the North, South and East. In a word, Modern Syria may be safely regarded a part of the Arabian world, with regard to language, customs and blood.*[35]

Obviously, since Syrians were Arabs and Arabs were the "purest type of the Semitic race," and had a "better claim upon the White Race than that of any modern nation of Europe," it followed, therefore, that a Syrian, that is, an Arab, was indeed a "free white person" within the meaning of the naturalization statute.[36] Unfortunately, Judge Smith was not convinced and the rehearing affirmed the previous decision.[37] On appeal, the decision was reversed, however, and Syrians/Arabs were once again eligible for citizenship.[38]

The discovery that Syrians were indeed Arabs did not mean that the

Arabic-speaking community suddenly and completely adopted a new identity. The evidence does not support such a conclusion. In fact, the community continued to think of itself and to be generally indentified as "Syrian"—until other factors intervened. Before discussing the other factors, however, we should reiterate the importance of one factor already mentioned, namely American prejudice against Muslims. Thus, even in the very document used to show the "oneness" of Syrians and Arabs, the author (and perhaps his publisher/patron) was cautious to exclude any reference to individuals toward whom Americans might feel strong antipathy. Thus, when Bishara made a summary statement in defense of his case, he wrote:

> *I most emphatically declare that our [American] national character needs the Semitic element in it. That 'pliability combined with iron fixity of purpose,' which has developed a Moses, an Elijah, a Hannibal, an Amos, a Paul, a Peter, a John, not to begin to enumerate that large host of Fathers, Prophets and Apostles.*[39]

Obviously, it is an impressive list of luminaries of whom any people would be proud. But the list is missing the specific name of one major prophet, namely Muhammad. This was no mere memory lapse, since the Arabic text of the same book includes Muhammad's name, just as the English text, I believe, intentionally excludes him.[40]

After World War I geographic Syria was divided into many parts and "administered" by two European powers, Britain and France. Also, France encouraged and/or reinforced divisions based on ethnic or religious sectarianism, emphasizing its own role as protector of Catholics in the Middle East, especially the Maronites in Lebanon. That development and the creation of an enlarged and independent Republic of Lebanon in the 1920s coincided with a definite realization on the part of Arabic-speaking Americans that they really had no intention of returning to their native lands and that they had struck roots in America. The realization did not come easily nor was it accepted willingly. It also often came after a serious attempt was made to resettle in the old country. Many then discovered that "you can't go home again." While almost all of the published memoirs make reference to that phenomenon, Dr. Shadid illustrates it best. Thus, in February 1927, Shadid wrote an article in *The Syrian World* titled "Syria for the Syrians," in which he argued forcefully that "Syria is the proper place, the best country in the world, for the Syrian people."[41] About a year and a half later, the same Dr. Shadid wrote in the same journal an article titled " 'Syria for the Syrians' Again: An Explanation and a Retraction." Why the change and why so quickly? During that eighteen months, the author went on a trip back home, taking along his oldest daughter, Ruth, who "would be my barometer, for from her reactions I would know how her sisters and brothers would take to the transplanting."[42]

It is worthwhile to note that while hardly any Arab-American authors reported culture shock upon coming to the United States, many, if not most, reported experiencing a major culture shock on their return home—especially if the trip was made many years after the initial emigration. The same was also true for Dr. Shadid. He expected to see a great deal of progress, especially after a thirty-years' absence and the coming of friendly France to Lebanon. Instead, "Beirut, and indeed the whole country, was as primitive as it had been when I had left it thirty years before."[43] According to him, Beirut harbored much chaos, cheating, bribery, and filth. It was as if he were seeing Lebanon with new eyes. In a way he was—through the eyes of his own children, born and raised in the United States. Thus, he wrote that "Ruth was visibly shocked and frightened. She didn't even want to land, and asked if we couldn't return to the United States at once."[44] Many others encountered similar problems—for which they were not prepared. Reverend Mansur wrote:

> *Syrian parents had been living with the hope of an early return to the homeland. The Great War now marks the dividing line between the old and the new in Syrian-American thinking. Syrian-Americans awoke to the fact that they had become accustomed to, and part of, American thought and life, and that a return to the homeland would be impracticable.*[45]

Once one made the decision to stay in America, many other questions had to be answered, including: How are the children to be raised? What traditions and values are to be retained? Which ones should be dropped or changed? Is Arabic to be forgotten or should special classes or schools be set up to teach the children Arabic? Should the churches also Americanize? If they do, and Arabic is no longer used in the liturgy, will the Syrians/Arabs lose their identity? These and related issues were discussed at length—often without reaching a satisfactory conclusion.[46] In particular, the identity question was not, and I believe could not be, resolved adequately and for good. Since this chapter treats the problem only to the late 1930s, I will take up the question in another study. Suffice it to say here that the identity of a people is not an innate characteristic but is, rather, shaped by many outside factors and elements of self-selection—such is the case with Arabic-speaking Americans.

GOVERNMENT, POLITICS, AND POLITICAL PARTICIPATION

To assess properly the issue of political participation, we should first begin by presenting the views of the early Arab arrivals concerning government, politics, and democracy. Practically all of them, Christian or Muslim, when asked why they came to America or what they found wonderful about America, mention freedom and the absence of oppression. Their response is understandable since almost all they had known under Ottoman rule was oppression and fear. The government was there to harass and exploit them. At times it even helped divide the population and get different factions to fight and kill each other. The major conflicts of the mid-nineteenth century, especially the massacres of 1860, were believed to be, in good part, the handiwork of the Ottoman authorities. The rulers plundered the land, discriminated against its Christian inhabitants, engineered or encouraged sectarian strife, and showed no justice or mercy.[47] Politics was the province and preserve of the leaders of each *millet,* or sect, whereas, the rest of the population avoided, like the plague, any contact with government and any semblance of political activity. Those who were not leaders did not identify with or feel an attachment to the government, the empire, or any particular country. As Rihbany put it:

> *I could claim no nationality and no flag. The rule of the Turk, especiallly during the reign of the ruthless Abdul-Hamid, was painfully repressive. Under it love of freedom and of progress was a crime against the state. The hawk-eyed detectives of the tyrant infected the land and haunted with fear the souls of our influential, forward-looking citizens. . . . [N]othing was really secure in a land where the ruler maintained a firm hold upon his subjects by promoting divisions and instigating massacres among them.*[48]

It was little wonder, therefore, that so many, especially Christians, were so bitter and disappointed—and ready to leave the "unbeloved empire." In Rihbany's words: "We left our 'mother country' with nothing but curses for her Government on our lips."[49]

It must be remembered that most of the early Arabic-speaking immigrants came to the United States primarily for economic reasons and, were not interested, therefore, in the civic or political spheres of their "temporary home"—except that they enjoyed the fruits of a democratic system, especially freedom from fear and oppression. Their idea of good citizenship was to obey the law and be patriotic. Indeed, the available evidence seems to indicate that in their citizenship and patriotism, Arabic-speaking Americans did extremely well and perhaps excelled most other ethnic groups. As an early study indicated: "In his love of law and order the Syrian cannot be excelled. . . . The universal testimony of the police authorities is that there is no more peaceful or law abiding race in New York City."[50] Louise Houghton, writing a few years later, reinforced that assessment using almost the same language.[51] Furthermore, in my interviews with older Arab-Americans, the one source of pride most often mentioned as a "contribution" to America is that people's respect for the law and the institutions of the United States.

Patriotism is another aspect of political participation in which Arab-Americans have excelled and of which they are extremely proud. As is the case with any other group or people, the persistent emphasis on patriotism and blind obedience is more often found among the military. Thus, Hawie's book, perhaps also because it was written during World War II, is replete with exhortations to patriotism—and declarations about how patriotic Syrian-Americans are. He himself was a much-decorated officer and was the recipient of the Purple Heart for his service and injury in World War I. He also reported that, according to the company commanders he interviewed, Syrians made good soldiers—and many of them served in America's armed forces.[52] That fact was indeed verified by military documents showing that "no less than 13,965 or about 7% of the whole Syrian community served in the United States army" in World War I.[53]

Among the most interesting books (and so far as I know the first book) written on the above-mentioned subject was *The Syrian Soldier in Three Wars,* published in Arabic in 1919.[54] The author, Lt. Gabriel Ward, primarily recounted his own military activity in the Spanish-American war, against the guerrillas in the Philippines, and in World War I. But he also included vignettes and/or short accounts and pictures of a number of other Arabic-speaking Americans who served in those three wars. The book begins with a picture of the American flag, which the author identifies as the symbol of freedom, democracy, and great glory. Also, throughout the book the author records his pride in serving his new country and heaps praise upon his fellow Syrians who also joined the U.S. armed forces and distinguished themselves in defending America.

In addition to serving the U.S. military with distinction, the Arabic-speaking community repeatedly reiterated its loyalty to America. Reverend Mansur wrote:

> *We Syrian-Americans stand for America first. We were made Americans first in our hearts, we have made America our permanent homeland, and we chose to be Americans first and nothing else. . . . We give first place to our American homeland, to the flag that guards our welfare, and to the Constitution that guarantees our freedom.*[55]

Over and over again, unquestioning loyalty was emphasized—and any aspects of dissent or new ideas were attacked as perhaps undermining the American system.[56] Thus, American democracy was greatly admired and staunchly, often blindly, defended. The system was almost too sacred to be tampered with. Besides, Syrian-Americans concentrated their full energies on other pursuits, primarily commercial. Perhaps the best account of Syrian-American political "activity" early in this century was provided by Lucius Miller, who wrote as follows about the "Syrian":

> *Born and bred under Turkish despotism, he appreciates the fruits of the democratic system without comprehending the nature of that system, or the individual responsibility inherent in it. He is usually sentimentally enthusiastic over the country and the President, boasts of his citizenship, papers his walls with lithographs of great Americans, and is most*

proud of his American-born son; but his real interest in the affairs of the country is that of self-interest.[57]

In his classic 1924 study of Syrians in America, Hitti devoted exactly two brief paragraphs to their political activities. According to him, "Syrians cut no figure in the political life of this nation. Very few of them interest themselves in politics or aspire to office."[58] It should be added, however, that that categorical statement referred only to an absence of participation in specifically American politics, since, within the Arabic-speaking community, political competition and infighting were rife.

Even when applied to the American political scene, however, Hitti's statement is more accurate and pertinent in reference to high elective offices on the state and national levels. Otherwise, while political participation by members of the early Arab-American community appears to have been limited, their role was not entirely passive. Thus, intercommunal conflicts arose occasionally and had to be dealt with, often with the help of the local priest acting as an intermediary.[59] Also, among those employed in factories, some did participate in strike activity. Lawrence, Massachusetts, for instance, which early in this century had the second largest Syrian community in the United States (after New York City), witnessed a major and violent strike in 1912 at the Wood and Washington Mills. Syrians participated in that labor-management confrontation, which lasted about three months. In fact, one Syrian was stabbed, and the Syrian band led the strike parade. According to Donald Cole, the "three Syrians on the strike committee were particularly important."[60]

Also, though few in number, the educated among the early Arabic-speaking immigrants did participate in American politics, but not as elected officials. Thus, Hitti and Rihbany, for example, were active in educating the public about the Arab world and various Middle East issues, including the Palestine question—in their writings, speeches, and policy statements. F. M. Al Akl and Michael Shadid, both medical doctors, demonstrated their concern for their fellow humans by being active in progressive and cooperative organizations. Specifically, Al Akl helped establish the Beacon Society, and then joined, and gave speeches on behalf of, the Edward Bellamy Society. His autobiography, *Until Summer Comes,* also criticizes society's lack of concern for the poor and the needy—both in the United States and throughout the world. He wrote:

Let us indeed labor to maintain the dynamism and virility of democracy. . . . Let us fight so that we can continue to be a healthy nation. Yet, let us never forget that we can hardly be a healthy member in the body of an unhealthy world.[61]

As for Shadid, "the founder of America's first cooperative hospital," his whole life was devoted to the idea of helping ordinary people receive good medical care at reasonable prices, through cooperative arrangements. In the process, he had to wage a long and bitter fight against the American Medical Association and its supporters in the Oklahoma legislature—a fight that he eventually won.

By and large, however, Arabic-speaking Americans did not participate much in politics, though they greatly admired the democratic process. Thus, both Rihbany and Rizk report how pleasantly surprised they were to see the losing presidential candidate gracefully accept his defeat and the victor not punish his opponents.[62] In any case, if and when Arabic-speaking Americans did join a political party, it was more likely to be the Republican Party. In general, however, the attitude was that politics was not for them, "not their bag," so to speak.[63] They avoided politics back home and were, to some extent, fearful of the consequences of any political participation here.

Perhaps Arab-Americans were also partly resigned to the futility of the whole political process. When interviewing an older Arab-American in Detroit, I asked him if he participated in politics and whether he was a Republican or a Democrat. Instead of giving me a direct answer, he proceeded to tell me a long and colorful story the purpose of which was to illustrate forcefully that, regardless of whether the Republicans or the Democrats won the elections, Arab-Americans got the shaft.[64]

It is worth noting that the early Arab community in the United States often confused "good citizenship" with avoidance of political activity, especially when such activity involved a challenge to specific laws or opposition to authority figures. Thus, especially when interviewed years after the event, Arab-American activists or their relatives would often deny or "forget" (consciously or subconsciously) their earlier political activity—perhaps in the belief that their "good citizen" image might be tarnished. For example, Ferris Marad's role in the 1912 strike in Lawrence, Massachusetts, is well documented. However, according to Cole, "When interviewed years later, Marad denied that he was influential in the strike and said he had done little more than lead one of the parades. Even then he had turned the strikers away from the mills and avoided possible use of force."[65]

SUMMARY AND CONCLUSIONS

The views of early Arab immigrants to America were shaped in part by the views they held about their own homeland as well as the views Americans held of them as a people or as individuals. Thus America was, in some respects, a mirror that reflected and sharpened the early Arab immigrants' views of themselves.

America unquestionably represented a new "promised land," a land of plenty and opportunity and freedom from oppression. People from the Arab world came to America to partake of that wealth and return to enjoy and share it with family and friends. It soon became obvious to early immigrants, most of whom were males, however, that wives and relatives would facilitate the accumulation of wealth and make life away from home more tolerable. As the realization dawned on them that "you can't go home again," an agonizing process of heart- and soul-searching was set in motion to determine a sense of identity and a relationship to the new, now permanent, environment. Several factors influenced that decision-making process, among them: 1. The experiences the Syrians/Arabs had at home and those that they brought with them to America; 2. The new political developments in the Middle East and the presence of two new Mandatory powers in the area, namely France and Britain; 3. The immigrants' religious and sectarian affiliations and the ability or inability of their churches and mosques to cope with a new environment; 4. The reaction of America and the Americans to the coming of the Arabic-speaking people to the United States; and 5. The immigrants' own personal characteristics, educational achievements, and philosophy of life. All these influences must be considered when discussing Arab views of America, especially in the areas of material wealth, freedom, religious affiliation, racial prejudice in America, and the development of an ethnic identity.

Briefly, early Arabic-speaking immigrants had learned much about America and developed a positive, almost fairy-tale image of America and the American people before they arrived in the New World. They were certainly impressed and awed by the wonders and tremendous achievements of America. Their participation in the civic and political life of the United States, at least on the national level, however, was rather limited. Their limited participation was mainly owing to their experience back home, where the family and/or the sect was the equivalent of a "nation" and where they developed an antipathy toward politics. When they discovered that America was to become their permanent home, they had to define their relationship to the new adopted mother. Their food and cuisine, their customs and social norms, were definitely Eastern or Arab and remained so without much change. Their ethnic identity and political affiliations, however, were neither definite nor secure and were, as a consequence, influenced by outside factors. They were all Arabic speaking, but were they Syrian or Lebanese or Arab? In part, at least, the response was dependent on tenuous and changing circumstances—and the response itself, therefore, was tenuous and pragmatic.

Notes

1. For a personal account of missionary activity, see Henry H. Jessup, *Fifty-Three Years in Syria*. 2 vols. (New York: Fleming H. Revell, 1910).

2. Henry Markham, *Siyahat Amrika* (Touring America), trans. Sa'ad N'am (Cairo: Dar al-Tiba'a, 1846). The original was H. Marquam, *Promenade en Amerique* (Paris: Librairie de l'enfance et de la jeunesse, 1838).

3. For a complaint that such a picture was misleading, see Abraham M. Rihbany, *A Far Journey* (Boston: Houghton-Mifflin, 1914), pp. 143–45. Thus, while the few memoirs and autobiographies written by Arab-Americans are useful research sources, they should be used with care since both by omission and commission they tell only part of the story and tend to give emphasis to particular favorite topics. They can be fruitfully supplemented by books written by Arab travelers to America and by the many articles that appeared in Arab-American journals and magazines in the early part of this century.

4. Salom Rizk, *Syrian Yankee* (Garden City, N.Y.: Doubleday, Doran & Co., 1943), pp. 70–72.

5. Ibid., p.72.

6. Ibid.

7. Saj'an A. Sa'adah, *Kitab dalil al-musafirin watarikh Amirka* (Travelers' guide and the history of America) (Ba'abda, Lebanon: Ottoman Press, 1896), pp. 82–85.

8. Ibid., p. 11.

9. Muhammad L. al-Batanuni, *Al-rihla ila Amrika* (The trip to America) (Cairo: Al-Sa'ada Press, 1930), p. 13.

10. Amir Boktor, *Al-dunia fi Amirka* (Life in America) (Cairo: Al-Matba'a al-asriyah, 1926), p. 30.

11. See the long, often dull but generally accurate description of America and Americans by a member of the Egyptian aristocracy: Muhammad Ali, *Rihlat Sumuw al-Amir Muhammad Ali Basha . . . ila al-jiha al-shamaliyah li-Amrika* (The trip of His Excellency Muhammad Ali Pasha . . . to North America) (Cairo: Al-Matba'a al-amiriyah, 1913).

12. Boktor, *Life in America,* p. 30.

13. Fu'ad Sarruf, *Mashahid al-alam al-jadid* (Views of the New World) (Cairo: Al-Matba'a al-Arabiyah, 1925), p. 19. See also Hassan Farid, *Sihir Amirka* (The magic of America), 2d ed. (Cairo: al-Matba'a al-asriyah, 1945), p 26.

14. Philip K. Hitti, *The Syrians in America* (New York: George H. Doran, 1924), p. 25.

15. Ibid., 25.

16. See, for instance, John P. Brennan's "An Interview of Hussien Hussien Ayad" (late 1970s, Mimeographed).

17. Bashara Kalil Forzley, *An Autobiography of Bashara Kalil Forzley,* ed. Philip Forzley (Worcester, Mass.: N.p., 1958), pp. 20–21.

18. Philip M. Kayal and Joseph M. Kayal, *The Syrian-Lebanese in America: A Study in Religion and Assimilation* (Boston: Twayne Publishers, 1975).

19. For various studies documenting this early anti-Muslim bias, see Helen McCready Kearney, "American Images of the Middle East, 1824–1924: A Century of Antipathy" (Ph.D. diss., University of Rochester, 1976); Edward W. Said, *Orientalism* (New York: Pantheon Books, 1978).

20. George Haddad, *Mount Lebanon to Vermont* (Rutland, Vt.: Tuttle Company, 1916).

21. Rizk, *Syrian Yankee,* p. 159; also pp. 131, 144–45, 157.

22. Ashad G. Hawie, *The Rainbow Ends* (New York: Theo Gaus' Sons, 1942), p. 62.

23. George Hamid, *Circus* (New York: Sterling Publishing Co., 1950), p. 156; see also p. 141.

24. Ibid., p. 149.

25. Michael A. Shadid, *Crusading Doctor: My Fight for Cooperative Medicine* (Boston: Meador Publishing Co., 1956), p. 35.

26. Ibid.; see also pp. 55, 57.

27. Shadid, " 'Syria for the Syrians' Again: An Explanation and a Retraction," *Syrian World* 3, no. 4. (Oct. 1928): 25.

28. Ibid. See the first article, "Syria for the Syrians," *Syrian World* 1, no. 8 (Feb. 1927): 21–24. For a brief report on the controversy and the special meeting of the American Syrian Federation of New York to discuss and resolve it, see "Discussing a Racial Problem," *Syrian World* 1, no. 11 (May 1927): 52–56.

29. Rev. W. A. Mansur, "Problems of Syrian Youth in America," *Syrian World* 2, no. 6 (Dec. 1927): 9. For a humorous treatment of this painful experience of prejudice, see William Peter Blatty, *Which Way to Mecca, Jack?* (New York: Bernard Geis Associates, 1960), pp. 27–28.

30. For a brief report on this issue, see Paul W. McBride, *Culture Clash: Immigrants and Reformers, 1880–1920* (Saratoga, Calif.: R&E Research Associates, 1975). For a condescending attitude toward "Arabs," see Edward Corsi, *In the Shadow of Liberty* (New York: Macmillan, 1935), who wrote: "About 1880 our country was deluged with numbers of fakers belonging to a group called 'Maronites', followers of Maron, a supposed saint who lived in the fifth century," pp. 265–66.

31. A good general survey is Roger Daniels, *Racism and Immigration Restriction* (Saint Charles, Mo.: Forum Press, 1974).

32. See, in particular, the "Races or Peoples" section of *Abstracts of Reports of the Immigration Commission*, vol. 1, 61st Cong., 3d sess., S. Doc. 747, vol. 7 (Washington, D.C.: Government Printing Office, 1911), pp. 217–83.

33. In Re Dow (District Court, South Carolina, 211 Fed. Rept. 486, Feb. 18, 1914).

34. Joseph W. Ferris, "Syrian Naturalization Question in the United States," pt. 1, *Syrian World* 2, no. 8 (Feb. 1928): 7.

35. Kalil A. Bishara, *The Origin of the Modern Syrian* (New York: Al-Hoda Publishing House, 1914), pp. 26–27, English section.

36. Ibid., p. 27. It should be noted here that the word "race" does not have quite the same meaning today as it did during the citizenship debates of the late 1920s, when people spoke of "blood" and other genetically oriented terms.

37. In Re Dow (District Court, South Carolina, 213 Fed. Rept. 355, April 1914).

38. Dow vs. United States et al. (Circuit Court of Appeals, Fourth District, 226 Fed. Rept. 145, Sept. 14, 1915), pp. 145–48. See also Joseph W. Ferris, "Syrian Naturalization Question in the United States," pt. 2, *Syrian World* 2, no. 9 (March 1928): 18–24.

39. Bishara, *Origin of the Modern Syrian*, p. 44.

40. Ibid., p. 69 of the Arabic text.

41. Shadid, "Syria for the Syrians," p. 24.

42. Shadid, *A Doctor for the People* (New York: Vanguard Press, 1939), p. 94.

43. Ibid., p. 96.

44. Ibid., p. 95. See also Haddad, pp. 91, 99.

45. Mansur, "Problems of Syrian Youth," p. 8.

46. For discussion of these and other issues, see *The Syrian World* for the few years it was in existence. In particular, the following articles are of some value: George A. Ferris, "Syrians' Future in America," *Syrian World* 3, no. 11 (May 1929): 3–8; Lila M. Mandour, "To Speak or not to Speak Arabic," *Syrian World* 2, no. 1 (July 1928): 40–41; E. K. Saloomey, "An Open

Letter to Mr. N. A. Mokarzel," *Syrian World* 2, no. 1 (July 1928): 37–39; and the following articles by Rev. W. A. Mansur, "The Future of Syrian-Americans," *Syrian World* 2, no. 3 (Sept. 1927): 11–17; "The Greatness of the Syrian Race," *Syrian World* 3, no. 3 (Sept. 1928): 10–17; "Our Syrian-American Fellowship," *Syrian World* 3, no. 8 (Feb. 1929): 16–22; and "Syrians' Loyalty to America," *Syrian World* 3, no. 10 (April 1929): 3–9. For delightful vignettes and many insights about Arab-Americans of that period, see Eugene Paul Nassar, *Wind of the Land* (Belmont, Mass.: Association of Arab-American University Graduates, 1979).

47. See the first seven chapters of Rizk, *Syrian Yankees*, pp. 1–116.

48. Rihbany, *Far Journey*, pp. 156–57.

49. Ibid., p. 172.

50. Lucius Hopkins Miller, *Our Syrian Population: A Study of the Syrian Communities of Greater New York* (New York: n.p., ca. 1904; San Francisco: R&E Research Associates, 1968), p. 41.

51. Louise Seymour Houghton, "Syrians in the United States: Intellectual and Social Status," *Survey* 26 (Sept. 2, 1911): 786–803, esp. pp. 795–96.

52. Hawie, *Rainbow Ends*, p. viii.

53. Hitti, *Syrians in America*, p. 102.

54. Gabriel E. Ward, *The Syrian Soldier in Three Wars* (New York: Syrian-American Press, 1919). In Arabic.

55. Mansur, "Syrians' Loyalty," p. 4.

56. Hawie, *Rainbow Ends*, p. vii.

57. Miller, *Our Syrian Population*, p. 40.

58. Hitti, *Syrians in America*, p. 89.

59. Cyril Anid, *I Grew with Them* (Jounieh, Lebanon: Paulist Press, 1967).

60. Donald B. Cole, *Immigrant City: Lawrence, Massachusetts, 1845–1921* (Chapel Hill: University of North Carolina Press, 1980), p. 188.

61. F. M. Al Akl, *Until Summer Comes* (Springfield, Mass.: Pond-Ekberg Co., 1945), p. 360.

62. Rihbany, *Far Journey*, p. 237; Rizk, *Syrian Yankees*, pp. 237–39.

63. Ward, *Syrian Soldier*, p. 41.

64. Interview with L. A. [Louis Ajami] in Detroit, Dec. 31, 1982.

65. Cole, *Immigrant City*, p. 188.

Dr. Michael Shadid and the Debate over Identity in *The Syrian World*

RAOUF J. HALABY

The "Letters to the Editor" and the "Readers' Opinions" segments of newspapers and magazines have traditionally provided a forum for readers to express, among other issues, their views regarding political, economic, and social concerns. First published in 1926, *The Syrian World*, the first English-language Arab publication in America, provided such a forum for its readers under the title the "Reader's Forum." This article will deal with a particular revelatory debate in *The Syrian World*'s "Reader's Forum," and the impact the debate had on the newspaper's intellectual development.

The Arab peoples' love for the spoken and written word is inherent to their culture and traditions. Hence, as the economic status of the early immigrants improved and they adjusted to American society, they attempted to unify both to combat the social, political, and racial ostracism they experienced and to share a cherished literary heritage. The different religious communities initiated the publication of Arabic newspapers in Boston, New York, Chicago, Detroit, Lawrence, Massachusetts, and other cities. The newspapers served as an important bridge between Eastern and Western ideas. They also served as a means of preserving the native tongue, and, more important, the propagation of vernacular rather than classical Arabic. The latter made a profound impact on the development of modern Arabic literature; especially significant was the emergence of modern Arabic vers libre and the simplification of newspaper language. Most significant, however, was the freedom the people found in expressing their political and religious views without fear of censorship, deportation, or execution. Newspaper issues attacking Ottoman corruption and atrocities frequently were smuggled into Syria. There is no doubt that the Arabic-language newspapers published in America influenced Syrian thought and sentiment, thus planting the seeds and fanning the flames that sparked the Syrian rebellion against the Ottoman Empire.

In America, moreover, the Syrian, through his newspaper, was able to keep up with the news of the village and country he left behind. He also found the written medium to be an excellent avenue in which a variety of topics could be addressed. Among those were issues of mercantile opportunities, the translation of the Constitution and other legal documents, general political events affecting his being, the problem-solving mechanisms to racial and social issues, as well as news about his fellow émigrés.

Beverly Mehdi has pointed out that in the thirty-one-year period between 1898 and 1929, a total of 102 Arabic-language newspapers and periodicals came into existence.[1] Obviously only a few survived and succeeded. But when one considers that the Syrians numerically represented one of the smallest immigrant groups, one must marvel at their significant number of publications. Marvel can also be expressed at the Arabs' ingenious ability to adapt a Western technology (geared solely to the use of the Latin alphabet) to the native semitic Arabic alphabet.

The most successful newspapers were sponsored by the various Syrian Arab religious groups. The earliest Arabic-language newspaper, *Al-Hoda* (The Guidance), was first published in 1898 by the Lebanese Maronites of New York City. A year later the Syrian Greek Orthodox community of New York started its paper, *Miraat al-Gharb* (The Mirror of the West), and in 1910 the Syrian Druze community started its paper, *Al Bayan* (The Statement), read also by Muslims.[2] The papers projected the religious views of each of the groups and served as a link between the Old and the New World. Other journals and magazines that merit recognition are those dealing exclusively with scholarly and artistic themes. These are *Al Muhajer* (The Emigrant), *Al Jamia* (The League), and *Al-Funoon* (The Arts), started in 1903, 1906, and 1911, respectively. By 1928 six Arabic dailies ran in New York City, one Arabic daily and one semiweekly in Detroit, one weekly in Lawrence, and two monthlies in both New York City and Detroit.[3]

Among these papers, *The Syrian World* made its debut in July 1926 under the ownership and editorship of Salloum Mokarzel and the assistance of two aides. By that time, a younger generation of American-born Syrians was emerging. The first English-language Arab newspaper therefore came into existence to satisfy a need that heretofore had been ignored; namely, writing about Syria and the Syrians in the English language. The editor explicitly stated in the first issue that his paper was not addressed to the older generation (nativists), but rather to their offspring (Americanists) who were "born and bred on American soil and under the influence of the ideals represented by the stars and stripes."[4] The label "nativist" refers to those Syrian immigrants who wished to return to Syria and/or those who demanded that Syrian customs and mores remain as they were in the Old World. They feared that assimilation would lead to amalgamation and ultimately to the complete destruction of the native values. The "Americanist" label is used in reference to those Syrian immigrants who felt that they should assimilate and become a part of the American mosaic. That group encouraged the acceptance of American values and stressed patriotism and devotion to the newly adopted land.

Also in the first *Syrian World* issue appeared the editor's strict rules for a nonsectarian stand. The paper was not to serve as a forum for propaganda or factionalism, or in any way be "subordinated to any faction, whether religious or political." He desired his paper to serve "as a forum for the discussion of the existing problems among Syrians in America in an effort to arrive at their best solutions," to air out the generational and cultural gaps of the up and growing first generation who were to "comfort themselves with a befitting sense of honor as citizens of this great nation."[5] (The Americanist point of view is explicitly stated.)

Examples of *The Syrian World*'s unbiased religious approach are seen in its treatment of religiohistorical, ethnographic, and cultural themes of Christian, Druze, and Islamic nature. It quoted sayings of the Prophet and Christ and wrote about Hindu religion and philosophy, Nordic sagas, and ancient classical philosophy and literature. It is, therefore, my opinion that the classification of the publication as a newspaper is erroneous. In the first place, it was of quarto rather than folio size, and second, it was primarily a scholarly publication, for in addition to the above-mentioned themes, it also published literary articles, short stories, poems, original plays (in serial form), and book reviews. Toward the end it printed the "Editor's Comments and Notes," the "Reader's Forum," "The Spirit of the Syrian Press" (a review of the editorials of the prominent Arabic-language newspapers in America), "About Syria and Syrians" (news items on Syrians in America and around the world), and last, a segment called "Political Developments in Syria" (a detailed account of all the political developments under the French and the British).

In February of 1927, Dr. Michael Shadid of Elk City, Oklahoma, found this English-language publication an appropriate medium in which to express his pent up feelings regarding the social and professional ostracism he experienced in a predominantly white Anglo-Saxon America. His prescribed remedy was simple: Syrians should return to their homelands. Thus his article "Syria for the Syrians" paved the way for a lengthy debate in the "Reader's Forum" segment of the paper between the nativists who vented their feelings on the issue of racial prejudice, and the Americanists who found Shadid and his co-nativists at fault in their predicament and advocated a change of attitude and a sense of devotion to America, its people, and their ways. The opinions were almost equally divided between the two factions, and, over a six-month period, each group presented, defended, and argued its case. To discover who this Shadid was, whence came this man of opinions, and what his reasons were, one must briefly discover the character behind the mask.

Born a posthumous child in the Lebanese village of Judaida circa 1882, Michael A. Shadid immigrated to New York City in 1898 whereupon he was "promptly outfitted with a satchel full of jewelry."[6] Having saved more than five thousand dollars from a two-year peddling endeavor throughout the Northeast, South, and Southwest,[7] Shadid enrolled at Tarleton State College in Stephenville, Texas, and was graduated in 1902.[8] In 1906 he was graduated from the Washington University School of Medical Sciences, and throughout his tenure in Saint Louis became an ardent supporter of one-time presidential aspirant Eugene Debbs and a strong supporter of the socialist movement.

Between 1906 and 1923 he practiced medicine in Maxville, Missouri, and in Oklahoma City and Carter, Oklahoma. From 1923 until the 1950s he resided in Elk City, Oklahoma, where he served as chief surgeon and medical director of the Elk City Farmer's Union Cooperative Hospital. His long service to the people of western Oklahoma earned him much respect and honor. More significant, however, Shadid's revolutionizing of health care and the role he played in establishing the then-novel prepayment health care plan have earned him the title of father of cooperative medicine in America—this despite a twenty-five-year legal battle (which he won) between the Elk City Farmer's Union Cooperative Hospital and the American Medical Association through its proxies, the Beckham County and the Oklahoma Medical associations.

In "Syria for the Syrians," Shadid addressed himself to the issues of racial prejudice and social ostracism, which he himself had experienced in Elk City. His thrust was on the notion that "of all countries Syria is the country of choice for Syrians to live in." He declared that he had reached this conclusion by assessing and comparing the cultural, social, and economic factors of the Syrians in America and in Syria. First he pointed out (in a theoretical and superficially simplistic way) that Syrians from America, with modern farming machinery and know-how, could make contributions to their country and its peoples. Next he claimed that cotton, rice, and wheat could be easily planted in Syria with great financial rewards. Once agriculture made headway, industrial and commercial enterprises were surely to follow. Next, based upon his experiences with racial prejudice, he detailed the reasons for returning to Syria as follows:

Syrians are subject to being ostracized not alone by native Americans but by all those peoples belonging to the Nordic branch of the white race. . . . Indeed it may be said that among native born Americans there is more prejudice against foreigners in general and

> *Syrians in particular than in any other country of the wide world. . . . It permeates the mass of Americans without regard to class or station in life. . . . The bulk of Americans is made up of the so-called middle class and this class is more emphatic in its prejudices than any other. . . . Across the street . . . live two doctors, two 'brother' physicians, both klansmen. They recognize me professionally but ostracise me socially. Next door to me lives (a second generation Swede, on the other side a banker, both members of the KKK). . . . I would not mind if this social ostracism affected me . . . but I do object to having my children feel they are being discriminated against, they being native born, on my account. I object very strongly to my children being looked down upon or considered inferior by snobbish children.*[9]

Shadid went on to state that despite his twenty-four-year membership in the Masonic order in other towns, his bid for membership to that order in Elk City was turned down. He also cited the case of two Syrian merchants, one who was threatened by the Klan to leave Greer County, Oklahoma, and another whose dry goods store was burned down "after he received a threat by mail ordering him to move away from town." He ended his article by stating that he believed in the American people and that there is "more good in the hearts of the American people than evil . . . [but] I would rather live on equality with any people than live on a basis of inequality. . . . My thesis," he concluded, "is that Syria is the proper place, the best country in the world, for the Syrian people."[10]

The same issue carried the "Editor's Comment" on the article and invited the readers to express themselves. In his three-page comment, the editor commended Shadid on his sincerity and deplored the regrettable bigoted attitudes exhibited by such people. But at the same time, the editor cleverly reminded his readers that America has drawn people from every race "to create the greatest experiment in history" and that they (Syrians) are newcomers who have contributed "to the well-being of the country" in a constructive way and "for that reason are more American" than the old stock group. The editor, therefore, saw no "wisdom in advocating the return of the Syrian immigrants to Syria" because it was inadvisable and impractical. He urged the Syrians to note that they were just "beginning to see the fruition of their early, hard efforts and [that they should] not forsake positive results to risk a doubtful experiment." Furthermore, in addressing himself to the older generation, he urged them to remember that their children's American "conceptions and ideals will be at variance" with Syrian values. His recommendation (typically Americanist), therefore, was twofold: for Syrians to dismiss the notion of return and to "give thought in all earnestness [to] the discovery of a means by which they could improve their standing as a racial unit in the land of their choice."[11]

No sooner had the readers read Shadid's article than the Americanist view was more forcefully heard from in the March issue. One reader took the doctor to task, accusing him of contracting "Elkcityitis" (prejudice), a contagious disease. He blantantly told Shadid that he could not forgive him "for his surrender and advice." The reader further stated that "America has been too benevolent for us to permit one or two hundred bigoted so-called Americans to cause us to lose faith in our adopted land." The reader emphatically told Shadid that as a child he sang " 'America' with fervor for we loved every word and phrase of 'America' and no one can persuade us that our childish conclusion was wrong, and that we did not have as much right to sing the anthem as any one else here."[12] Another Oklahoma reader chided Shadid for his reflections on American attitudes and suggested that Shadid go back to Syria where he could "sow the seeds of liberty and advanced civilization which [he had] experienced in America."[13] The last view was expressed by a young Syrian chemist from Syracuse, New York, who was in agreement with Shadid. He stated that his experiences had been of a negative nature in that he was denied the position of chief chemist in a steel mill because of his national origin.[14]

The Arab press in America also seemed to have taken an interest in the budding conflict between the nativist and Americanist views. The Greek Orthodox *Miraat al-Gharb* had formerly rebuked the nativist sentiments by stating the following:

> *Bearers of American citizenship should observe the laws of their country, and not limp between the two sides. They should not forget their obligation to the country which was good to them; which treated them as she did its own children not distinguishing between them and her original ones. Let us be one hundred percent Americans, and take pride in that we are a part of this free and just nation.*[15]

Three weeks after Shadid's article appeared, *Miraat al-Gharb*'s editor commented in his "Practical Patriotism" editorial that long may the American flag "wave over our heads. It was the flag for which our brave sons fought in the World War, the proud flag that ever returned victorious from the battlefield."[16]

The Maronite *Al-Hoda,* on the other hand, representing the nativist view, maintained that the Syrian "stands in need of everything that the new land can give. . . . It is our duty" the editor told his readers, "to transfuse into the veins of the old the blood and vigor and energy which animates the new, and this we shall do."[17]

In its second month (April 1927) the debate became more heated. A pioneer Syrian resident of Oklahoma (as he referred to himself) listed the names of ten successful Syrians throughout the state as proof of their social acceptance. Shadid was included in the list and his success as a physician and his popularity among the voters in his district were cited. The Syrian resident in question presented a simple formula: as long as Syrians "maintain their loyalty to their adopted country, attend to their own business and discharge their duties as true citizens," they should not fear any prejudice. A second comment voiced in the debate was from one who remarked that while he abhorred the prejudicial attitudes, he was saddened by the "pitiful defeat manifested in his [Shadid's] article." A third reader criticized Shadid for his stand and attitude and responded to the previously mentioned young chemist's charge by stating that he was probably denied the position either because of his inexperience or his youth,[18] thus adding a new dimension to the debate by isolating the two groups and displaying personal attacks on Shadid that bordered on the facetious side.

Worried about the personal ridicule and its negative effects on both sides of the debate and about the seriousness and validity of the charges and countercharges, the editor, together with leaders of the Syrian Lebanese Club of New York City, held a public discussion on April 15, 1927, to air out the controversy relating to discrimination against the Syrians in America. Joseph Ferris presided and Dr. F. I. Shatara started the discussion by reading a paper in which he "analyzed the various social ailments of the Syrians and, while he lauded them for their many virtues, pointed out some faults which he hoped would be corrected." He emphasized the "distinct mission" the Syrians had to perform in their new country: "to contribute [their] best."[19] The five members of the panel (editor Mokarzel included) agreed that unity and harmony must be promoted among the two groups and that education, cooperation, and organization were roads to the desired goal as the Syrians in America were to trudge through the times of "transition,"[20] a euphemism for assimilation. The discussion was printed in its entirety in the May 1927 issue.

The "Reader's Forum" for the May 1927 issue included a response by Shadid in which he answered his attackers and stated that the disease was "Americanitis," a disease that "discriminated against" people of "swarthy color and . . . racial extraction." He adamantly emphasized that "Syrians, like Jews, are socially ostracised and cannot be assimilated." He also insisted that he lost the congressional race owing to racial prejudice as illustrated by a letter he received from a physician who attacked his "farmer labor, socialist rot" and that "he was not competent to tell Americans what [they] should do." He concluded his letter by telling Shadid that if he was bent "on governmental change [he should] go back where he came from and tell them."[21]

Evidence confirms Shadid's charges, for when he ran for Congress many rumors were spread about him. He was called an atheist, a Turk, a Jew, an enemy of America, a communist, a Nazi, a chronic drunkard, and finally, he was accused of drowning his daughter because she married an American.[22] The most vicious attack, however, appeared in an article titled "The Peddler of Rugs" in the *Vici Beacon:*

Down the street he comes, a man apart, knowing no friend; his queer dress, his hooked nose, his broken speech and queer mannerisms set him aside from the rest—the peddler of rugs.

On his arm a gaudy display of rugs and scarfs, gleaming like jewels in the sunlight. Sparkling tinsel and glistening silk, yet alas, they bear no blessing of a known manufacturer, a thing made only to sell thru picturing of the faults of others. Bearing a guarantee of a foreigner whom you will perhaps never see again.

Nor are the political rugs exemplified by the candidacy of Dr. M. Shadid of any better quality. These rugs, too, glisten in the light of hard times, they are smooth; but what lies under the surface?—Will they, like the peddler's rug, fade, will they become a thing forsaken, dirty, unfit to have around?

After the first washing what will we have?

They carry not the blessing of a Washington, Jefferson, Lincoln, Wilson, or Coolidge. They do carry the blessing, however, of every socialist, or ex-socialist I know. You count them over—every one you know—no preamble of the Constitution teaches class hatred and the 'down with the rich' doctrine that Shadid does—but the old Socialist newspaper 'Appeal to Reason' did.

No American parentage glorifies this person, and no American philosophy blesses his doctrine. We need no off-color capital-baiting lines of thought in our national makeup.[23]

The editor of *The Syrian World* was apparently concerned about the subjectivity of the letters and the personal attacks on Shadid. He stipulated, therefore, in his May 1927 editorial that all letters on the topic, starting with the June 1927 publication, address themselves to the issues—racial discrimination and the return to Syria—without any personal criticisms. Thus the June 1927 newspaper contained only two letters addressing the topic. One letter exhibited a remarkable turnabout and advised Syrians not "to maintain the clannishness of [their] fathers." The author advised them to absorb "the Spirit of America" without sacrificing their "ideals to achieve Americanism." The other reader thought that the discrimination was a "case of personality and locality." He warned that "pessimism and dissatisfaction never lead to any constructive results. Agitators are not popular," he concluded.[24] With these two letters the debate on the issue subsided in the "Reader's Forum." As will later be pointed out, the debate had far-reaching implications on the subsequent content of the paper. First, though, an ironic twist needs mention.

Fourteen months after the last letter appeared in *The Syrian World*, Shadid sent the magazine a letter termed "Explanation and Retraction." The reaction was prompted by the following event: having stated that Syria was the place to go back to, Shadid, with his daughter, visited Lebanon in the summer of 1928. His daughter's "reactions toward living in the Near East were most violent and [he] knew that her five brothers and sisters would feel as she did." Thus giving up "all thought of returning to Lebanon," Shadid, in a complete reversal, "decided to spend the rest of [his] days in the United States."[25]

In his retraction, Shadid stated that economic conditions in Syria were not what he claimed them to be in his article "Syria for Syrians," and that he was wrong on that issue. He refused, however, to retract his stand on racial prejudice, and he reiterated his reasons for believing in that fashion.[26] The editor again invited the readers to respond, but no further comments on the Shadid issue were printed in any of the succeeding issues of the paper. Was the controversy dead? Far from it.

In a 1929 Senate debate over an amendment relative to the Armenian, Greek, and Syrian immigrant quotas set forth in the 1924 Quota Law favoring immigrants of European and English stock, David Reed, the Republican Senator from Pennsylvania, referred to the Syrians as the "trash of the Mediterranean, all that Levantine stock that churns around through there and does not know what its own ancestry is, . . . the penitentiary group let out on condition they emigrate to America."[27] For the first time in its history the Syrian community in America united and rallied behind Democratic Senator David Walsh of Massachusetts, who led the opposition on the Senate floor. *The Syrian World* also deplored Reed's attitude and urged its readers to combat the anti-Syrian sentiments. The Senate debate was, in effect, Shadid's sweet revenge against those who disputed his belief that racial prejudice existed against the Syrians in America.

Thus two and one half years after his first letter appeared in *The Syrian World*, Shadid sent in his last letter, one of vindication, in which he stated:

> *Editor,*
> *The outburst of Senator Reed only substantiates what I have repeatedly asserted in what I have contributed to a previous issue of* The Syrian world [sic], *that the Syrian people are discriminated against in this country on account of racial prejudice. Let me repeat, therefore, that the Syrian is better off in his own country living on bread and milk and enjoying the good opinion of his neighbor, than to live sumptuously in a place and be socially ostracized and discriminated against as a citizen.*[28]

It goes without saying that Shadid did experience racial prejudice and he was, in fact, ostracized. It is my belief, however, that the negative behaviors were exhibited toward him because Shadid set out to revolutionize medical care. The physicians of Elk City feared that a cooperative approach to health care would cut into their businesses. They fought Shadid with all their weapons and, because they could not discredit his excellent medical abilities, attacked the most conspicuous aspects about him: his dark complexion and his background. The issue of racial prejudice itself is not of great significance here. What is significant is that Shadid had indirectly influenced the subject matter of *The Syrian World* (as well as other Arabic language newspapers in the U.S.) for several years in the following manner:

1. On a regular basis articles dealing with agriculture and agricultural developments in their various aspects were published for the first time.

2. Also published were articles dealing with the need to develop dairy farms and hydroelectric facilities for the purpose of industrial development and irrigation in Lebanon, Syria, and Palestine.

3. In the segment "Syria and Syrians," news of the achievements of the Syrian community were published on a regular basis, with such comments as "His appointment [to assistant city attorney] to his present position is proof of ability recognized without regard to foreign extraction."[29]

4. *The Syrian World* published a series of articles dealing with the moral and social behavior of the Syrian immigrants, and their marital, cultural, and national concerns. The articles also dealt with the dating habits of the younger generations, the generation gap, and the values of the "Syrian" home, and the education of the younger generation and its need to learn the mother tongue. While emphasizing the Americanist (assimilationist) views of patriotism, good citizenship, and hard work, the views paradoxically emphasized Syrian values and mores. The strongest proponent of the Americanist views was the Rev. W. A. Mansur, minister of the First Methodist Church of Wineside, Nebraska. He authored several articles under such titles as "Problems of Syrian Youth in America," "What Every Syrian Boy and Girl Ought to Know: Timely Advice to the Syrian-American Generation," "Our Commission to Posterity," "Our Pride in Our Syrian World," "Our Pride in Our Country," and "The Future Syrian Americans." In the latter, he reminded the Syrian Americans that they "owe it to America, to [their] ancestors and to posterity to be and become the best Americans possible," and he encouraged them to vote, obey the law, pay their taxes, have a good home life, acquire an education, and develop good health habits. Editor Mokarzel's commentary on this article encouraged the readers to heed the "enthusiasm and optimism of the Rev. W. Mansur" and hoped that it would "prove contagious."

5. Finally, Shadid's article and the debate it initiated signaled another series of articles, letters, and debates in the "Reader's Forum" that dealt with all facets of Syrian life.

In reviewing the causes and effects of the newspaper debate of the "Americanists" versus the "nativists," one character, namely Shadid, clearly rises steadfastly above all others. Ironically, "Shadid" translates from the Arabic as "steadfast." In an interview with Salom Rizk, Shadid expressed his gratitude toward America in the following manner:

> *When I was peddling jewelry from door to door those first years in America, I saw a lot of America . . . [and] the more I saw, the more I loved it. But some things disturbed me. Here and there were injustice, oppression, and discrimination. I knew they didn't belong here. . . . I met people who were busy making this country, already the best in the world, even better. I decided I ought to do my share. I owed a debt to America for the opportunities she had given me, and I felt I ought to repay it in some concrete way. This hospital is part of my payment. Let's say it's the down payment.*[30]

Rizk answered that he had met many people who knew of Shadid's contributions and that if he had to answer for them, he would give him a receipt marked "paid in full."

Notes

1. Beverly T. Mehdi, *The Arabs in America 1492–1977* (New York: Oceanea Publications, 1978), p. 17.

2. Ibid.

3. *Syrian World,* 2, no. 1 (July 1926): 54.

4. Ibid.

5. Ibid., 2–3.

6. Michael A. Shadid, *Crusading Doctor: My Fight for Cooperative Medicine* (Boston: Meador Publishing Co., 1956), p. 29.

7. Ibid., p. 31.

8. Ibid., p. 32.

9. *Syrian World* 1, no. 8 (February 1927): 22–23.

10. Ibid., 23–24.

11. Ibid., 47–48.

12. Ibid., no. 9 (March 1927): 54–56.

13. Ibid., 56.

14. Ibid., 57.

15. Ibid., no. 6 (December 1926): 69.

16. Ibid., no. 7 (January 1927): 55.

17. Ibid., no. 8 (March 1927): 52.

18. Ibid., no. 9 (April 1927): 48–51.

19. Ibid., no. 11 (May 1927): 52.

20. Ibid.

21. Ibid., 47–49.

22. Shadid, *Crusading Doctor,* 231–32.

23. Ibid.

24. *Syrian World* 1, no. 12 (June 1927): 56–57.

25. Shadid, *Crusading Doctor,* p. 77. While Shadid did not go back to Syria, as he had preached in 1927, he was instrumental in the construction of a one-hundred-bed hospital in his native village of Judaida.

26. *Syrian World* 3, no. 9 (October 1928): 24–28.

27. Adele Younis, "The Coming of the Arab Speaking People to the United States," Ph.D. diss., Boston University, 1961, pp. 291–305.

28. *Syrian World* 3, no. 12 (June 1929): 44.

29. Ibid. 2, no. 1 (July 1927): 61.

30. Salom Rizk, *Syrian Yankee* (Garden City, N.Y.: Doubleday, Doran & Co., New York, 1943), pp. 316–17.

PART TWO

COMMUNITY STUDIES

"Colored" and Catholic

The Lebanese in Birmingham, Alabama

NANCY FAIRES CONKLIN AND NORA FAIRES

Like most early Lebanese communities in the United States, that in Birmingham was established in the years following 1890, up until the immigration restrictions of the 1920s.[1] Most Birmingham residents had migrated first to the Norteast or to cities in the Great Lakes area, and thence to Alabama. The founding Lebanese families in Birmingham originated in the farming villages in the area around Zahleh in the central region of the Syrian province of Mount Lebanon; many came from the village of Wadi-el-Arayeche. A small but steady flow of immigrants from that area to Birmingham led to a Lebanese community totaling sixty-five families by 1915.

The Lebanese who came to Birmingham entered one of the fastest-growing, most rapidly industrializing cities of the United States. The immigrant pioneers, and most of those who followed, carved a familiar niche in the expanding economy; like some of their counterparts elsewhere in America, many took up peddling and other commercial enterprises. Their economic success and the subsequent institutional development of the Lebanese community, however, took place within the strictures of an aggressively racially bifurcated and Protestant society. Hence, part of understanding the saga of the Lebanese of Birmingham is appreciating what it has meant to be sometimes regarded as "colored" and to be saliently Catholic in segregated, Protestant Dixie.

The development of the Lebanese community in Birmingham cannot be understood as a separate entity from the complex of ethnic communities that came to distinguish that industrial city. This essay, therefore, first examines migration and immigration to Birmingham, particularly the social, economic, and occupational development of the Mediterranean groups. It then analyzes the political and social climate of the city in which the Lebanese were to make their home, a climate dominated in the early years of this century by issues of race and segregation. The reaction of the Lebanese to the stresses of economic change and social ostracism was not to assimilate, but to establish and maintain strong, stable community institutions. The institutions, and particularly the Maronite church, which formed the focal point for the community, are described in the concluding section, bringing the history of the Lebanese in Birmingham up to the present day.

This essay makes use of both documentary and oral history materials. To sketch out the formation of the Birmingham Lebanese community, it relies primarily on local histories, government documents, and scholarly studies of the city and region; to portray the experience of the process of community formation, the article draws on the testimony of contemporary community members.

THE ETHNIC MOSAIC IN DEVELOPING BIRMINGHAM

The immigrant Lebanese were a small part of a much larger flow of people into Birmingham in the late nineteenth and early twentieth centuries. Indeed, Birmingham had been nothing more than a cornfield when in 1871 a group of industrialists and speculators rallied to establish a village at what they hoped would be the junction of two railroads. Lying in the heart of a fabulously rich mineral region, the new city was christened Birmingham after the English industrial power the promoters sought to emulate.[2] Despite a series of critical setbacks in its growth, Birmingham achieved sustained industrial and commercial success by 1910. Accordingly, the city's population, little more than three thousand in 1880, climbed to nearly 179,000 in 1920 (see table 4). In those forty years, Birmingham's growth rate matched the growth rates of other burgeoning regional centers, such as Atlanta, Houston, Kansas City, and Los Angeles. From the 1920s on, the city's expansion resembled the pattern of more mature industrial economies like Pittsburgh and Detroit. By 1930, Birmingham housed 260,000 residents, but during the depression, which badly hurt the city, population growth slowed to a trickle; recovery came to the "hardest hit city of the nation" in the 1940s as war production boomed, pushing the population to more than 326,000 by 1950.[3]

Many of the migrants to Birmingham came from the surrounding countryside as both rural blacks and rural whites flocked to the iron and steel city. Interestingly, the percentage of blacks in Birmingham's population remained remarkably stable through the main years of the city's growth: 42 percent in 1890, 43 percent in 1900, and 39 percent in both 1910 and 1920.[4] While the percentage of whites in the community hovered at roughly

Table 4.
Population Growth of Birmingham, Alabama, 1880–1950

	Total Population	Percent Increase
1880	3,086	—
1890	26,178	748.3
1900	38,415	46.6
1910	132,685	24.5
1920	178,806	34.8
1930	259,678	45.2
1940	267,583	3.0
1950	326,037	21.8

Source: United States Census Bureau.

sixty percent, the composition of the "white" population changed. Birmingham and its surrounding area of mines and mills attracted Alabamian and other southern workers but also workers from northern states and from foreign nations. In the four decades following 1880, immigrants of many nationalities, including Russians, Hungarians, Greeks, German and Eastern European Jews, Italians, Irish, Germans, and many Slavic peoples, settled in Birmingham, making it one of the most ethnically complex cities in the region.[5]

The lure of Birmingham and its environs for those newcomers, both black and white, was the promise of jobs, and, by the turn of the century, a biracial, multiethnic working class had been formed in the area. Blacks held the lowest-paid, lowest-status jobs and formed the core of the city's industrial work force, holding 65 percent of the iron and steel industry jobs in 1900 and 75 percent of them ten years later.[6] According to a federal survey reported in 1911, blacks were also the largest group among the district's nearly seven thousand coal miners.[7] They were followed in number by Anglo whites, southern Italians, "Scotch," Slovaks, and a variety of other European immigrant groups.[8] In the city, perhaps a quarter of the adult male workers were first- or second-generation Americans at the turn of the century.[9]

Alabama's Lebanese, Greeks, and Jews are largely absent from the federal government's roster of coal miners. None of Alabama's miners was listed as being of "Syrian" birth. Similarly, only seven of Alabama's coal miners were listed as Greek and none were listed as "Hebrew."[10] The groups, with the addition of a substantial segment of the more numerous Italians, were part of the commercial sector of the area's economy. Acting as peddlers, wholesalers, and retailers to the diverse nationality groups and to both blacks and whites in Birmingham and its hinterland, the groups comprised a second tier in the occupational hierarchy.

As early as 1887, according to local historians of the day, the "Jewish inhabitants of Birmingham were among its most substantial trades people."[11] Hailing primarily from Germany and numbering about 250 persons in the 1880s, Jews held various occupations in the city, but, as a contemporary study relates:

> *Above all . . . the Jewish merchants rapidly and successfully established themselves as prominent storekeepers, clothiers, jobbers, bankers, and owners of some of the city's most notable department stores and mercantile establishments.*[12]

By 1917 the Jewish community had swelled to more than thirty-five hundred persons, largely owing to the outpouring of Eastern European emigrants. The newer immigrants, with less capital and more "foreign" ways, faced greater resistance from the Anglo community. A ghetto soon formed in the city, wherein most Eastern European Jews conducted the bulk of their personal and public relations through the 1920s. Despite their segregation, many took up commercial activities, and some gained positions in the professions, consolidating and widening the Jewish niche in the city's economy.[13]

The Italian immigrant community in Birmingham had a more complex occupational profile. Italians were the largest European immigrant group to settle in Birmingham, numbering more than five hundred in the city area in 1900 and totaling more than twenty-one hundred two decades later. Ninety percent of those immigrants were from Sicily, and many, like the Lebanese in the city, were chain migrants from a single village.[14] Most took jobs as laborers in industry upon arrival, but many left such toil, as soon as their savings allowed, to open up family-run grocery stores. The success of their enterprises rested partially on the Italians' willingness to go where the market was: to open up stores in black neighborhoods, where other whites would not do business. "By the 1930s," concluded a local history of the immigrant group, "Italians owned more than three hundred grocery stores in the Birmingham area. They sold fresh meat, staples, and canned goods, but usually no produce."[15]

A few Italians did become succesful selling fruits and vegetables, but that economic specialty fell mostly to yet another of the city's small ethnic enclaves, the Greeks. Throughout the first two decades of the century, many of Birmingham's five hundred Greek residents sold fruits and vegetables from stands set up along city streets.[16] Indeed, the immigrant group's virtual monopoly of that lucrative business prompted an unsuccessful petition to the city council aimed at revoking the Greeks' vending licenses. Over time, some Greeks expanded their produce sales, opening up stores; a city survey taken in 1908 revealed 125 food-related enterprises owned by Greeks, including groceries, restaurants and cafés, bakeries, confectionaries, drink-bottling companies, meat markets, and coffee importers. By the 1920s other Greeks had entered the ranks of the Birmingham entrepreneurs as proprietors of hotels, laundries, and other small businesses, such as shoeshine and barber shops.[17]

Within Birmingham's ethnically specific occupational hierarchy the Lebanese established their own niche. Peddling, the trade adopted by the Birmingham Lebanese, expressed the group's cultural inclinations while fitting into the spectrum of jobs open within the hierarchy of occupations in the city. Like their Italian, Jewish, and Greek counterparts, the Lebanese traded with both blacks and whites; unlike the majority of the other immigrant merchants, the Lebanese traded throughout the countryside of Alabama. The immigrant Lebanese, both men and women, carried a stock consisting mainly of goods for personal use that were difficult for farm families to make themselves or to procure from nearby stores. On their backs they carried such items as dry goods, notions, tinware, combs, and handcrafted goods (especially fine linens and laces made by Lebanese women). A handful of Lebanese families started the network of peddling, setting the newer arrivals up in stock and establishing their routes for them. By the 1920s most had been able to give up their peddling to establish stores. Trade with farmers had often brought them foodstuffs in exchange for their wares; consequently, as they moved up from peddling some became wholesalers and retailers of groceries and produce. Birmingham's Southside alone came to house twenty Lebanese groceries. Other Lebanese set up shops to sell linens and dry goods. Their success in climbing the occupational ladder was impressive.[18]

In two decades, the Lebanese community in Birmingham established itself as a middle-class, entrepreneurial group. The Lebanese shops retailing groceries and specialty goods joined the many Jewish department stores and clothiers, the numerous Greek produce and other food-related firms, and the plentiful Italian corner grocery stores to complete the intricate web of ethnic specialization in commercial Birmingham. Together with the more numerous migrant and immigrant industrial workers, the immigrant merchants helped to fill the city's growing demand for labor.

THE POLITICAL AND SOCIAL CLIMATE OF BIRMINGHAM DURING THE ERA OF LEBANESE IMMIGRATION

Labor shortage was a persistent problem that limited the South's economic expansion, as entrepreneurs in Birmingham and throughout the region recognized; to ease the situation, some employers, investors, and real estate speculators urged the active recruitment of immigrants. As Birmingham's economy blossomed after the turn of the century, the Alabama legislature endorsed that strategy, enacting a law in 1907 that established a commissioner to promote immigration.[19] Here Alabama was following the precedent of several other Southern states,[20] and doing so while the rate of increase of immigrants to the state for the decade was 32.1 percent, higher than in other Deep South states and slightly exceeding the national average.[21]

As swelling numbers of immigrants settled in Birmingham, the state's strategy for filling the labor gap would seem to have succeeded: as we have seen, the foreign-born provided labor for both commerce and industry. And yet the southeastern European immigrants who toiled in the city's mills and the Mediterranean immigrants who came to own many of the city's shops were not the immigrants that Alabama's legislators had in mind. Section 8 of the state statute of 1907 declares:

> *That immigrants shall be sought from desirable white citizens of the United States first, and then citizens of English-speaking and Germanic countries, France and the Scandinavian countries, and Belgium as prospective citizens of this State.*[22]

But citizens of those countries were unlikely candidates for migration to industrializing Dixie. Emigration from those nations ebbed in the late nineteenth century, while the so-called new immigration—the exodus of souls from outside northwestern Europe—surged after 1900. Hostility, not hospitality, greeted the "new immigrants," including the Lebanese, who came to Birmingham. By 1924 they would be virtually excluded under a new federal immigration code established with the fierce backing of Alabama legislators.

Alabama's commissioner of immigration took office in the midst of a nationwide rising tide of feeling against the flood of newcomers of the "new immigration," a sentiment that became particularly adamant and vicious in the South. The anti-immigrant fervor was symptomatic of broader cultural conflicts in the early decades of the twentieth century, an era in which racial, religious, and class antagonism swept through the South.[23]

Fundamentalist Protestantism, which had surged in the 1890s, continued to rule in Dixie after the turn of the century. Violence was common, especially in the growing cities.[24] A reorganized Ku Klux Klan (KKK) soared in membership, and Birmingham provided one of its most fertile soils. A single Klan organization in the city boasted ten thousand members, reputedly the largest Klavern in the South. Perhaps another ten thousand residents of Birmingham belonged to other, rival KKK factions. The local chronicler of the Jewish experience quotes a member of his community who lived through those days:

> *[M]ost Jews were "horrified but they felt helpless in the face of the Klan whippings, floggings and kidnappings that were commonplace" in Jefferson County. Klan members were "somewhat psychopathically concerned with drinkers, Negroes, friends of Negroes, Catholics, friends of Catholics, immigrants, Sunday movies, divorce, and nonconformity in general."*[25]

Birmingham was also the site for racially explosive labor conflict in those years. The United Mine Workers (UMW) had been active in the area since 1893, organizing both white and black workers. The union's racial policies angered many Alabamians and frustrated local employers' attempts to keep wages down through traditional practices of segregation. The high tide of UMW activity came in 1908, when coal operators mounted a vicious counterattack to a major strike. In the midst of the successful campaign to smash the UMW, a group of Birmingham citizens articulated their stand on the race issue: "The people of Alabama [will] never tolerate the organization and striking of Negroes along with white men."[26]

It was in that culturally charged atmosphere that Southern politicians began to champion the fight to limit the "new immigration," with Alabama legislators in the forefront of the battle, in Washington and at home. Birmingham's own Representative, Oscar W. Underwood, raised the immigration question in the House in 1905, lecturing his colleagues on the dangers of allowing those without pure "white" blood in their veins to enter the United States. His fellow Southerner, Sen. S. M. Simmons of North Carolina, left little doubt who the purveyors of race suicide were. The new immigrants, according to Simmons:

> *are nothing more than the degenerate progeny of the Asiatic hoards* [sic] *which, long centuries ago, overran the shores of the Mediterranean . . . the spawn of the Phoenician curse.*[27]

When the bill proposing to restrict immigration by the imposition of a literacy test appeared in Congress in 1912, sixteen Southern Senators supported it and one opposed it; the figures for Southern votes in the House were sixty-eight to five.[28]

Notably, it was Alabama Rep. John Burnett who reported the bill to the House for its approval.[29] Burnett was a member of the House of Representatives' Committee on Immigration and Naturalization; it was out of this committee that in 1912 he entered the unsuccessful bill to establish the literacy test. A sample of the testimony before the committee provides a sense of the racist views in support of immigration restriction presented to the committee.[30] Mr. T. J. Brooks, representing the Farmer's Educational and Cooperative Union, claiming to have half its three million members in Southern states, presented a resolution that had been passed at the organization's national meeting in Birmingham in 1909. The Farmer's Union resolution

> *called upon our State and particularly our Federal officials, to exclude the present foreign influx by means of an increased head tax, a money test, the illiteracy test, and other effective measures.*[31]

At one point in his testimony, Brooks declared:

> *Perhaps we feel that we are encroaching upon a sentiment in denying the immigration of anybody that wants to come here, because our ancestors came here from somewhere, and of course lots of good men are not born in this country. Jesus Christ, for instance.*[32]

And, when questioned directly about which immigrants he objected to, Brooks answered:

> *The Sicilian, the Southern Italian, the Greek, the Syrian, and some from that belt of Africa and Asia surrounding the Mediterranean Sea, and farther east, including all Mongolians and Hindus.*[33]

It was just such attitudes that Congressman Burnett promulgated in his home state. In 1907, following his return from a tour of Europe he had conducted in his role as a member of the committee investigating immigration, Burnett stated, "I regard the Syrian and peoples from other parts of Asia Minor as the most undesirable, and the South Italians, Poles and Russians next."[34]

Later that fall Burnett spoke to the Birmingham Commercial Club about his support for a literacy test to limit immigration and evidently repeated his racial views. The Congressman's comments brought a sharp reaction from a noted member of the city's Lebanese community, Dr. H. A. El-Kourie. El-Kourie wrote two letters to local newspapers, and they ran with the titles "Dr. El-Kourie Defends Syrian Immigrants" and "El-Kourie Takes Burnett to Task."[35] The two letters, together with a fragment of an essay, were collected (and presumably distributed) in a document with the telling name "In Defense of the Semitic and the Syrian Especially," accompanied by a photograph of the handsome, urbane author on the front page.[36] The writings of the immigrant physician, worthy of investigation in their own right, provide a penetrating criticism of the viewpoint represented by Burnett and other nativists. El-Kourie details the positive attributes of the Syrian immigrants to America, pointing to their rapid advancement, educationally and economically; he cites their patriotism in serving in the nation's armed forces; and he declares that the Syrians have been quick to adopt American ways.[37] But El-Kourie provides more than a list of the achievements of his fellow immigrants; he attacks Burnett's racial views directly. It is here that this Lebanese immigrant offers a remarkable and sweeping denunciation of the bigotry of his age as it was lodged against his particular ethnic group and those of kindred cultural origin.

El-Kourie traces the origins of the "Semitic family of the white race" and concludes that the "direct descendants" of that race are the "Syrians, Hebrews, German Jews, Spanish Jews, Polish Jews, Russian Jews, Bedouins and Sedentary Arabs." He claims that Burnett is simply wrong in his declaration that those people are not "white."[38] In stressing that the Semitic family is of the white race, El-Kourie does not seem to imply that as such they are superior to the black race, at least in the writings available to us. He does, however, movingly chronicle the contributions to world civilization of those of the Semitic family. Rather than the "Phoenician curse" the North Carolina Senator had railed against, El-Kourie points to advances in navigation, to the origin of the alphabet, and to achievements in art that stem from the "Phoenicians." His broad analysis of interethnic ties stands in stark contrast to the ethnocentrism he was combating. Of Burnett's remarks regarding the racial inferiority of those outside his narrow definition of the white race, El-Kourie has this to say:

> *I have no doubt that the racial hatred that is developing is due largely to such unguarded and unconservative utterances which are practically daggers stabbing the hearts of the people attacked.*[39]

At this point, we do not know the full extent to which the racism manifested by the city's and state's political leaders, the rise of the KKK, the increasing resistance to local workers, the mounting pressure put on the black community, or the militance of fundamentalist Protestantism shaped the Lebanese experience in Birmingham. Fragmentary data provide clues to the impact of that environment on the Lebanese community.

Philip K. Hitti's *Syrians in America,* published in 1924, presents a telling example of bigotry toward the Lebanese in Birmingham in a political campaign. Hitti quotes the text of a handbill circulated in the city in 1920:

For Coroner

Vote For

J. D. GOSS

The White Man's Candidate

> *They have disqualified the negro, an American citizen, from voting in the white primary. The Greek and Syrian should also be disqualified. I DON'T WANT THEIR VOTE. If I can't be elected by white men, I don't want the office.*[40]

Race hatred directed at the Birmingham Lebanese did not end with rhetoric. They, as well as other Mediterranean peoples, report exclusion from "white only" restaurants and from public facilities. A second-generation Lebanese American describes discrimination in the city in both racial and religious terms.

> *[For the first Lebanese] it was a very hazardous life because they went into [the] country and sold to these people who, back in those days aliens were nil, you know. They were persecuted. And they didn't know the language and might say the wrong word. . . . See, people here were even afraid to say they were Catholic at one time. Down South. You know that is a Baptist country. If you said you were Catholic, you got it. My father had*

to go to court one time. We had a cow in the yard and somehow the cow—I don't think it bothered her, that woman, or anything; she just made a big suit out of it. Well, he—see that cross he's wearing on his lapel [pointing to his portrait]—the lawyer told him to put that cross away because they, they're going to, it might make him lose the case. He said, "Well let me tell you buddy, this is going to help me . . . win the case, don't worry about it. I ain't putting away no cross. It's going to stay right here." Sure enough he won the case.[41]

Undoubtedly the Lebanese community was not a distinct entity in the minds of many Birmingham residents. Goss, the "white man's candidate," knew the Lebanese were a separate group, but he lumped them together with the Greeks as nonwhites. A Greek American resident of Birmingham remembers that many Anglos regarded foreigners, particularly those from Mediterranean areas, as a common, alien element.

In the South, there weren't too many ethnic groups. The only [groups were] Italians, Greeks, very few Greeks, very few Italians, and the Jewish people. And we were looked down upon. In fact, they called us "dagos" in those days [group laughter]. They did! They called the Italians and the Greeks "dagos." And everybody would murmur if they wanted to speak to somebody in their native tongue. They would go secretly to speak so they wouldn't be ridiculed.[42]

Even today a Birmingham Lebanese American father prepares his children to face verbal abuse. But, after four generations in the South, he argues a different response:

I'm sure [my wife's family] had a rough time in Mississippi growing up. I know my mother and father did, in this area. I think they got so tired of defending and having people not understand [that they gave up their language and culture]. Me, I consider it ignorance if they do not understand. I just feel like they should look at their own background. You know, who are they to judge me? . . . And that's what I tell my children. And I tell them if anyone calls you anything bad—and I tell them what the words that are bad—you have my permission to pick up a brick and hit them. I don't like violence, but they do. And we're in 1982 now and those days are gone, you know, where you have to defend your religion and your background.[43]

The legacy of the climate of racial and religious hostility is complicated and confusing for Birmingham's Lebanese. Certainly they, especially the darker-skinned Lebanese, experienced painful moments: every time they used public facilities they faced possible challenges to their race; similarly, each farmhouse that a peddler approached required the reestablishment of racial identity and the possibility of antiforeign and anti-Catholic prejudice. At the same time, the Lebanese benefited from segregation: racial bifurcation promoted their economic ascendance.

INSTITUTIONAL DEVELOPMENT AND CULTURAL MAINTENANCE IN THE BIRMINGHAM LEBANESE COMMUNITY

Within the context of economic success and cultural marginality the Lebanese established a cohesive organizational life. The community's small size, relative homogeneity, and position on the periphery of white society contributed to the fashioning of a strong ethnic consciousness that blended considerations of religion with nationality. The Birmingham Lebanese community has sustained vigorous religious, social, and service organizations over eight decades. Those institutions have evolved with the developing community, adapting to its changing needs and aspirations.

At the close of immigration in the 1920s the Birmingham Lebanese community boasted two churches—Saint Elias Maronite Catholic Church and Saint George Melkite Greek Catholic Church—and a twenty-year-old service and social organization, the Phoenician Club.[44] The Phoenician Club was created as a burial society by the earliest, male settlers, evolving into a community and welcoming center and coffeehouse. Today it continues as the Cedars Club, a social and recreational center for Lebanese families and the locus for secular activities related to traditional feast and holyday celebrations for Saint Elias and Saint George congregationalists.

By 1910 the tiny community had raised sufficient funds to bring a Maronite priest from Lebanon and rent a space where the Saint Elias Maronite Catholic Church, named after their home church in Wadi-el-Arayeche, was consecrated. Together with their Syrian, Greek, and Palestinian coreligionists, Lebanese Melkites established Saint George Melkite Greek Catholic Church in 1921. The two churches, whose present-day buildings are just a few blocks apart, have maintained a close, cooperative relationship throughout their history. The churches and their secular counterpart, the Cedars Club, have provided the critical institutional focus of the Birmingham Lebanese community's cultural life in the isolation of the Deep South.

Saint Elias Maronite, the larger and exclusively Lebanese congregation, is an outstanding institution, regionally and nationally. It has been the largest and, until the 1960s, one of only two Maronite churches in the South.[45] Saint Elias experienced considerable attrition in its membership over its first thirty years—owing in large part to hiatus in the occupancy of the priesthood and to the opening of Saint George—but its loss does not appear ever to have reached the 50 percent estimated for Maronite congregations nationally.[46] Today the parish numbers 260 families, totaling eight hundred to one thousand people, more than 80 percent of whom are Lebanese or of Lebanese descent.[47]

In 1939, as the youngest of the early immigrant generation came to adulthood, Saint Elias secured the services of a charismatic and visionary leader, Fr. Joseph Ferris Abi-Chedid.[48] An ardent and articulate Lebanese nationalist, Abi-Chedid galvanized community self-awareness. While many of his ambitious projects met with success, Abi-Chedid's plan for a Maronite school at Saint Elias foundered on misplaced opposition from the Latin Rite bishopric under whose jurisdiction the Maronites had been placed. Not comprehending the ancient, liturgical distinction in Rites that was the basis for the Maronites' (and Melkites') insistence on religious autonomy, the Latin Rite diocese made every attempt to assimilate what it regarded simply as an especially recalcitrant ethnic group. Maronite and Melkite children—as well as Greek and Russian Orthodox young people—attended the Birmingham diocesan parochial schools, a practice that diluted, Abi-Chedid and his parishioners feared, the distinctions between the Rites and threatened Lebanese ethnic identity. Beleaguered by virulent anti-Catholic fanaticism, Birmingham's Roman Catholic leadership could afford to pay little attention to the peculiar demands of its Lebanese minority.

While efforts to establish a school with an Eastern Rite and Arabic language and culture failed in fact, the community activities dedicated to raising funds for the project and the debate about the school served to unite the Birmingham Lebanese at a period during which Lebanese communities in other cities were experiencing declining interest in institutional and cultural affairs. Unlike the rivalry that has characterized Maronite and Melkite congregations in other Lebanese settlements, Birmingham's Saint Elias and Saint George have worked jointly to further the welfare and sustain the ethnic identity of the city's Lebanese. Throughout the decades they have cosponsored after-school classes in Arabic language and culture. Many of the more secular holiday activities are conducted jointly, often through the Cedars Club. The Birmingham chapter of the American-Lebanese League alternates its meeting place between the two churches.[49]

Their Catholicism contributed in setting apart the Birmingham Lebanese from the black and white world, making the Lebanese more suspect but enabling them to avoid raising some of the thorny questions about which side of Alabama's strict color line they belonged on. By establishing their own burial society, the Lebanese did not face possible exclusion of their dead from "white only" city cemetaries. Attendance at Latin Rite parochial schools—a practice not paralleled elsewhere in the United States[50]—shielded Lebanese children from confronting racial segregation.

Birmingham Lebanese are informed and articulate about their heritage and proud of their success in the face of difficult circumstances. The priest of Saint Elias, Fr. Richard Saad, compares Birmingham's religious and ethnic consciousness favorably with that experienced in his own childhood in Detroit's far-larger Lebanese community.

I think the Birmingham community has always been very aware of itself. I really believe that. And I've heard compliments about them, nationally, you know, throughout my time as a priest. . . . They've always stayed close to their traditions and their identity and their church. Haven't gone too far away and had to pull them back, I mean, they know, they have had that awareness. And I think that is due to the churches which promote that and to the [Cedars] Club.[51]

THE LIMITS OF ADJUSTMENT

The development of the Birmingham Maronite parish, of the other local Lebanese organizations and institutions, and of the ethnic group itself parallel, in part, the experience of the Lebanese elsewhere in America. Yet the adjustment of the Birmingham Lebanese was not as simple or swift as has been posited as the norm.

Referring in particular to early Lebanese communities, a leading scholar of Arab-American assimilation recently concluded that

the attempts of the immigrant generation to maintain Arab culture ran afoul of their eagerness to succeed in the United States; the requirements of success relegated tradition to second place. . . . The participation of the early immigrants in American life was somewhat cursory; coupled with their prosperity, however, it was nevertheless sufficient to allow their children to enter the larger American society with relatively little psychological stress.[52]

The evolution of the Birmingham Lebanese community indicates the degree to which the structure of the host society could thwart such easy adjustment. The key issue for white society in Birmingham, as for the rest of the developing South in this period, was how to facilitate economic expansion while maintaining the color line. The growing ranks of immigrants complicated that already difficult problem. As an area Greek put it:

We had the monied people who settled Birmingham, then we had the foreign people. And they looked on them more or less in the same classification as blacks.[53]

The foreigners, then, inhabited an uneasy position definitely below the white elite group, but "more or less" like blacks. The Lebanese in Birmingham carved out an economic niche in the city, and their commercial success made them less like Birmingham's working-class blacks. But religion, nationality, and color separated them from the Anglo majority. In this era of deepening cultural conflict, the economic importance of the Lebanese was not enough to offset the racial and religious feeling against them. As champions of the caste system sought a clearer color line and a narrower religious spectrum, the "colored" and Catholic Lebanese in Birmingham turned to the organization of their own communal life, forging strong and enduring bonds and institutions.

Notes

1. This paper draws extensively on field research conducted by Nancy Faires Conklin and Brenda McCallum documented in their unpublished ms., "Final Report: Greek School, Holy Trinity—Holy Cross Greek Orthodox Cathedral, and Lebanese Arabic School, St. Elias Maronite Catholic Church, Birmingham, Alabama," Project on Ethnic Heritage and Language Schools in America, American Folk Life Center, Library of Congress, 1982. We gratefully acknowledge the contributions of Brenda McCallum, Head, Popular Culture Library, Bowling Green State University; Robert Jefferson Norrell, Department of History, University of Alabama; and the informants in the Birmingham community.

2. Paul B. Worthman, "Working Class Mobility in Birmingham, Alabama, 1880–1914," in *Anonymous Americans: Explorations in Nineteenth-Century Social History,* ed. Tamara K. Hareven (Englewood Cliffs, N.J.: Prentice-Hall, 1971), 174; and Robert S. Allen, *Our Fair City* (New York: Vanguard Press, 1947), 105. On the growth of Birmingham, see also Zane L. Miller, "Urban Blacks in the South, 1865–1920: The Richmond, Savannah, New Orleans, Louisville, Birmingham Experience," in *The New Urban History,* ed. Leo F. Schnore (Princeton, N.J.: Princeton University Press, 1975), 184–204; and Blaine A. Brownell, "Birmingham, Alabama: New South City in the 1920s," *Journal of Southern History* 38 (February 1972): 21–48.

3. On Birmingham's population growth, see Howard P. Chudacoff, *The Evolution of American Urban Society,* 2d ed. (Englewood Cliffs, N.J.: Prentice-Hall, 1971), 103, 205; Howard N. Rabinowitz, "Continuity and Change: Southern Urban Development, 1860–1900," in *The City in Southern History,* ed. Blaine A. Brownell and David R. Goldfield (Port Washington, N.Y.: Kennikat Press, 1977); Blaine A. Brownell, "The Urban South Comes of Age, 1900–1940," in *The City in Southern History,* ed. Brownell and Goldfield, 124–26; and Edward F. Haas, "The Southern Metropolis, 1940–1976," in *The City in Southern History* ed. Brownell and Goldfield, 173. The quote is from Allen, *Our Fair City,* 105.

4. Miller, "Urban Blacks in the South," 188–89.

5. Conklin and McCallum, "Final Report," 22–28; Worthman, "Working Class Mobility in Birmingham," 180.

6. Worthman, "Working Class Mobility in Birmingham," 175.

7. U.S. Cong., *Report of the Immigration Commission,* 61st Cong., 2nd sess., "Bituminous Coal Mining in the South," Report on Immigrants in Industry, pt. 1, S. Doc. 633, 1911. The study used data collected in 1902.

8. Bituminous Coal Mining in the South," 141–42.

9. Worthman, "Working Class Mobility in Birmingham," 175, 180.

10. "Bituminous Coal Mining in the South," 139, 141–42. Some of the thirty-five Russians enumerated may have been Jewish, as may some of the other Eastern European nationals, but the numbers are probably negligible.

11. W. F. Teeple and N. Davis Smith, *History of Jefferson County and Birmingham, Ala.* (Birmingham: Teeple and Smith, 1887), 242; as quoted in Mark H. Elovitz, *A Century of Jewish Life in Dixie: The Birmingham Experience* (University, Alabama: University of Alabama Press, 1974), 22.

12. Elovitz, *A Century of Jewish Life in Dixie,* 23.

13. Elovitz, *A Century of Jewish Life in Dixie,* 22–23, 35, 59, 66–67, 98.

14. All information on Italians in Birmingham is from "The Italians: From Bisacquino to Birmingham," a *Birmingfind* pamphlet (Birmingham: no publisher), n.d. (publication of an ethnic history project funded by the National Endowment for the Humanities); and R.J. Norrell, "Steelworkers and Storekeepers: Social Mobility Among Italian Immigrants in Birming-

ham," paper delivered at the annual meeting of the American-Italian Historical Association, New York, 1982.

15. The Italians: From Bisacquino to Birmingham," n. p.; see also Norrell, "Steelworkers and Storekeepers," 3–4.

16. On Birmingham's Greek community, see Conklin and McCallum, "Final Report," 11–21, 28–36, and "The New Patrida: The Story of Birmingham's Greeks," a *Birmingfind* pamphlet, n.d.

17. Conklin and McCallum, "Final Report," 13.

18. Conklin and McCallum, "Final Report," 24; "Birmingham's Lebanese: 'The Earth Turned to Gold,' " a *Birmingfind* pamphlet, n.d.

19. U.S. Cong, *Report of the Immigration Commission,* 61st Cong., 3d sess., S. Doc. 758, 517–19.

20. Senate Doc. 758, 517–19.

21. L.S. Overman, *Amendment of Immigration Laws,* 61st Cong., 2d sess., S. Doc. 251, 1912, 9. Figures are for the decade 1900 to 1910.

22. Senate Doc. 758, 519.

23. In the 1890s, the South had largely opposed efforts to restrict immigration. The reasons for the region's decided shift to a position of leadership in the battle for immigration restriction are complex, lying beyond the scope of this paper, but are clearly related to the surge of racism and tightening of segregation against blacks during the early twentieth century. On the rise of Southern nativism, see John Higham, *Strangers in the Land: Patterns of American Nativism, 1860–1925* (New York: Atheneum, 1971), 164–71.

24. David R. Goldfield, "The Urban South: A Regional Framework," *American Historical Review* 86 (December 1981): 1020–22. Goldfield points out that Southern urban murder rates exceeded those for other cities in the nation.

25. Elovitz, *A Century of Jewish Life in Dixie,* 85. The Klan also harassed Italians in the city; see Norrell, "Steelworkers and Storekeepers," 11.

26. As quoted in Brenda McCallum and Cliff Kuhn, "Unionization in Birmingham," unpublished ms., Archive of American Minority Cultures, University of Alabama, April 1983, 2.

27. As quoted in Higham, *Strangers in the Land,* 164–65. See also the discussion of Underwood in Norrell, "Steelworkers and Storekeepers," 11.

28. Higham, *Strangers in the Land,* 164–67.

29. J.L. Burnett, *Report on Immigration of Aliens into the United States,* U.S. Cong., 2nd sess., House Rept. 851, 1912.

30. Overman, *Amendment of Immigration Laws,* 20–38.

31. Overman, *Amendment of Immigration Laws,* 21.

32. Overman, *Amendment of Immigration Laws,* 30.

33. Overman, *Amendment of Immigration Laws,* 31.

34. This account of Burnett's remark appears in an unpublished ms. by Dr. H.A. El-Kourie entitled, "In Defense of the Semitic and Syrian Especially"; see below. This document was made available by Robert Jefferson Norrell.

35. The articles appeared in the Birmingham *Ledger,* September 20, 1907, and the Birmingham *Age-Herald,* October 20, 1907.

36. The essay bears the title "Facts Establishing That the Semitic is the Equal of Any Race and Superior to Many." All future references will be to the title of the document as a whole, "In Defense of the Semitic and the Syrian Especially."

37. "In Defense of the Semitic and the Syrian Especially," n. d., n.p.

38. "In Defense of the Semitic and the Syrian Especially," n. d., n.p.

39. "In Defense of the Semitic and the Syrian Especially," n. d., n.p.

40. Hitti, *The Syrians in America* (New York: George H. Doran Company, 1924), 89.

41. Quoted in Conklin and McCallum, "Final Report," 79.

42. Quoted in Conklin and McCallum, "Final Report," 79.

43. Quoted in Conklin and McCallum, "Final Report," 80.

44. Conklin and McCallum, "Final Report," 24–26.

45. Conklin and McCallum, "Final Report," 24.

46. Philip M. Kayal, "Religion in the Christian 'Syrian-American Community,' " in *Arabic-Speaking Communities in American Cities*, ed. Barbara C. Aswad (Staten Island: Center for Migration Studies of New York, 1974), 125.

47. Conklin and McCallum, "Final Report," 24–26.

48. Conklin and McCallum, "Final Report," 38–41.

49. Conklin and McCallum, "Final Report," 22–27, 37.

50. The attendance of Birmingham's Lebanese at parochial schools stands in contrast to the general Syrian pattern, as reported in Hitti, *The Syrians in America*, 91.

51. Conklin and McCallum, "Final Report," 82–83.

52. Alixa Naff, "Arabs in America," in *Arabs in the New World: Studies on Arab-American Communities*, ed. Sameer Y. Abraham and Nabeel Abraham (Detroit: Wayne State University Press, Center for Urban Studies, 1983), 22.

53. Quoted in Conklin and McCallum, "Final Report," 79.

From the Near East to Down East

Ethnic Arabs in Waterville, Maine

ERIC J. HOOGLUND

The immigration of Arabs to Maine began around 1890, reached a peak between 1906 and 1914, then continued intermittently until 1940. During that fifty-year period approximately four hundred Arabs came to the state. The majority of them had emigrated from villages in what is now Lebanon. They had set out for the United States and then made their way Down East in search of work opportunities or to join family members who already were established in Maine. By the time World War I broke out, 50 percent of the estimated three hundred Arab immigrants then in the state had chosen to settle permanently in Maine.

Arab individuals and/or families resided in more than a dozen cities and towns throughout the state by 1915. In only one place, however, was there a large enough concentration to constitute a distinct Arabic-speaking ethnic community. This was in the small city of Waterville, located on the west bank of the Kennebec River in the south-central part of the state. By 1915 two-thirds of all Maine's Arabs lived in Waterville and in the adjacent towns of Fairfield and Winslow. The Waterville area was an important textile manufacturing center during that period. The prospect of jobs in the cotton and woolen mills had served as a major attraction for the immigrants. After 1915 the Arabs established firm roots in Waterville; they married, raised families, and gradually gave up any dreams of returning to their home villages. In effect, Waterville became their home. In the process, Waterville became the major center for Arabs in Maine as various business and cultural establishments were set up to serve the specific needs and interests of the local community.

The purpose of this article is to describe the formation of the Arabic-speaking community in Waterville, Maine, up to 1940. The paper is divided into two parts. The first part covers the years 1890 to 1915, the period when most of the actual immigration took place. The origins of the immigrants and their reasons for settling in Waterville are examined. The second part focuses upon the transformation between 1915 and 1940 of the immigrant community into an ethnic community.[1]

ARAB IMMIGRATION TO MAINE, 1890–1915

Informants do not agree upon the precise date that the first Arab arrived in Maine. The earliest dates are generally given as between 1885 and 1888. Arabs were first officially recorded in Maine in the census of 1900, listed as natives of "Syria." However, barely one-dozen "Syrians" were enumerated by census takers for the whole state. Even in Waterville, which soon would become a center for Arabic-speaking immigrants, only three persons of "Syrian" origins are known of: a man, his wife, and their Maine-born infant son.[2] The major influx of ethnic Arabs thus began after 1900. An estimated five persons per year arrived in the state between 1901 and 1905. Beginning in 1906, however, the number of Arabs coming to Maine significantly increased. At the time of the 1910 census more than 150 Arabs lived throughout the state. During the next four years the number of immigrants nearly doubled.

By 1915 an estimated three hundred Arabs lived in Maine. They resided in the state's largest cities, such as Portland, Lewiston, and Bangor, and in the many mill towns, such as Bath, Biddeford Caribou, Eastport, Fairfield, Fort Fairfield, Madison, Millinocket, Old Town, Pittsfield, Sanford, Van Buren, Vasalborough, Waterville, and Winslow. In some places, such as Bangor, Fairfield, and particularly Waterville, several Arabic-speaking families resided. In other towns, for example Bath and Eastport, only a single family in each is recorded.

The Arab immigrants shared several characteristics, all of which helped to nurture a distinct ethnic identity: 1) They all spoke the same language, Arabic. Even more significant, they all spoke the same or closely related dialects of Arabic; 2) They tended to come from the same geographical area, the historic province of Syria, which was then a part of the Ottoman Empire. In particular, they came from districts that are now part of the states of Lebanon and Syria; 3) The overwhelming majority of the immigrants were of peasant origins. Specifically, they came from villages in south Lebanon, to the northeast of Beirut, and in the Latakia and Damascus areas of Syria; 4) The immigrants were relatively young. More than 75 percent were twenty-five years or younger when they left their native villages to come to the United States; 5) The majority, when they immigrated, were

Two girls pose in costume in this 1920s photograph from a play sponsored by Saint Mary's Syrian Orthodox Church in Pawtucket, Rhode Island. The Syrian Ladies' Aid Society of Boston and similar organizations in other communities put on plays with traditional Arab themes in order to raise money for charitable projects. Photo courtesy of Robert Laffey.

illiterate in their native language, as well as in English, but had a deep respect for learning and placed a high value on education after settling in Maine; 6) At least 80 percent of the adult males became wage laborers in factories or in small work shops, and thus tended to have similar occupations, incomes, interests, and aspirations. Finally, they were virtually all Christian: two-thirds were Maronite (Syriac-rite Catholics); about 20 percent were Greek (Antiochian) Orthodox; some 10 percent were Melchite (Greek-rite Catholics); and the rest included Protestant sects and a few Muslims.

The Arabic-speaking immigrants generally did not consider themselves Arabs, nor were they called Arabs by other ethnic groups in Maine. Legally speaking, those who had arrived in the United States before 1918 were subjects of the Ottoman Empire, commonly referred to as Turkey. Thus, some Americans called immigrants from the area "Turks." None of the Arabic-speaking Christians, however, thought of themselves as Turks. Before World War I, they had identified themselves upon the basis of religious affiliation, and not upon the basis of nationality. Thus, in the old country they were Maronite or Orthodox or Melchite or Protestant. In a new country, where they were surrounded by different peoples who identified themselves on the basis of ethnicity, it became necessary for the Arabic-speaking immigrants to find a similar identity. As early as the 1890s they had begun to refer to themselves as "Syrians."

The term "Syrian" conveyed both a geographic and an ethnic meaning. In a broad sense, a Syrian was a native of the Ottoman Empire's province of Syria, which included Syria proper, Mount Lebanon, and Palestine. More specifically, "Syrian" designated a speaker of Arabic who was not a Muslim but a follower of one of the ancient Syrian Christian churches that still existed in the Near East. In contrast, the term "Arab" generally was used by Christians to refer to native Muslims of Syria, although among the educated urban population of Syria the growing tendency was to use "Arab" as an all-inclusive, secular term of national identity.

The use of "Syrian" as an ethnic designation was also encouraged by United States immigration officers who preferred to have nationality categories for the diverse peoples arriving from the Ottoman Empire and the other multiethnic empires, such as Austro-Hungary, Germany, and Tsarist Russia. It even became common practice to list the language spoken by the "Syrians," that is, Arabic, as "Syrian." In 1899 the term "Syrian" was officially adopted by the U.S. to identify Arabic-speaking immigrants from Ottoman Syria. In Maine the term Syrian came to be associated not just with the people and their language, but also with their food, music, customs, and institutions. It was not until after World War I that some of the more politically conscious members of the Arabic-speaking community in Maine tried to encourage a new "Lebanese" identity. Nevertheless, "Syrian" continued to be the most widely used ethnic term up to 1940. For that reason it will be used in the remainder of this article to refer to the Arabic-speaking immigrants in Maine.

The Syrians had left their native villages and traveled across the ocean to find work and establish new lives. They were part of the mass migration of thousands of Syrians to North and South America between 1890 and 1914. Of course, the three hundred who came to Maine during that period represented but a tiny fraction of the overall movement. The development of the Syrian community in Maine shared, nevertheless, many similar patterns with the formation of larger Syrian communities, and even with other ethnic communities, throughout the northeast and midwest. For that reason an examination of the Syrians in Maine provides valuable insights into the transformation of immigrant settlers into ethnic Americans.

It is natural to inquire why the Syrians chose to come to Maine, a state still predominantly rural during the fifteen years beginning in 1900. In fact, approximately two-thirds of Maine's population lived on family farms at the turn of the century. Maine also was beginning to experience, however, the effects of the industrialization that was transforming the United States into a major world power between 1870 and 1914. Even though the state was relatively isolated from the areas of major manufacturing and population growth, the establishment of textile, leather, pulp, and canning factories was proceeding in scores of small towns and villages. The mills needed workers, so, like their larger counterparts in the booming cities of the industrial heartland, they recruited immigrants for their labor force. Maine did not become a major industrial state, nor did it become a major center for immigrants, but several thousand jobs were created in the generation leading up to World War I, and several thousand immigrant workers were hired to fill those positions. The greatest number of immigrants came from Quebec; in addition to French Canadians, many English and Scottish Canadians arrived from the maritime provinces. Other immigrants included Armenians, British, Chinese, Danes, Finns, Germans, Greeks, Irish, Italians, Poles, Russian Jews, Slovaks, Swedes, Turks, Ukranians, and of course, the Syrians.

It is likely that the first Syrians came to Maine quite by chance, but after 1905 those who had become established in the state acted like a magnet to draw brothers, sisters, cousins, other kin and nonrelated friends from the same villages. By 1915, Syrians were living in more than a dozen Maine towns. With one exception, however, the numbers of Syrians in any one community were small, ranging only from three to thirty persons. The exception was the city of Waterville, where more than one hundred immigrants and more than sixty of their Maine-born children lived in 1915. In addition, most of the towns in which ten or more Syrian immigrants resided were adjacent to Waterville (e.g., Fairfield and Winslow) or relatively close by (e.g., Madison and Vasalborough).

It is probable that the primary reason for the concentration of Syrians in Waterville was the greater availability of work there. As late as 1900 only two Syrian immigrants had lived in Waterville. But the decade from 1900 to 1910 was both a period of major Syrian immigration into Maine and a period of major development for Waterville. Indeed, its prosperous and expanding factories drew sufficient workers to make Waterville the fastest-growing city in the state. Its population increased by 21 percent, three times more than the statewide average of only 7 percent. The population continued to grow by approximately 2 percent annually until 1915, when it reached 12,500. The fact that Waterville's era of relatively fast growth coincided with the heaviest Syrian immigration to Maine fostered the conditions that attracted the Arabic-speaking migrants to the city.

In 1915, Waterville was a manufacturing center. Its factories produced cotton and woolen textiles, paper products, machines, cast-iron stoves, small boats, and various consumer goods. But it was a small city, and its transformation from a semirural town of little significant industry had occurred within one generation. Waterville was located on the left bank of the Kennebec River opposite the place in the river where large boulders created natural falls. Originally the site had been occupied by an Indian village known as Ticonic. The Indians of the Kennebec Valley were accomplished agriculturalists. Their productive lands began attracting European settlers during the last half of the eighteenth century. By 1802, when Ticonic and a large area extending up to ten miles to the west were incorporated as the Town of Waterville, the native Indians had been largely displaced. Throughout most of the nineteenth century Waterville grew steadily but gradually. As late as 1880 half of its population, then only forty-seven hundred, lived on farms. The compact village along the river was the home of about two thousand people. It had one factory, the Hathaway Shirt Company, which had pioneered the production of ready-made shirts for men as early as 1837, and several saw mills. Waterville, however, primarily served as a service center for the agricultural hinterland.

Waterville's growth after 1880 was relatively rapid. In the twenty years up to 1900 its population doubled to ninety-five hundred. Several new factories were established: the Lockwood Cotton Textile Company, the Wyandotte Worsted Woolen Mill, the Lombard Power Traction Company, and the Hollingsworth and Whitney Paper Company (actually on the right bank of the river and legally within the municipal boundaries of Winslow). Many smaller workshops were set up and the old Hathaway Shirt Company was expanded. Accompanying the influx of jobs and people were constant construction projects: farmland was converted to residential streets; tenements were built near the factories; and, most significant, Main Street was completely transformed, as blocks of three- and four-story masonary buildings replaced the old wooden clapboard homes and businesses. After 1900 the factories continued to expand their labor forces, if not their physical plants (which actually had been built large to allow for growth in productive capacity); the Maine Central Railroad established its rail car maintenance and repair shops in Waterville; residential development northward resulted in the physical merger of Waterville and Fairfield; and considerable "public" construction—the city hall, schools, hospitals, and the like—was undertaken. By 1915, Waterville was not just one of the state's principal manufacturing centers, but was also one of its major commercial centers.

The description of Waterville given above is meant to provide background on the kind of community in which the Syrians settled. Now it is appropriate to examine some of the social characteristics of the immigrants. The most complete information comes from the 1910 census for Waterville.[3] The raw data—nearly three hundred printed pages for Waterville—provide information for each individual living at an address on the date that census enumerators visited. Thus, the name, gender, age, marital status, place of birth, date of immigration to the United States if non-native, language spoken, occupation, place of employment, education, and other miscellaneous information are recorded for each person. The total population of Waterville in 1910 was 11,458. Of that number, eighty were listed as having been born in Syria.[4] A careful study of the names reveals that three of the Syrian immigrants were erroneously counted twice, at different addresses.[5] After adjusting for that error, seventy-seven Syrians are correctly counted as being in Waterville at the time of the 1910 census.

The total population of those of Syrian origin was 55 percent greater than the Syrian immigrant population, since the 1910 census included forty-one children who had been born to the Syrians in Maine (thirty-eight) or in Massachusetts (three). Thus, 118 ethnic Syrians actually were in Waterville. That figure represents 1 percent of the city's total in 1910.

The census contains interesting data on the male-to-female ratio among the seventy-seven immigrants. Forty-eight of them, or 62.3 percent, were males; forty-six were men fifteen years or older, and two were boys under the age of ten. There were twenty-nine females, all fifteen years or older. Women thus constituted 37.7 percent of the Syrian immigrants.

Twenty-two married couples are counted among the immigrants. In addition, three women were listed as widows, and one man was married to a non-Syrian. Four of the women were single, as were twenty-three of the adult males. Those figures illustrate that eighty-six percent of the women and 50 percent of the men were married.

Table 5 presents a summary of the age categories of the Syrians when they first arrived in the United States. It was derived by subtracting the number of years each Syrian had been in America from column 7 (age at last birthday). The former figure was determined by subtracting the date given in column 15 (year of immigration to the United States) from 1910, the actual census year. Thus, if a Syrian was recorded as twenty-three on the census sheet (1910) and as having immigrated in 1906, it was assumed that he or she would have been nineteen at the time of immigration. Applying the same method to all seventy-seven immigrants, we can see, as shown in table 5, that more than half—56 percent—of all Syrians were between the ages of fifteen and twenty-four when they arrived in the United States; a total of 84.5 percent were under thirty.

Among the seventy-five adult immigrants, forty-four were employed at the time of the census. Forty-one of the employed were men, and three were single women. None of the twenty-five married or widowed women were gainfully employed outside of the home. Table 5 provides a summary of the occupations of the employed Syrians. It is noteworthy that 86 percent of all the employed Syrians were laborers. More than one-third of the employed—sixteen persons—worked in one factory, the Lockwood Cotton Textile Company, the largest mill in Waterville. It was located on the Kennebec River

Table 5.
Age of Waterville's Syrians at Date of Their Immigration to the United States

Age in Years	*Number of Immigrants*	*Percentage of Immigrants*
Under 10	3	4
10–14	11	14
15–19	21	27
20–24	22	29
25–29	8	10.5
30–35	7	9
Over 35	5	6.5
TOTAL	77	100

Source: Derived by author from data in 1910 Census of Waterville, Maine.

below the Ticonic Falls and immediately south of Main Street. It employed an estimated five hundred workers in 1910.

The second largest employer in Waterville was the Wyandotte Worsted Wollen Mill with approximately 350 workers. It, too, was located along the river, but above the falls and near the approximate site of the old Indian village of Ticonic. At least seven Syrians worked at the Wyandotte; in addition, it is likely that the dye house, where one Syrian was employed, was part of the woolen mill (see table 6). More than one-half of all the employed Syrians, a minimum of twenty-three persons, thus worked at one or the other of the city's two principal factories.

Less than 12 percent of the employed Syrians were engaged in business. Those individuals included three retail merchants, one "traveling salesman," who actually may have been a peddler, and one person listed as "peddler". Finally, the occupation of one Syrian was given as "barber." His place of work was a barbershop, but the data does not specify whether he was a proprietor or an employee.

The five adult males who were unemployed in 1910 included three young men who had arrived in the United States in 1909 or 1910 and were living in households headed by employed relatives. The three household heads were all laborers. It is probable that they hoped to find employment at their workplace for their brothers/brothers-in-law. The other two unemployed men were both over forty and headed households in which grown sons were employed as laborers.

We can conclude the analysis of data from the 1910 census by looking at the residential patterns of the immigrants and their families. Syrians lived in three of Waterville's seven wards. Their greatest concentration was in

Table 6.
Occupations of Syrian Immigrants in Waterville, Maine, 1910

Occupation	*Number*	*Percentage of Total Employed*
Barber	1	2.2
Laborer	(38)	86.4
cotton mill (includes 3 women)	16	
woolen mill	7	
railroad yard	6	
coal yard	1	
dye house	1	
odd jobs	1	
farm hand	1	
unspecified or illegible	5	
Merchant	(3)	7.0
groceries	2	
dry goods	1	
Peddler	1	2.2
Traveling salesman	1	2.2
TOTAL	44	100.0

Source: Derived by author from data in 1910 Census of Waterville, Maine.

Ward Four, which included the Head of Falls neighborhood. Occupying part of the site of the Indian village of Ticonic, Head of Falls was a section of tenements across Temple Street from the Wyandotte Worsted Woolen Mill. The area, which has been redeveloped as a park since the 1960s, was wedged between the railroad tracks and the Kennebec River just below the intersection of Front and Temple streets. In addition to the cross-track continuation of Temple Street, which ended at the footbridge crossing the river to the pulp mill on the opposite bank, two small streets, Head of Falls Court and King Court, extended off Temple and paralleled one another. Several hundred people lived in the crowded, wooden tenement homes in Head of Falls. The majority of inhabitants were of French-Canadian origins, the predominant ethnic group in Waterville by 1910. But nearly half of the city's total Syrian community—fifty-eight of 118 immigrants and their American-born children—also lived in Head of Falls.

Two Syrian families totaling eleven persons lived immediately adjacent to Head of Falls on Front and Temple streets. The northern continuation of Front Street was in Ward Three but within a ten-minute walk of Head of Falls. In one sprawling, clapboard home, which the census enumerator designated the "Syrian tenement house," lived twenty-seven Syrian immigrants and their Maine-born children. The remaining twenty-two members of the Syrian community also lived within ten minutes walking distance of Head of Falls, in the tenement neighborhood adjacent to the Lockwood mill.

The data discussed above does not reveal any unique characteristics of Waterville's Syrian community in comparison to other Maine towns where Syrian immigrants lived in 1910. In those localities in which at least ten Arabic-speaking immigrants were enumerated, whether genuine urban centers such as Portland or semirural mill towns like Fairfield and Vasalborough, one finds similar patterns with respect to the immigrants' relative youth at the time of immigration, the male-to-female ratio, the marriage rate, the high percentage of adult males employed as laborers, and the tendency of Syrians to reside in close proximity. What does stand out about Waterville's community is its relative size. By 1910 three times as many Syrian immigrants lived in Waterville as lived in the town with the next highest number of immigrants; and half of all Syrian immigrants in the state were in Waterville.

From the completion of the Thirteenth Census in June 1910 until the early months of 1915 when Syrian immigration virtually ceased on account of the travel difficulties associated with World War I, the number of Syrian immigrants in Waterville increased by at least 80 percent. In this four-and-one-half-year period an estimated sixty-five Syrians, over one-third of whom were females fourteen years of age and older, arrived in the city.[7] During those same years, an additional twenty children were born to the immigrants. Thus, the Arabic-speaking community had grown to two hundred by 1915. It also had become part of Waterville's ethnic mosaic and constituted the largest and most important Syrian community in the entire state of Maine.

THE SYRIAN COMMUNITY OF WATERVILLE, 1915–40

In October 1914 the Ottoman Empire joined the European war on the side of the German and Austro-Hungarian Empires against Great Britain, France, and Tsarist Russia. The hostilities in Europe and in the Middle East virtually cut off the flow of immigrants from Syria as well as elsewhere. The United States entered the conflict in 1917 but did not declare war on the Ottoman Empire and never participated in the hostilities between the British/French armies and the Ottoman Turkish troops. During the war a major famine ravaged Syria. It was precipitated by a combination of drought, Anglo-French policies of blocking Turkish-controlled ports, and Turkish policies of requisitioning grains and punishing the Arabic-speaking population for suspected disloyalty to the imperial government based in Istanbul. Syrian immigrant communities throughout the United States collected medical supplies, foodstuffs, and clothing to send to Syria to aid the victims of the famine. In Waterville, nine of the immigrant men served in the U.S. army, and the Syrian community as a whole bought generously of the Liberty Bonds sold to finance the war.

The Ottoman Empire was on the losing side in World War I. After the war, its territories were divided up among the British, the French, and their European allies. Syria was carved into four separate colonies: Lebanon and Syria under French administration, and Palestine and Transjordan under British administration. Emigration from these new "countries" resumed in 1919. During the five years that followed, however, only twenty persons immigrated to Maine; at least an equal number returned to the Middle East to test living conditions under the new political order.

In the years immediately after World War I the United States was swept by an ugly wave of antiforeign prejudice. In response to the "nativist" bigotry, Congress enacted a series of restrictive immigration laws, culminating in the 1924 Immigration Quota Act that effectively brought an end to more than a century of relatively open immigration policies. The 1924 law limited the number of immigrants to 150,000 per year, and established an unabashedly racist national origins quota for determining who could be admitted to the country. The number of immigrants of any one nationality were henceforth to be based upon the actual percentage of that ethnic group in the 1890 census. For Syrians, initially defined as nationals of the new French-controlled states of Lebanon and Syria, the quota was one hundred persons per annum.

The 1924 law meant that virtually no possibility existed for the Syrian community in Waterville or elsewhere in Maine to continue to grow through the arrival of new immigrants. In effect, the immigrants who had arrived up to 1915 were responsible for ensuring the survival of their traditions Down East. The immigrant generation apparently was determined to pass on cherished aspects of their culture to their American-born children. Between 1915 and 1940 the Syrians made conscious efforts to transform their community from an immigrant one to an ethnic one with solid roots in Waterville.

In the period 1915 to 1940 the number of Syrian families in Waterville doubled from about thirty to about sixty. The size of the community increased 50 percent, from two hundred to three hundred persons. During the same twenty-five-year period, Waterville's total population increased by one-third, from 12,500 to 16,700. The faster growth rate of the Syrian community means that the total population of Syrian-origins had increased from 1 to almost 2 percent of the city's population since 1910.

Up to 1940 the majority of Syrians continued to live in the Head of

Falls neighborhood. Beginning in the early 1920s, however, several families moved out of Head of Falls proper and into more solidly constructed houses along Front Street and the side streets between Temple and Union that connected Front Street with Main Street. The expanded residential area was still within walking distance of Head of Falls. During the 1920s and 1930s the larger neighborhood was served by Syrian groceries, restaurants, coffeehouses, clubs, a bakery, a church, and a primary school. The Syrians confronted a dilemma during the process of transforming themselves from a Syrian immigrant community into a Syrian ethnic community: how to maintain their district identity while simultaneously trying to become American and dealing with antiforeign prejudice.

The Syrians in Waterville sought to preserve their identity through both institutional and informal means. Arabic remained, informally, the principal language in the homes right up to 1940. The foods prepared, the social customs observed, and the family traditions honored were all similar to those that the immigrants knew in their native villages, albeit with some adaptations necessitated by the different demands of an urban, working-class lifestyle in a foreign country. More-formal efforts to maintain their distinct heritage were attempted through the creation of both religious and secular institutions.

The first secular institution was the Lebanon Youth Society (LYS), founded in November 1916 by eight of the immigrant men. The LYS initially rented a room in a house on Front Street and conducted regular meetings there, but eventually moved to larger quarters on Main Street. The LYS was an all-male social club with a membership of about one hundred by 1940. It raised money for various charitable causes, both to benefit the community as a whole and to help individual needy families. The members of the LYS included the most influential men of the Syrian community. Thus the LYS played a more active role in its affairs during the 1920s and 1930s than one would normally expect of a social club.

A second secular institution was the Syrian Athletic Club (SAC). It was established in the 1930s by young men who had been born in Waterville to immigrant parents before 1915. They were the first generation to go to the public schools, the oldest ones having graduated from high school as early as 1922. The SAC reflected the interests of the single, bilingual men of the period: an ethnic consciousness combined with an enthusiasm for American popular music and sports. The SAC members organized a football team, which played games with the teams of other social clubs in Waterville and in the surrounding area. It also had a large room in one of the tenements in Head of Falls. Informants recall that many dances were held at the SAC premises.

A third secular "institution" was short-lived. This was a newspaper that was printed in both Arabic and English for one year in the late 1920s. It was started by four of the younger immigrants who had acquired literacy in both languages, an unusual accomplishment for that time. Indeed, most of the immigrants born before 1890 were not even literate in Arabic. The paper apparently was a monthly and was typeset in Boston. Informants who remembered the paper recall that it contained articles about political developments in Lebanon and Syria, which by then had been set up as two separate entities both dependent on France. It featured, in addition, general-interest articles about other Arabic-speaking communities, especially in New England. The paper ceased publication when the owner of the Arabic-language printing shop in Boston died, and it proved difficult to find another shop that provided typesetting in Arabic.

A final institution that should be mentioned is the "school." In the late 1920s regular Arabic classes were held in a private home in Head of Falls. The purpose was to instruct the American-born youths to read and write the language of their parents. One informant who attended the school recalled that two immigrant men literate in Arabic were the teachers.

For most of the Syrian community in Waterville the principal influence for maintaining cultural identity was not through secular institutions but through religious ones. The immigrants were not, however, unified in terms of religious beliefs. About 70 percent of them were Maronites, while another 20 percent were Greek Orthodox. A few were Melchites (Greek Catholics), and at least one was Muslim. Since the denominations in Waterville in the early 1900s lacked members of the clergy, the immigrants who wanted to pray in congregations had to rely upon already-existing churches. The Maronites generally attended services at the Catholic church, whereas the Greek Orthodox went to one of the several Protestant churches. By the 1920s about ten families of Greek Orthodox origins were parishioners at Saint Mark's Episcopal Church. For occasions of significant rites of passage, however, the families continued to import Greek Orthodox priests from Boston, despite their nominal affiliations with, and even financial support for, their adopted church.

Before World War I only a single Catholic Church was established in Waterville. The Maronites regularly attended services there, but apparently never felt comfortable. The church, Saint Francis De Salles, served primarily the large numbers of French-Canadians who had immigrated to Waterville after 1880. Its priests and their sermons were French, which tended to alienate the Maronites who believed that the foreign language they most needed to learn was English. In addition, by 1915 a certain degree of antagonism between the French-Canadians and the Syrians was evident; undoubtedly it stemmed from competition over jobs. Thus, when a second Catholic church, staffed by Irish priests who presented their sermons in English, was opened after the war, the Maronites joined that new parish, Sacred Heart, en masse.

Even though the Maronites found the Sacred Heart Church more congenial, their own rite differed from the Latin one in several respects. Thus, after 1920 they were determined to establish their own parish. At that time, about fifty families, including those who had converted from the Greek Orthodox or the Melchite denominations, were Maronite. In 1924 they were granted a Maronite priest from Lebanon through the help of another Maronite priest who had visited the Waterville community and knew of their hopes. Thus, Waterville's Maronite parish came into existence. Church services were initially held in private homes and rented rooms. Finally, in 1927, the parish succeeded in buying a property on Front Street, right in the heart of the Syrian ethnic section. The house was appropriately remodeled and dedicated as Saint Joseph's Maronite Church.

Saint Joseph's quickly emerged as the most important social institution for the Arabic-speaking community. The Maronite rite services were a direct link to a religious heritage that the children born in Maine had not experienced before 1924. The public dinners of Syrian food, organized by the women of the church to raise money for church projects, attracted Syrians, both Maronite and non-Maronite, from other Maine towns. Beginning in 1934 the church became the principal sponsor of an annual three-day summer fair, or *mahrajan,* which was held at the Central Maine Fairgrounds in the then-underdeveloped western part of Waterville. Among the regular exhibits was a replica of a Lebanese village, set up by the youth of the church. Arabic food, music, and dancing were displayed, and entertainers were hired to perform sword and belly dances. The *mahrajans* of the late 1930s attracted people not only from all over the state of Maine but also from as far away as Massachusetts, New Hampshire, and New York.

A major project of the church during the 1930s was to establish a primary school for the education of the many children who had been born to the immigrant parents (the average family had six children by 1940). The young priest who arrived in the 1930s was instrumental in setting up a school. Rev. Philip Nagem, born in the city to immigrant parents in 1904, was a son of the Waterville Syrian community. After graduating from Waterville High School in 1922, he entered a Catholic religious order. In the late 1920s he was sent to Lebanon, where he studied the ancient Syriac rite at a Maronite seminary. He reputedly placed a high value both on education and pride in heritage, and persuaded the community leaders of the desirability of a Maronite school. Property was finally acquired near the church and a small parochial school opened in the autumn of 1938.

Nagem is also remembered as the first Syrian to insist upon using "Lebanese" as a term of ethnic identity. He had been educated in Lebanon in the 1920s, a period when France was in the process of creating two separate countries, Lebanon and Syria, out of the old Ottoman province of Syria. It was a time of heady political and intellectual debate over identity:

were the people of Lebanon considered Arab, Syrian, or Lebanese? The people never reached a national consensus on that important question; Nagem evidently was influenced by the faction that argued for a Lebanese identity. When he returned home to Waterville he initiated a campaign to make the parishioners aware of the distinction between Lebanon and Syria. Since some of the immigrants had come, however, from villages in the "new" Syria, and since the immigrant generation had lost touch with the political currents of the old country, his efforts met with only limited success. "Syrian" continued to be the most widely used term up to 1940.

Even while the Syrian community made conscious efforts to preserve its ethnic identity, it was simultaneously pressured to "Americanize." The pressures affected the immigrants and their American-born children in divergent ways. Among the immigrants the pressures tended to be subtle. The immigrants accepted that they were different from Americans, yet, once they had decided to stay permanently in Waterville, they gradually began to consider themselves Americans as well as Syrians. Being American became associated with owning a home and educating one's children; the means to those goals were perceived, at least by the men, to be having a steady job and acquiring a functional knowledge of spoken English. One might reasonably argue that the immigrants absorbed the American dream after 1915 and became preoccupied with trying to achieve it, but they did not necessarily feel any pressures to adopt broader aspects of American culture; indeed, they disapproved of certain American social customs, convinced that their own traditions were superior.

The children of the immigrants who were born in Waterville between 1900 and 1925 perceived their ethnicity differently than did their parents. The difference was owing primarily to the fact that they attended public schools and thus were socialized in a proassimilation environment during their formative years. Consequently, they were more concerned with the broader aspects of American culture and tended to feel self-conscious about their family customs, which non-Syrian peers might judge to be strange. At the same time, the American-born Syrians, especially during the 1930s, were less inclined to share their parents' confidence in the American dream. They tended, for example, to be critical both of working conditions and of wages in the factories. Most of them, especially those who graduated from high school, hoped to avoid working in the mills.

During the 1920s and 1930s the factories continued to serve as the primary source of employment both for immigrants and for their children who were becoming adults. Significantly, it was considered appropriate for unmarried daughters to work. By 1940 approximately 80 percent of all American-born Syrian women had worked for at least one year while they were between the ages of sixteen and twenty-four. A small number of the married women also worked. The preferred work was in the woolen mill, where wages averaged about five cents more per hour than in the cotton mill and where overall working conditions were better than they were elsewhere. By 1930 many more Syrians were employed at the Wyandotte mill than at the Lockwood; Syrians constituted nearly 10 percent of the Wyandotte's entire working force (forty out of 410 workers), and most of them had learned the specialized trade of a weaver.

Working hours were long in Waterville's factories, as in factories throughout the country. The average work day was ten and one-half hours, and wages as late as 1933 were rarely more than thirty-five cents per hour. The unionization of workers for the purpose of improving conditions was resisted by the Yankee establishment that still dominated the city. Two Waterville-born sons of Syrian immigrants nevertheless played key roles in organizing unions in the Wyandotte and other mills. In 1934, in the midst of the Great Depression, George Jabar and Bernard Ezhaya helped to persuade most of Waterville's textile workers to join the nationwide textile strike for a uniform forty-hour work week and a minimum wage.

The strike in Waterville lasted for three weeks during September 1934. The owners of the Lockwood mill tried to break the strike by hiring unemployed workers to cross the picket lines. Their action led to a violent confrontation between some three hundred strikers and state police personnel who had been called upon to protect the mill. The Maine National Guard was eventually sent to Waterville to help maintain order.[8] The strike ended ten days later, following President Roosevelt's announcement that a special Textile Labor Relations Board would be set up to study working conditions throughout the textile industry.

The two Syrian union activists, Jabar and Ezhaya, used their experience to help organize textile workers throughout the state after the 1934 strike. In their careers up to World War II, they exhibited high motivation, a willingness to undertake risks, and a conviction in the possibility of change. In such respects, the men were typical of the children, especially the males, born in Maine to Syrian immigrants between 1900 and 1915. More than 50 percent completed high school, often while simultaneously working. While at least 80 percent of the men worked in the factories in their youth, by 1940 three-quarters of them were actually undertaking efforts to move up to other occupations in sales, management, and the professions. In other words, attempts to achieve upward social and economic mobility was becoming a main characteristic of the generation.

Even while the American-born Syrians were making progress in terms of assimilation, they tended to be sensitive about their heritage. The primary reason for their sensitivity was the general prejudice against the community during the 1915–40 period. The Arabic speakers and their children were perjoratively referred to as "black Syrians." Yankees of British and Irish stock whose roots were in preindustrial Waterville (i.e., pre-1880) tended to look down upon all the immigrants, not just the Syrians. The prejudice rarely involved blatant discrimination; rather, it was more subtle. The immigrants themselves generally were unaware of the extent of the prejudice because their limited knowledge of English tended both to discourage contact with the Yankees and to cause them to miss linguistic cues. Their children, however, grew up fluent in English and readily comprehended speech nuances and gestures that were intended to express insults and/or disdain.

Anti-Syrian prejudice was much more openly expressed among the French-Canadians than among the Americans. Approximately fifteen hundred French-Canadians had immigrated to Waterville from farms and villages in Quebec between 1880 and 1915. By World War I, they constituted the single largest ethnic community in the city. Since the French were predominantly mill workers, they competed with the Syrians for the small number of more-prestigious and better-paying jobs, such as that of a weaver. The result was that a degree of mutual distrust and dislike formed between the French and the Syrian youth in the 1920s and 1930s. Their rivalries often were expressed through derogatory ethnic slurs, and sometimes through fist, snowball, and rock fights. At the same time, however, the prevalence of anti-French prejudice in Waterville permitted Syrians and French-Canadians to identify with a common enemy: bigotry. Members of the two communities sometimes put aside their mutual suspicions to cooperate, as happened during the textile strike of 1934.

CONCLUSION

By 1940 the original Arabic-speaking immigrants to Waterville had succeeded in establishing a genuine Syrian ethnic community in their adopted city. Their children, the American-born second generation, had multiplied to comprise the largest component of the community. The younger Syrians were beginning to join their parents in leadership positions in the Church and in clubs. Born, reared, and educated in the Elm City, members of the second generation spoke English fluently, albeit with a distinct Down East accent, and identified themselves as Americans. But they also knew they were Syrians, and some even wrestled with the distinction between "Syrian" and "Lebanese." The children of the immigrants also had begun to marry and to raise their own families, and some third-generation Syrians were already preparing to enter secondary school. Thus, within forty years, the Syrian community had taken root in Maine.

World War II would stimulate major changes within the Syrian community as it would for other ethnic communities throughout the United States. After the war, Lebanon and Syria both became independent countries, stimulating renewed interest in how to define ethnicity. During the 1950s and 1960s the term "Lebanese" gradually replaced "Syrian," especially among those in the community born after 1920.

Notes

1. The primary research for this article is based upon interviews with more than twenty immigrants and their American-born children. The interviews were conducted in Waterville and in Belgrade Lakes, Maine, between 1976 and 1986. In addition, in the spring of 1983, I obtained copies of transcripts of interviews with twenty other immigrants and second-generation Americans recorded in the winter and spring of 1976. A Waterville attorney, Joseph Ezhaya, initiated the effort for the Waterville Oral History Project, which was sponsored by the Maine Commission on the Humanities as part of the state's celebration of the bicentennial of the signing of the Declaration of Independence. I am grateful to Joey Ezhaya for helping me to get access to the valuable interviews and also for providing insightful comments on some of the data they contain. The original tapes and typed transcriptions are deposited with the Waterville Public Library.

In the spring of 1983, I circulated questionnaires within Waterville's ethnic Arab community. It was designed to elicit information on the origins of pre-1925 immigrants and their educational backgrounds, occupations up to 1940, and other social data. I am grateful to Marie Deeb of Thomas College in Waterville for assisting with the project and also for sharing with me over the years her own considerable knowledge about the Arabic-speaking immigrants throughout the state of Maine.

Many other people have assisted my research efforts during the past decade. Unfortunately, it is not possible to thank them all individually in a note. I must acknowledge, however, special gratitude to Amelia Azar, John Jabar, Anna and Cynthia Mitchell, and Sadie Nasrallah.

Finally, any study has its beginning. The original inspiration to undertake this research was provided by Mrs. Joseph George and her five daughters, Louise, Annie, Matilda, Janet, and Celia. To each of these special women I am lovingly indebted.

2. See "Kennebec County," *Twelfth Census of the United States, 1900: Maine,* vol. 10 (microfilm, reel number 594, National Archives, Washington, D.C.). The three persons of "Syrian" origins are enumerated in Waterville in Ward Six.

3. By law the federal decennial census records are sealed for seventy-two years. The actual census sheets filled out by hand by enumerators for the 1910 census were microfilmed and made available to the public in 1982–83. They can be viewed in the special reading room at the National Archives, Washington, D.C. For the 1910 census of Waterville, see "Kennebec and Knox Counties," *Thirteenth Census of the United States, 1910: Maine,* vol. 19, pp. 1–233, (microfilm, ED's 118–33, roll 542).

4. In 1910 the city of Waterville was divided into seven wards, each of which was canvassed by a separate enumerator. The enumerators for wards Three, Four, and Six counted Syrians in their residence-by-residence enumeration. The Syrians were identified under the "Nativity" column on the census sheets where space was provided for writing in the place of birth of each individual and the place of birth of his/her father and mother. The enumerators used the following terms to identify Syrian nativity: "Syria"; "Syr."; "Syrian"; and "Turkey Eu Syria."

5. Not only were the census takers for each ward different, but the actual door-to-door enumeration was undertaken over a period of several weeks. One family, consisting of a man, his wife, and their daughter, all of whom had been born in Syria, plus five additional children born in the United States, apparently moved from Ward Four to Ward Six during the course of the enumeration and was counted at both residences.

6. One hundred twenty-six Syrians are actually listed on the census sheets, but I have deleted eight names that were erroneously counted twice. See note 5 above.

7. No precise data exists for this period. I have estimated the figures based upon collected information about 110 Syrian immigrants known to have come to Maine after the 1910 census was completed. By 1912 a community of Syrian immigrants was established at Madison, a small Kennebec River mill town about twenty miles north of Waterville. Virtually all of them, both men and women, worked in the woolen mill, which was then in Madison. By 1918 many of the Syrians in Madison had resettled in Waterville. Also by that date, some of the Syrians who had been in Waterville in 1910 relocated to other Maine towns or moved out of the state.

8. For a description of the strike and riot, see *The Waterville Morning Sentinel,* September 18–20, 1934.

Arabic-Speaking Immigration to the El Paso Area, 1900–1935

SARAH E. JOHN

At the end of the nineteenth century, El Paso, Texas, and Ciudad Juarez in Chihuahua, Mexico, were quiet frontier towns. Yet the recent arrival of railroads—which linked El Paso to both coasts and Ciudad Juarez to Mexico City—had begun to attract new residents from the eastern United States and from many foreign lands. The development of rail service and the resulting population growth created many new economic opportunities for established residents as well as newly arrived immigrants. Businesses catering to the needs of the growing population, especially the Mexican community in both El Paso and Ciudad Juarez, offered room for growth. Those immigrants who wished to work long and hard would be able to find many opportunities in El Paso. For many, the best chance for economic success lay in peddling and selling groceries, dry goods, and other similar merchandise. The early Arabic-speaking immigrants in El Paso took advantage of those opportunities.[1] Since the term "Syrian" has traditionally referred to a people with a shared history, cuisine, language, and culture, the term in this chapter will refer to Arabic-speaking immigrants to the El Paso area from what are now Syria and Lebanon.

Understanding the experience of the early Syrians in El Paso requires consideration of family and kinship ties.[2] Social, religious, and economic life for the Syrian immigrant centered on the extended family and included the protective attitude an individual felt toward his kinsmen. That attitude prevailed to the extent that the kinsman would perform specific services and favors for his family. It was somewhat expected by the new Syrian arrivals that family members would help them once they came to the United States.

Many families in El Paso and Ciudad Juarez followed the same pattern, with one or two family members arriving first, then sending for brothers, sisters, wives, children, and cousins as soon as possible.[3] The pattern is illustrated, for example, by one early El Paso Syrian who lost some of his brothers and sisters in a flu epidemic in Syria after World War I. Following the tragedy, he "took parental responsibilities for many of his nieces and nephews and later brought them to El Paso."[4]

The idea of the extended family was most important to early Syrian immigrants, especially in economic terms. Advancement depended upon the family. In the peddling trade, each member participated in some aspect for the good of the whole. Family members knew that if they all worked together, concentrating wholeheartedly on developing their economic base, they would have a better chance to survive economically and become successful. Thus Syrians followed the pattern of being self-employed, working for the most part in family groups.

In many cases, Syrians helped one another, regardless of blood ties, simply because they were from the same country. The fact that they were paisanos (Spanish for "compatriots") was enough to warrant mutual assistance.[5] Aid took the form of providing merchandise for the newer arrivals to peddle, finding a place for them to stay, and in some cases forming business partnerships. In one case, for example, an early immigrant who was Muslim and who was not part of a family group in the El Paso area was given help by local Christian Syrians.[6] Thus, it is not difficult to see how Syrian business and social life developed along family and ethnic lines.

It is probable that a few Syrians were in the El Paso area by the mid-1860s, and by 1885 surnames such as Elias, Issacs, and Abraham appear in city directories for El Paso and Paso del Norte (Ciudad Juarez), suggesting Middle Eastern backgrounds for those persons.[7] By the early twentieth century, Syrians in El Paso had made their way to Texas from the east coast, and others had begun to use the Mexican border as an alternative entry port.[8] The latter persons included itinerant peddlers who drifted in and out of the border region on their way to other destinations in the United States and Mexico. Eventually many of them settled in the El Paso–Ciudad Juarez area. By the turn of the century, just over thirty Syrians lived in El Paso, as listed in the city directories and in the *1900 Name Census.* They lived between the four-hundred and six-hundred blocks of South El Paso Street, where their businesses were located.[9]

Early Syrian families clustered within a three-block stretch of South El Paso Street. Most of the later arrivals settled in the same area, thus following urban clustering patterns observed among other ethnic groups. Syrians also tended to have their businesses at the same place where they lived; in the early part of the century, most Syrian families lived above or behind their places of business. Thus they saved money by paying rent on only one space.[10] All of the Syrians in El Paso around 1900 were self-employed. Moreover, all were in the same business—selling groceries.

South El Paso offered several advantages to Syrian immigrants. First, living and having their businesses in the downtown El Paso zone assured them of attracting a great number of local prospective customers on the street. Similarly, the fact that they settled in an area where produce dealers in the Mexican-American community congregated afforded the Syrians the opportunity to meet and mingle with members of that ethnic group, and to increase their own clientele.[11] Furthermore, with South El Paso Street just a short distance from the international bridge, the downtown location was also within easy reach of shoppers from Mexico.

The Syrians of El Paso at the turn of the century lived in family groups, which appears to be typical of the pattern found in the Syrian immigrant community in general.[12] Given the dates of marriage listed in the 1900 census, most of the couples in El Paso were married before they came to the United States, and the husbands either brought their wives with them or were joined by their families soon afterward.[13]

It is easy to understand how the Syrian population grew from these few families in the El Paso area. Once the early immigrants began writing home or returning for short visits to the old country, relating stories of the opportunities to be found in El Paso, they began to bring or send for more of their relatives and friends.[14] Likewise, newer immigrants were eager to take advantage of the orientation and translation assistance from their compatriots already here.[15] For example, at least three of the immigrants who came to El Paso between 1900 and 1905 came from the town of Zahleh and probably were instrumental in attracting others to El Paso from the same place.[16]

It is difficult to estimate the number of Syrians who came to El Paso from Mexico in the early 1900s, but evidently there were many. In addition to several government immigration reports citing crossings by Syrians into the United States via Mexico, El Paso city directories of the period list Spanish first names with Arabic last names, hinting that those Syrians came through Mexico.[17] No doubt, by 1905 a significant number of Syrians were crossing into El Paso from Mexico, as a Syrian named Salim M. Mattar was hired that year as an interpreter for the Immigration Service in El Paso.[18] Another Syrian, Esau Malooly, was hired about a year later in the same capacity.[19] Presumably, there would have been no need for an Arabic-speaking translator unless the number of immigrants from Syria at the entry port warranted such attention.

While only one of the Syrians found in the *1900 Name Census* actually was listed as a peddler, it is generally accepted in the local Syrian community that the early immigrants peddled before and after they opened small stores.[20] As the Syrian population grew, however, Syrians branched out into other areas. By the 1910s, selling of dry goods, notions, general merchandise, and clothing were the most favored of the new endeavors.[21] By 1915 the Syrian community boasted of a confectioner, a carpenter, a chauffeur, and at least one restaurant owner. Only one Syrian in that year was listed in the city directory as a peddler (huckster).[22] Those who had opened stores, however, were still involved in peddling, and they used the store not only as a business place but also as a storage area.[23]

The selling of fruits, dry goods, and clothing presented challenges. Making oneself understood was probably the biggest difficulty, but learning money values and how to give change also presented problems. At first some Syrians used sign language to get their ideas across. One Syrian woman used to point to a specific coin when a customer brought a piece of merchandise to the counter to pay for it, showing that person how much the merchandise cost. One can imagine the comical scenes played out when early Syrians tried to sell their items. One man remembers how one of his compatriots used sound effects, such as buzzing like a bee, to explain to the potential customer that he sold honey.[24] Eventually, however, the Syrians learned English and Spanish and were able to support themselves quite well.

There is no doubt that Syrians who learned Spanish—and most of them did—had a definite advantage. Those who had come from Mexico already knew Spanish to some extent, then learned English. Others learned both languages at the same time, mainly because they lived and had their businesses in a predominantly Spanish-speaking neighborhood. Syrians recognized a market in the Mexican community in El Paso, and they capitalized on that trade. Making the most of that opportunity was the key to their relatively quick achievement of economic stability in El Paso.

Many of the early Syrians peddled in working-class neighborhoods such as Smeltertown (a settlement composed of Mexican-American laborers of the American Smelting and Refining Company) and South El Paso.[25] Those who had stores in the downtown area automatically attracted the Mexican trade. Some Syrians peddled merchandise on both sides of the border, whether they lived in El Paso or Ciudad Juarez.[26] The term *arabe* was generally used by the Mexican community when speaking of Syrians.[27] For many, the term became synonymous with that of merchant. As one Mexican-American recalled:

> *The only payment one had to make was to the* arabe *who came by once every so often for the installment, Montelongo. He was a man who used to sell clothing. He was American, but he had the demeanor of an* arabe.[28]

Although the person described was not a Syrian, he had the *estilo de arabe*—the characteristics of a Syrian—because he was a peddler of clothing in the Mexican community. He went by to collect a payment every once in a while, a common practice among Syrian peddlers. For example, one Syrian used to collect his payments at Smeltertown every Thursday, the day after the workers were paid.[29]

The Syrians were called *arabes* by the Mexicans to distinguish them from the *americanos* (mostly Anglo-Americans). Generally the Mexican and

Syrian communities got along well with each other in the early part of the century. They had daily contact since they lived in the same neighborhood, and many of the children of the Syrian immigrants learned Spanish before they learned English because they grew up and played among Spanish-speaking children.[30] Growing up in a trilingual environment did not seem unusual for the children, thus making it easy for them to move relatively freely among the different ethnic groups in El Paso.[31]

By the middle and later 1910s, the pattern of family businesses was becoming well established. For example, at least seven family businesses—among them, grocers, sellers of general merchandise, confectioners, produce dealers, and restaurant owners—were prospering in the Syrian community at that time. Similarly, business associations between Syrians outside nuclear family groups also began to appear.[32] During the 1920s, occupations dealing with produce were still the most common, but dry goods were becoming more popular with Syrian businessmen.[33] Furthermore, some were beginning to branch out into the wholesale business, supplying to others on a large scale; their expansion added to the Syrians' sound economic base in El Paso. In the twenties, at least three Syrians dealt in the wholesale dry goods business, while two others owned wholesale produce establishments.[34]

The growth of Syrians' business interests in El Paso accompanied that of the El Paso area population in general and in the Syrian community as well. In the teens and early twenties, people from other parts of the United States, in addition to Mexican refugee families fleeing from the Mexican Revolution, arrived at El Paso. Syrians made up part of the refugee group. Many of the revolution's leaders frowned on foreigners who lived in Mexico at that time, and they pushed out Syrians as well as other groups.[35] Quota legislation introduced at that time forced additional Syrians to find routes other than through traditional ports of entry to the United States, thus leading more Syrians to use the Mexican border for their entry and join those already in the El Paso area. Evidence of the growth of the Arabic-speaking population from Mexico is illustrated by the rise in the use of Spanish first names with Arabic last names. Examples of these, listed in the El Paso city directory of 1920, include Felipe, Miguel, and Salvador Ayub (the Spanish spelling of the name Ayoub); José Azar; Domingo David; Antonio Dipp; Juan Habib; José Karam; Alejandro Nassar; Antonio Maluff; and Luís Shaar.[36]

In addition, by that time many businesses owned by Syrians had Spanish names, underscoring the desire of business people to continue to attract the Mexican community's trade. Stores such as La Norma (dealing in dry goods, notions, and shoes), La Unión Fraternal (a restaurant and pool hall), the Casa de Oro Lunch Room, and La Morena (a grocery store) were all owned by Syrians.[37]

In the 1920s, the Syrians continued to enjoy the opportunities offered to them by having their businesses in South El Paso, especially around the Syrian cluster on South El Paso Street. Other popular streets for Syrian businesses included nearby South Stanton, South Santa Fe, San Francisco, and San Antonio. Some Syrians had left the early Syrian neighborhood by the 1920s and lived or had their businesses away from the downtown area. They were, however, in the minority; for the most part, Syrians continued to live at their places of business or very close by, clustering around their compatriots in apartments sometimes owned by other Syrians.[38]

By the mid-1920s, the majority of those Syrians who were not self-employed worked for other Syrians. Their close ethnic ties were characteristic of the community. It was also common for Syrian businessmen to hire young Syrian men who wished to work after school or upon graduation from high school.[39] Business associations were formed outside the family, but for the most part continued to be with other Syrians.[40] At least two business associations, however, were made between a Syrian and a member of the Mexican community.[41] The relationships were not unusual, given the close relations Syrians and members of the Mexican community had during those years.

During the 1930s, Syrians branched out into other pursuits besides the early produce and dry goods businesses. Although not listed consistently in the city directories, many Syrians had begun to deal in real estate.[42] In addition, at least two office buildings, the Abdou Building and the Nebhan Building, were owned by Syrians in 1930.[43] Other new associations in businesses between Syrians included a candy manufacturing and pecan shelling business, and a garage.[44] Syrian wholesaling in dry goods and produce continued in the 1930s, and at least two more Syrians had begun selling wholesale produce in El Paso at that time.[45]

One important change that can be noted in the Syrian community of the 1930s is that families were beginning to move their homes away from the business district. Syrians settled in what is now considered west-central and central El Paso. They continued to live in extended family units to some degree, and many times brothers and first cousins, together with their wives and children, shared a common dwelling.[46] Second-generation Syrians were listed in the directories of the 1930s. Many were students, while others worked outside the family, most for Syrian firms.[47]

During that period, new peddlers appeared in the city directories. Many had recently come into El Paso after having resided in Mexico, especially in Ciudad Juarez. They were related to or knew Syrian families who had lived in El Paso for some time.[48] The new residents started as grocers and peddlers, just as their older, established compatriots had done.

When the depression reached its depth in El Paso around 1932, it had a twofold effect on the Syrian population. On the one hand, some Syrians lost their property, stores, and money. For example, one family, having become well established in the dry goods and real estate business, went bankrupt and lost their home, and had to rent a place in which to live. To get back on their feet, the whole family took up peddling goods and candy from a truck. The sons in the family left school to peddle and took night jobs to help the family become economically stable again.[49] On the other hand, other Syrians were able to make money during the depression. Having enough capital, they were able to buy property, thereby increasing their wealth and holdings by the 1940s and 1950s. In one case, a Syrian purchased many small properties during that era and furthered his career as a realtor.[50]

One fact is evident: Syrian families helped one another. Those who could gave jobs to others who were unemployed. According to one second-generation Syrian, few Syrians during the depression had to receive government help.[51] The Syrians who remained in the produce and dry goods businesses, traditional areas of Syrian employment in El Paso, were best able to survive.[52] While most of the Syrians did not prosper, they were able to stay in business after some initial losses. With the help of their entire families, most Syrians were able to overcome their setbacks and to maintain an adequate economic base.

Besides their economic life, another important aspect of the Syrian experience in El Paso includes the Syrians' social life. In the early years, their social life consisted almost exclusively of relationships with other Syrian families. The size of the community was small, the families lived close together, and Syrians worked side by side in businesses run by other members of their ethnic group. People saw each other daily. According to one member of the community, Syrian homes were open to other members of the group at all times.[53]

Most often, Sundays were the days when Syrian families visited each other, bringing out food and drink and engaging in conversation.[54] Even the Syrian families who lived in Ciudad Juarez would come to El Paso to visit, since they could cross the border easily using local crossing cards.[55] Much of the same type of visiting occurred on religious holidays such as Christmas and Easter. Women prepared special foods for those occasions.[56]

Often the Syrian communities of El Paso and Ciudad Juarez gathered for all-day picnics. Families in El Paso formed a caravan to go to Ciudad Juarez, met the members of the Syrian community there, and then proceeded to Palo Chino, a picnic area that was then outside the Ciudad Juarez city limits. The families took food; sometimes men hunted small game. Often the people visited surrounding ranches and farms where they purchased corn, mangoes, and other fruits and vegetables for the picnic.[57] The Syrian families also gathered on the United States side of the border. Places outside the El Paso city limits, including farming areas in El Paso County, were popular picnic spots. On those occasions the Syrians could enjoy each others' company and the outdoors as well. Men could talk to other men, women could socialize with other women, and teenagers and children had a chance to meet and congregate in their own groups.[58] Such gatherings reinforced the closeness of the Syrian community in El Paso and Ciudad Juarez in the early years.[59]

The religious life of the Syrian community in El Paso varied slightly from the almost ethnically exclusive life they led. Since Syrian religious backgrounds were diverse, the Syrians in El Paso attended a variety of churches. The overwhelming majority of the early El Paso Syrians were Christians; however, since few Eastern rite churches existed in the United States and none were in El Paso, they looked for the religions most similar to their own.[60] For those who were Maronites, the smaller Christian segment in El Paso, the choice was easy. Being part of the Roman Catholic Church, the Maronites attended Catholic churches, most often Sacred Heart Church in South El Paso.[61] As they began to move out of the South El Paso area, they attended churches such as Saint Patrick's Cathedral and Saint Joseph's, both in central El Paso.[62]

Attending Catholic churches reaffirmed the Syrian community's relations with the *mexicanos,* most of whom were Catholics, by providing more social contact between the two groups. Later, when the Catholic Syrians attended Saint Patrick's, they met more Anglo-American Catholic families. Thus their adherence to the Catholic faith helped the acculturation process of Syrians in El Paso and at the same time reinforced business contacts with both the Mexican and Anglo-American communities.

Lacking a church of their particular Christian persuasion, Orthodox Syrians were forced to find other ways to worship. Many times they attended whatever church was nearby. Some were able to find a regular meeting place at Saint Clement's Episcopal church. The Episcopalians welcomed the Syrians and allowed them to use the church's facilities for meetings and an occasional mass that was performed by the itinerant Orthodox bishop who periodically came to El Paso to perform religious rites such as baptisms and marriages.[63]

Having had contact with the Episcopalians both in the old country and in the United States, many Syrians eventually became members of that faith.[64] Not owing its allegiance to Rome, and yet retaining enough ritual to attract worshipers of the Orthodox faith, the Episcopalian Church in El Paso was a logical choice for many of the Orthodox Syrians. As early as 1911, Syrians were confirmed in the Church of Saint Clement in El Paso.[65] At least one baptism performed for a Syrian family in that church included the ritual of triple immersion as used in the Orthodox Church, but was performed by an Episcopal minister.[66] Even when they did not become members of Saint Clement's, many Syrians attended services there.[67] By the 1930s more and more Syrian families had had contact with Saint Clement's, and many of them became Episcopalians. Members of at least a dozen Syrian families were listed in the 1920s and 1930s as members of the Church of Saint Clement.[68]

In various ways attendance at the Episcopal Church led to the acculturation of many of the Syrians, just as attendance at the Catholic churches did with others. Through their churches, Syrians made contacts with other ethnic and social groups, and thereby promoted their general acceptance by the different population groups in El Paso. By the 1930s, Syrians were recognized at least on a social level by all segments of the El Paso community.

The few Jewish and Moslem Syrians in El Paso and Ciudad Juarez were generally accepted by the larger Syrian population, given the cultural ties that existed among the subgroups. For example, at least two families of Syrian Jews living in El Paso had cordial social contacts with many of the Christian Syrian families.[69] The same can be said for the one Muslim family living in the area.[70] When the head of that family first arrived in Ciudad Juarez, he came with a group of Christian Syrians from his hometown, one of whom had loaned him money for the trip. Once at the border, they lived together, peddled together, and later formed business associations.[71] On a social level, then, both Jews and Muslims shared in the social activities of the greater Christian Syrian community of El Paso and Ciudad Juarez.[72] Thus, because of their strong ethnic heritage, most Syrians were able to live together and relate to each other socially and culturally.

In sum, between 1900 and 1935, the El Paso Syrian community grew from a few families to a thriving ethnic community. Starting out as peddlers and store owners on a small scale, Syrians became well established in business, mostly along family lines. Syrians showed a preference for produce and dry goods, and for trading with the Mexican community on both sides of the border. They were just beginning to branch out into different economic pursuits by the time the Great Depression hit. The new business activities would become important for them and for the El Paso community in the 1940s and 1950s.

Having found a home in the El Paso area, Syrians attracted other members of the group—from Mexico, from such other states as Pennsylvania and New Mexico, and from other parts of Texas.[73] Their church attendance helped them become accepted by other El Pasoans, while they kept close relations within their own group.[74] The second generation became Americanized enough to be able to move freely within the different elements in El Paso, while the close relations with other members of the Syrian community reinforced their traditional cultural heritage.[75]

Notes

1. For convenience the author combined information gathered on the Ciudad Juarez Syrian community with that on the El Paso community. They generally shared the same experiences and had close ties in the early years.

2. Information presented in this chapter concerning family and cultural heritage is partially based on oral history interviews. "The Cultural Heritage and Preservation of Syrian-Lebanese Traditions in the Southwest," an unpublished paper written by Dr. Najim A. Bezirgan and Rosemary Gillette Karam (ca. 1973), was especially helpful in the research for this paper. The manuscript is on file in the archives of the Institute of Texan Cultures, University of San Antonio, Texas (hereafter cited as Institute of Texan Cultures Archives).

3. "Abraham Haddad Dies; Services Scheduled Tonight," *El Paso Herald-Post,* 5 March 1982, Sec. D, p. 4.

4. Folders on the Helou and Ekery families, Institute of Texan Cultures Archives.

5. Personal interview with Abed Esman, 4 May 1982. The word "paisano" is still used quite extensively in the Syrian community when referring to another Syrian or Syrian American.

6. Ibid.; and personal interview with Zacchia Ayoub, 19 February 1982.

7. *El Paso, Texas and Paso del Norte, Mexico Business Directory for 1885* (Albuquerque: Rackliff and Wainley, 1885), p. 88; *General Directory for the City of El Paso for 1886–87* (Dallas: A. D. Aldridge and Company, 1886), pp. 83, 113; *Directory of the City of El Paso, 1888* (El Paso: El Paso Directory Company, 1888), pp. 48, 63; and Keith Humphries, "Sudden Death Made El Paso Politics Lively in 'The Good Old Days,' " *El Paso Herald-Post,* 31 October 1941, p. 13, which is written about a family named Abraham.

8. As many Syrians were being barred from entry to the United States during this period, they began to find alternative routes to this country, one being through Mexico. For more information on this migration pattern, see " 'Trade Will Lead a Man Far': Syrian Immigration to the El Paso Area, 1900–1935," by Sarah E. John, M.A. thesis, University of Texas at El Paso, 1982.

9. *Worley's Directory of the City of El Paso, Texas, 1898–99,* (Dallas: John F. Worley and Company, 1898), pp. 184, 265, 273 (all city directories published by F. Worley are hereafter cited as *EPCD* followed by its year of publication); and U.S. Department of Commerce, Bureau of the Census, *Twelfth Census of Population, Texas, Vol. 35, El Paso County, 1900* [hereafter cited as *1900 Name Census*] (Microcopy No. T623, Rolls 1630 and 1631).

10. *EPCD 1900,* pp. 276, 303; and personal interview with Halem Ayoub, 16 February 1982.

11. At least six individuals with Spanish surnames also had their grocery stores on South El Paso Street, and the majority of the remaining grocers in South El Paso had Spanish surnames. *EPCD 1900,* pp. 276, 303; and interview with Halem Ayoub.

12. Both Abdo A. Elkholy, "The Arab American Family," in Charles H. Mindel and Robert W. Habenstein, *Ethnic Families in America: Patterns and Variations* (New York: Elsevier Scientific Publishing Company, 1976), p. 153, and Philip K. Hitti, *Syrians in America* (New York: George Doran, 1924), p. 57, claim, however, that most early Syrian immigrants to the United States were young males desiring to make money and return to their homeland.

13. *1900 Name Census.*

14. Folders on the Helou, Ansara, and Ekery families, Institute of Texan Cultures Archives; "Abraham Haddad Dies; Services Scheduled Tonight," *El Paso Herald-Post,* 5 March 1982, Sec. D., p. 4; and interview with Halem Ayoub.

15. Interviews with Halem Ayoub and Abed Esman.

16. Interview with Halem Ayoub; "Joseph Nebhan Rosary Services Slated Sunday," *El Paso Times*, 27 June 1971, Sec. A, p. 9; and Gilbert Malooly, "The Syrian People in El Paso" (Texas Western College, unpublished seminar paper, 1953), pp. 48, 54, 55. A few years later, people from Jwakhat, Syria (now in Lebanon) would bring many of their relatives to join them in El Paso and Ciudad Juarez.

17. *EPCD* 1904 p. 109; *EPCD* 1905, p. 177; and *EPCD* 1907, p. 185. Some of these were José Assad, Jorge David, and Eduardo Elias.

18. *EPCD* 1906, p. 318; and *Seraphic Report re Conditions on the Mexican Border*, National Archives Immigration File No. 51423–1, p. 14.

19. Folder on the Malooly family, Institute of Texan Cultures Archives. The *Historical Encyclopedia of Texas* states that Malooly himself came through Mexico.

20. *EPCD* 1905, p. 399; and interviews with Halem Ayoub, Zacchia Ayoub, and Abed Esman. Also, many of the author's relatives who came from Syria started as peddlers in El Paso and Ciudad Juarez.

21. *EPCD*, 1910 (Dallas: John F. Worley and Company, 1910), pp. 121, 123, 324, 342, 358. During the 1910s, South El Paso, around the area of the earlier Syrian cluster, continued to house the Syrians in El Paso, and "grocer" remained the most popular occupation.

22. *EPCD*, 1915 (Dallas: John F. Worley and Company, 1914), pp. 130, 150, 305, 314, 344.

23. Interview with Zacchia Ayoub.

24. Interviews with Abed Esman and Zacchia Ayoub.

25. Interview with Zacchia Ayoub.

26. Articles about Abraham Haddad in *El Paso Times*, 11 September 1979, Citizen's Vertical File, El Paso Public Library.

27. Interview with Halem Ayoub. The term is still used today.

28. Interview with Felipe Rodriguez by José Gutierrez, 20 November 1976. On file at the University of Texas at El Paso Institute of Oral History, No. 287, author's translation.

29. Interview with Zacchia Ayoub.

30. Interviews with Zacchia Ayoub and Halem Ayoub; and comments by Marie Barker during the interview with Abed Esman, her father.

31. Interview with Halem Ayoub; additional comments by Marie Barker.

32. *EPCD* 1915, pp. 130, 149, 150, 280, 306, 314, 386, 453, 506.

33. *EPCD*, 1920 (El Paso: Hudspeth Directory Company, 1920), pp. 324, 331, 349, 352, 414, 418, 443, 459, 488, 520, 549, 586, 587, 588, 599, 600, 607, 636, 642, 699, 701, 787, 810, 841 (city directories published by Hudspeth are hereafter cited as *Directory* followed by its year of publication).

34. Ibid., pp. 810–936, 941; *Directory* 1925, pp. 284, 880; and interview with Halem Ayoub.

35. Folder on the Karam family, Institute of Texan Cultures Archives. It is known that records exist from the Catholic Church concerning the help the Church gave refugees, including Syrians, fleeing during the Mexican Revolution. However, the author was denied use of these materials because of their sensitive nature.

36. *Directory*, 1920, pp. 352, 445, 459, 466, 599, 642, 701, 810.

37. *Directory*, 1925, pp. 284, 534, 546.

38. Ibid., pp. 284, 313, 372, 497, 535, 642, 734, 745, 752, 880; and interview with Halem Ayoub.

39. *Directory*, 1920, pp. 599, 607; *Directory*, 1925, p. 553; and interview with Halem Ayoub.

40. *Directory*, 1920, pp. 352, 600; *Directory*, 1925, p. 546.

41. *Directory*, 1920, p. 488; and *Directory*, 1927, p. 685.

42. *Directory*, 1930, pp. 485 and 534; *Directory*, 1935, p. 110; and Ayoub, Malooly, Nebhan, and Shamaley family folders, Institute of Texan Cultures Archives

43. *Directory*, 1930, pp. 174 and 604.

44. Ibid., pp. 174, 208, 600. Mr. Klink was Mr. Abdou's stepson, so this relationship can also be considered a family business association.

45. Ibid., p. 1017.

46. For example, the Abraham family lived at the Abraham Apartments, 502 1/2 N. Piedras, owned by Samuel Abraham. *Directory*, 1930, p. 175; and *Directory*, 1935, p. 82.

47. *Directory*, 1930, pp. 175, 208, and 537; *Directory*, 1935, pp. 109, 110, 322, and 520; and interview with Halem Ayoub.

48. *Directory*, 1930, p. 175; and *Directory*, 1935, pp. 82, 284, 422, 618.

49. Interview with Halem Ayoub; and folder on the Ayoub family, Institute of Texan Cultures Archives.

50. Folder on the Malooly family, Institute of Texan Cultures Archives.

51. Interview with Halem Ayoub. Only by checking the records could one be sure about the absence of Syrians on the welfare rolls, but Mr. Ayoub and others give the impression that few Syrians were on welfare during the depression. At least one Syrian who was a young man during that period, however, remembers that he worked on construction at Texas Western College (now University of Texas at El Paso) in a government-sponsored program.

52. While the *Encyclopedia of Texas* states that Salim N. Abdou was the "only individual man to survive the dryness and the competition of corporations" during the depression, it is probable that other Syrians in the produce and dry goods businesses were able to remain economically stable during that era. *The Encyclopedia of Texas,* vol. I, Ellis A. David, ed. (Texas Historical Society, ca. 1951), p. 229.

53. Interview with Halem Ayoub. Even in the 1950s, gatherings held by the author's family included Syrians almost exclusively.

54. Ibid.

55. Interview with Abed Esman.

56. Interview with Halem Ayoub.

57. Interview with Abed Esman; and comments by Marie Barker.

58. Interview with Abed Esman.

59. The fact that many Arabic-surnamed individuals remained in Ciudad Juarez is evidenced by the following surnames found in the *Directorio Telefónico No. 42, Juarez, Mayo 1979* (Mexico City: Imprenta Nuevo Mundo, S.A., 1979), pp. 17, 23, 25, 38, 44, 53, 65, 71, 77, 78, 83, 84, 89: Abud, Bitar, Elias, Ganem, Jalil, Nahmad, Najar, Nassri, Rafful, Rousette Ferris, Saad, Said, and Yanar.

60. Interviews with Zacchia Ayoub and Halem Ayoub.

61. *Ibid.*

62. This pattern may be illustrated by the many Syrian and Lebanese Americans who remain members of the Catholic Church.

63. Betty Pierce, "St. George Orthodox Church Started with a Syrian Club," *El Paso Herald-Post,* 25 April 1971, Sec. A. p. 7.

64. Many of the missionaries in Syria were Episcopalian.

65. *St. Clement's Parish Register,* No. 3, p. 177.

66. *Ibid.*, p. 28.

67. *St. Clement's Parish Register* No. 4, p. 16.

68. *Ibid.*, pp. 6, 46, 52, 62, 70, 78, 80, 84, 86, 92, 96, 104, 108, 114, 116, 122, 126, 128, 130, 136, 168, 172, 174, 178, 180, 184, 192, 196, 200, 348, 350, 356, 360, 362, 366, 368, 370, 376, 380, 382, 384, 392, 424, 438, 440, and 444. It is interesting to note that many Syrian business partnerships were made between men who were members of the Episcopal church. When St. George Orthodox Church was established in El Paso in the early 1950s, many Syrians left the Episcopal church and returned to their original faith.

69. Interviews with Halem Ayoub and Abed Esman; comments by Marie Barker during interview with Abed Esman, her father.

70. Interview with Abed Esman; comments by Marie Barker during interview with Abed Esman.

71. Interview with Abed Esman.

72. Interviews with Halem Ayoub and Abed Esman. Interestingly, the Moslem family would consult with the Jewish rabbi in El Paso on certain religious questions such as circumcision, diet, and the like.

73. Mansour Farah made his way to El Paso from Canada by way of Las Cruces, New Mexico; some of the Helous, Ekerys, and Abrahams came to Ciudad Juarez after residing in Pennsylvania for some time; the Abdous came from Denison, Texas. See folders on Abdou, Farah, and Helou families, Institute of Texan Cultures Archives.

74. When Salim N. Abdou passed away in 1953, his honorary pallbearers included well-known El Pasoans from several different ethnic groups: Sam D. Young, Fred Hervey, Jesus M. Quevado, Leo Momsen, R. E. Thomason, R. E. McKee, Ciro Caldarella, and W. S. Crombie. "Funeral Rites for Mr. Abdou Set Friday," *El Paso Times,* 12 November 1953, p. 26.

75. A few cases of interethnic dating and marriages had occurred by the 1930s, and proceeded on a larger scale in the 1940s and 1950s. For example, two of Salim N. Abdou's daughters married English-surnamed individuals. "Funeral Rites for Mr. Abdou Set Friday," *El Paso Times,* 12 November 1953, p. 26.

Yemenite Jewish Immigration and Adaptation to the United States, 1905–1941

DINA DAHBANY-MIRAGLIA

The immigration of Middle Easterners to the United States over the past one-hundred years has gone virtually unnoticed by most Americans, and no wonder. European migrants, originating from Ireland to the Urals, arrived in the hundreds of thousands each year. When these figures are compared to those of Middle Easterners who entered the United States at the rate of a few thousands per year and, after 1924, only a few hundred annually, we begin to see why American Middle Easterners—Jews, Christians, and Muslims—were "invisible." By 1941 the total number of Yemenite Jewish immigrants floated somewhere around 250 individuals: one-hundred or so Oldtimers and approximately 150 children. During the first sixty years of this century, their minute numbers helped Yemenite Jews to resist America's concerted pressures to assimilate them.

The numerical smallness of the first wave of Yemenite Jews allowed the immigrants to establish a community in the United States much like Jewish communities in Yemen. Their internal cultural diversity, the acculturation processes they underwent in Turkish (Ottoman) Palestine, and the move from the preindustrial Middle East into industrial America initially had little effect on the First Wavers' former cooperative kinship and friendship networks and patterns of association. Their traditional communal patterns had survival value. They cushioned the incoming Yemenite Jews from the disorienting impact of a strange host country by allowing them to internalize—gradually and selectively—American mores, beliefs, attitudes, practices, and language.

Aspects of Yemenite Jewish life in the United States that are directly related to this group's immigration and that are discussed in this paper are immigration patterns, community locations, education, occupations, and social organization.[1]

MIGRATION PATTERNS

Although more than half of the Oldtimers were born on the Yemeni plateau (North Yemen) and a few in Aden (South Yemen), nearly all of them grew up and married in Turkish and later British Mandate Palestine. About thirty-five to forty of the Oldtimers were "orphans" whose mothers fled Yemen with their children between 1850 and 1910.[2] They migrated to Turkish Palestine from the mid-nineteenth century until after World War I to avoid losing their children through forced conversion to Islam. By 1912 between fifteen hundred and two-thousand Yemenite Jews lived in Jerusalem.[3] By 1919, Turkish Palestine was home to an estimated 12,976 individuals from Yemen out of approximately fifty-seven thousand Jews from all over the world.[4] Only about 160 of the nearly thirteen thousand Yemenite Jews in Turkish Palestine immigrated to the United States before 1941.

For the Oldtimers, Turkish Palestine was an incubator, a place of transition. This pluralistic society was at once similar to Yemen and yet different. In Palestine the Oldtimers lived among a much greater variety of Middle Eastern peoples than existed in Yemen. Many came into daily contact with Western customs, and that familiarity was helpful to their survival in the United States. In Palestine they encountered the Western class system, and institutions such as political parties and corporations, as well as fraternal and cultural organizations, all unfamiliar nonkin patterns of associations.

Turkish Palestine was similar enough to Yemen in terms of languages, occupations, residence patterns, and strategies of association and interaction to allow for a fairly smooth adaptation. Both countries' Muslims depended on their *dhimmis,* or peoples of the book, to provide all sorts of manufactured goods.[5] Residential separation based on religion was characteristic of both Yemen and Turkish Palestine.[6] In addition, in both countries all religious populations depended on coreligionists for aid, resorting to nonmembers only when no other alternative existed. An additional advantage was the closeness of regional variations of Judeo Yemeni and Yemeni Arabic to Palestinian Arabic. They are sister languages and are for the most part are mutually comprehensible.

The Yemenite Jews who arrived to Turkish Palestine before World War I seemed to experience very little difficulty adjusting to life in Jerusalem's and, later on, in Tel Aviv's Jewish quarters, even when the other inhabitants were Jews from elsewhere in the Middle East and from Europe. No doubt one reason was that about half were born or else spent some time in Sanaa, North Yemen's capital city and in Aden.[7] Most of Yemen's Jews, however, were full-time craftspeople in occupations that are usually practiced in urban areas. The skills of craft manufacture—with their emphasis on production and on problem solving, their amenability to individuals' innovations, their dependency on supply and demand, and their portability—require a different mindset from agricultural skills, which do not transfer well to an urban milieu.[8]

It was the Sephardim (Judeo Spanish and Judeo Portuguese speakers) and the Ashkenazim (Yiddish speakers), Jews from Europe, who were the Oldtimers' primary sources of Western ideas and behaviors. This was especially true for the women who worked as housekeepers and babysitters in the houses of well-to-do Ashkenazim and Sephardim. In contrast, the Oldtimer men associated primarily with each other. Many of them prayed together twice daily, were apprenticed to the same Yemenite masters in construction and jewelry manufacture, and daily or weekly studied the Old Testament and some of its commentaries under the tutelage of a *mori,* a rabbi/teacher. It was not until some of them joined the British Army's Jewish Brigade during World War I that a few Yemenite men came into continuous, long-term contact with non-Yemenites.

Just as Jewish immigration from Yemen to Turkish Palestine during the mid-nineteenth and early twentieth centuries ranged from tens of individuals to one or two hundred a year, so, too, did the emigration of Yemenite Jews from Palestine to the United States. Yemenite Jewish immigration to America began almost imperceptibly between 1905 and 1907, when two couples, one accompanied by their three young children, arrived from Turkish Palestine. It was not until after World War I that other Yemenite Jews arrived. Then, in 1917, my father arrived by way of Egypt. Honorably discharged from the Jewish Brigade, he had been given a choice of free passage to England or to the United States. A few months later he was followed by another Yemenite Jewish Brigade soldier who had not made his decision to emigrate until he had returned to Palestine. Until 1922 the entire Yemenite Jewish population in the United States consisted of those six adults and the three children, nine people in all.

Between the end of 1923 and until 1931 virtually every ship leaving Palestine's port of Jaffa carried a handful of Yemenite Jews. The first shipload to arrive consisted of several men traveling together. Nearly all were married; some of them were already parents. More than half of the Yemenites following them in the ensuing years were, more often than not, the wives and children of men already in America, or else families emigrating together. All the Oldtimers were part of each others' open-ended networks. That is to say, although several met and became fast friends only after they arrived here, they shared mutual friends and acquaintances in Tel Aviv and Jerusalem.

Almost all the Yemenite Jews who emigrated before World War II married other Yemenite Jews, and most of the marriages took place in Turkish or British Mandate Palestine. None of the Oldtimer women married non-Yemenites, and only eleven or twelve of the wives of Oldtimer men were non-Yemenites. Of those, six were Sephardic, two were Syrians from Damascus (ash-Shamm), two more were Moroccans, and one was an Ashkenaziyah.[9] By 1931 between 150 and 160 Oldtimers and their children were living in the United States.

The flow of Yemenite Jewish immigration slowed considerably between 1931 and 1941, during the Great Depression. Only fifteen to twenty more arrived: the parents, siblings, and two more Yemenite wives of men who married—one in what was then British Mandate Palestine and the other in Egypt. Until 1959 no more than two more Yemenite women, both of them married to Oldtimer men in Palestine/Israel, arrived here.

As few as they were, the Oldtimers were as diverse culturally as members of populations many times more numerous. About half of them were from Sanaa, with a substantial minority from the towns of as-Saddah, Rada, Yarim, and Manakha on the central and southwestern/south-central ends of the Yemeni plateau. Another segment originated in east-central Yemen, from the Sharab and the Sharaf. A few came from Aden. Nearly all were raised in Turkish Palestine, and a number of the Oldtimer women were born there or else in Lebanon/Syria and Egypt.

As diverse as they were, the overwhelming majority of the Oldtimers nevertheless shared a preference for their familiar patterns of interaction and association, which their meager numbers actually encouraged. Indeed, although they entered the United States during its most intensive period of assimilation, the Oldtimers maintained the kinds of social ties that they enjoyed in Yemen and that continued during their stay in Palestine. They established a community based on cultural ideologies of self-help, resourcefulnees, and *miswoh,* or helping others.[10]

These beliefs found pragmatic expression through economic interdependence and economic self-sufficiency by making use of the combined efforts of every member in a family. They sought each other by means of a multitude of frequent interactions. These included chats several times a day from windows across a street or an alley, daily and weekly visits to each others' homes, and get-togethers, such as picnics or the more formal men's daily and/or weekly meetings for ritual prayer. Some also interacted in twice or thrice weekly gin, pinochle, and poker games. Other, more intermittent, kinds of interactions included rites of passage and affairs organized by the women to raise money for a variety of charitable projects. All of these interactions involved large and small kinship and friendship networks within the community. Much of the success in maintaining the former patterns was based on a high degree of residential proximity.

COMMUNITY LOCATIONS

With few exceptions the Oldtimers chose to live as close to each other as they could. They were accustomed to the ancient Middle Eastern practice whereby people of the same religion, from the same region, or speaking the same language reside in the same section of a city or a town. Whether they debarked at Ellis Island or at Providence, Rhode Island, between 1922 and 1928 almost all the Oldtimers lived within a few blocks of each other on New York's Lower East Side. Most lived on Norfolk and Suffolk streets, in the five- and six-story walk-up tenements between Rivington and Delancey streets. There were, of course, exceptions.

One couple took the train for Los Angeles within a few days of stepping off the ship. Another, a single male, headed for New Orleans. One of the first two families to arrive between 1905 and 1907 ran a launderette in Williamsburg, Brooklyn. In 1928 six families found the congestion and noise of the Lower East Side unbearable and moved to Boro Park in Brooklyn within a few days to a few weeks of their landing. One reason they chose Boro Park rather than another Brooklyn neighborhood was because a year or so earlier another couple and their two preschoolers were offered a free apartment in a Boro Park apartment house if they would janitor the building. Unhappy with their isolation they made frequent trips to the Lower East Side to visit friends and to advertise their new neighborhood. Their plan succeeded. By 1931 more than half of the Yemenite Jews in the United States were living in Boro Park.

Until the early 1950s the Yemenite Jewish community was split geographically between Manhattan's Lower East Side and Brooklyn's Boro Park. In spite of a distance of about ten miles and the physical demarcation of the East River, they remained a cohesive community. They worked together in the same occupations and commuted back and forth for events by means of trains, trolleys, and buses, and occasionally by private car. The few who had telephones called each other, often on a daily basis, and with few exceptions the Oldtimers interacted with each other at least weekly, meeting at parties, outings, and other kinds of get-togethers.

OCCUPATIONS

How did those first Yemenite Jewish immigrants, ignorant of the language and practically penniless, find lodgings and jobs? Whether they came before or after World War I, they all made use of at least two ancient and no doubt universal strategies: they exchanged information and favors with kindred, friends, and coreligionists, and enlisted the aid of anyone they found who was willing to help them find a job or a place to live.

I do not know how the first two families "found their feet," so to speak, but I can describe how my father and some of the others who arrived during the 1920s helped themselves and each other to survive. By dint of listening to and asking questions of Ashkenazi soldiers in the Jewish Brigade my father discovered that a particular group in New York always had someone at the piers to help other Jews find a place to stay or even a job. A few of the Oldtimers took advantage of the assistance offered by HIAS, the United Hebrew Immigrant Aid Society, founded in 1909 to help newly arrived Eastern European Jewish immigrants.[11]

Shipboard culture was another source of contacts and information. Initially, the Yemenites and Ashkenazim who boarded at Jaffa tended to keep apart, but as the ships stopped to pick up passengers from other ports, Jaffa embarkees began to differentiate themselves from the later arrivals. A monthlong trip in close quarters forces socialization between people who, under less physically restrictive conditions, would avoid each other.

The first couple to move to Boro Park were offered the free apartment by the Ashkenazi who owned both the Lower East Side apartment house in which they had lived and the Brooklyn one in which they superintended. The woman was a close friend of the wife of one of the two brothers who followed that first couple to Boro Park. The brothers had decided to settle in Brooklyn long before the brothers's wives and their small children left British Mandate Palestine, the result of more than a year's correspondence that sailed back and forth between the two women. The upshot was that the two brother-husbands rented apartments in Boro Park well before their families debarked from their ships. The elder of the two brothers had spent a year in an Ashkenazi *yeshiva* in Turkish Palestine and was fluent in Yiddish.[12] He became an especially useful resource. He generously helped other Yemenites find apartments as well as jobs in the garment trade, in which he spent all his working life as a presser.

When they stepped off the ships most of the Oldtimers took the first jobs they were offered or could find. Nearly all the men became peddlers, their wares supplied on consignment by Syrian Jews from Aleppo (Halab) and Damascus who operated dry goods stores. Pushing carts or, more often, carrying packs, these men sold sheets and towels, handkerchiefs and scarves. Their customers were primarily Italian immigrants from Calabria and Sicily. They could not sell to other Jews, especially the Europeans, because the Ashkenazi peddlers had the advantage of being culturally the same as their customers and speaking Yiddish as well. An even greater barrier was skin color. A large number of the Oldtimers were dark skinned, in a range from olive to black. The United States differs from the Middle East in regard to skin color. In the latter region, skin color is a criterion of social and not racial ascription, a matter of taste and not one of status. This difference in perception no doubt derives partly from degrees of physiognomic variety. Skin color is historically much more homogeneous in Europe than it has ever been in the Middle East. The Middle Eastern counterpart to the European and American black/white dyad is a continuum that ranges from black to brown to red to yellow to white.

In some ways these Oldtimers were prepared to fit into an industrialized society. Although pre–World War I Palestine and Yemen were essentially preindustrial, the factory system was not entirely unknown. My mother's father's mother ran a small weaving factory in as-Saddah, a town on the southern end of the Yemeni plateau. Her sons and a few other weavers plied their trade in a single room. When she was busy she "jobbed" the excess work to independent weavers. Her future daughter-in-law, my mother's mother, was the floor girl.[13] Twelve years later, in Jerusalem, she worked again as a floor girl for a time in that city's only cloth-making factory.

Several of the Oldtimer women, having learned their trade in post–World War I Jerusalem, were skilled operators of sewing machines. British introductions of cheap factory-made cloth and clothing to the Middle East during the late nineteenth-century all but destroyed the handweaving and tailoring crafts everywhere but in Yemen, forcing their practitioners to seek other ways of making a living. Many Yemenite Jewish men in Turkish Palestine went into the building trades and a few into jewelry manufacture, both of which were, at that time, resistant to industrialization.[14]

Prepared as they were psychologically to adapt to an industrialized society, the Oldtimers' lack of a Western education and its concomitant lingual and cognitive skills, and their poverty severely limited their occupational options. They did have the advantage of coming from a culture that places a high value on entrepreneurship, an economic perspective that American society values, at least ideologically. Accustomed to being craftspeople, they were not attracted to the retailing and wholesaling that distinguishes the Syrian Jewish economy. Only three Oldtimer couples opened stores from which they sold dry goods or jewelry, silver, china, and gewgaws. Those women who rejected sewing machine operation took the only options left open to them: housekeeping and babysitting. In common with their stay-at-home friends, the Yemenite women who worked in the service occupations saw themselves as independent entrepreneurs who were in control of their workplaces. Only one Oldtimer woman who earned a degree at a teaching seminary in Jerusalem worked as a teacher. She was qualified to teach kindergarten in Ashkenazi *yeshivas,* which she did for thirty years and more.

Those few women who were trained in Turkish and British Mandate

Palestine in jewelry design and manufacture, by male relatives or at the newly established Betsalel trade school in Jerusalem, eventually opened their own shops and factories in Manhattan. Initially, nearly all of them worked for established jewelers, European coreligionists, until they amassed enough capital to become independent. Most pooled skills and money and went into partnerships with a brother, a son-in-law, or their wives. Although the wives were, in terms of labor, equal partners, to my knowledge none of them had her name on the business papers.

EDUCATION

The Oldtimers' experiences in the American education system were mostly limited to night-school attendance during the 1930s and 1940s, in Boro Park and on the Lower East Side. Only a few attended those schools during the 1950s. The only Oldtimer to complete high school was a woman. Unlike the others, she had gone to a lycée in Egypt for several years during World War I; there she learned to read and write in both Arabic and French. She was prepared, psychologically and intellectually, to endure the long years necessary to acquire a diploma. The responsibilities of feeding, clothing, educating, and housing their families, and the long hours of work for very little money, left little free time, and most of the Oldtimers preferred to spend their leisure time with each other. The overwhelming majority attended night schools for six months to a year because they needed to fulfill the minimum requirements for citizenship. Being adults, compulsory universal education did not oblige them to stay in school, but it did require their children to do so.

The American school system did have some small influence on the Oldtimers and on their communal life. Its greatest impact was on their children, the majority of whom attended New York City public schools and Ashkenazi Talmud Torahs afterward.[15] Many of the boys learned from their fathers or from a *mori,* to pray in the Yemenite Jewish tradition, usually on Saturday afternoons. About half the boys but only four of the girls attended Ashkenazi *yeshivas* from between one and eight years.

Of the approximately sixty girls, about thirty finished high school, the later-born among them the majority of those who graduated. Fifteen or so left or were taken out of school before the eighth grade, and only about ten had more than one year of college. One of the older girls never went to school. Her father forced her to remain in their Lower East Side apartment and sew the piecework that he brought home to her every evening from a nearby clothing factory. Few of the Oldtimers encouraged their daughters to go to college, for marriage and a home were the life goals they and American society had, during the 1930s, 1940s, and 1950s, set for females. Some of the boys were pushed to go to college.[16] About twenty completed two or more years. Most of them attended and the then tuition-free colleges in what is today the New York City University system; one attended Julliard for three years. The American education system was one, but not the only, important mechanism that helped to draw the Oldtimers' children away from the community and into the American mainstream.

THE COMMUNITY

Separated by a river and twice ten miles of winding railroad and trolley tracks, these 250-odd people constituted a community in every sense of the word.[17] They carried with them from the Middle East a way of life that they continued to maintain in the United States. As it has for about two-thousand years in Yemen, Jewish law and practice continued to shape Oldtimer communal life in America. Shabboth, the Sabbath, defined the week, and the many fast and holy days peaked and rounded out each year. Few Oldtimers during the 1920s and 1930s worked in the factories; those twelve-hour shifts and seven-day weeks conflicted with keeping Shabboth. The credo of those Yemenites forced to work on Shabboth must have been *oseh shabbothikhoh hol wial titstarekh labiriyoth,* meaning "Better to violate Shabboth than to beg others for help."

The importance of Shabboth in American Yemenite Jewish communal life cannot be overstated. Shabboth was the one day a week when the Oldtimers interacted intensely with each other. The men congregated in the *kanis,* the synagogue, for more than three hours each Shabboth morning and afternoon to pray and to study, and to eat the obligatory third meal in the early afternoon. They gathered in groups and talked, exchanging information and relating anecdotes and stories as well as using genealogies to identify and define relationships. Occasionally they sang from the *Diwan,* a book of men's poetry, discussed commentaries on the chapter of the week, and consumed many traditional Yemenite foods.[18] Unless a circumcision or a bar mitzvah (a rite of passage commemorating a boy's coming of age) was scheduled, or a major holy day was celebrated, hardly any of the women attended Saturday or weekday morning services. In the Yemenite Jewish tradition, religious ritual is the province of men, and the *kanis* their version of a New Guinea men's house.

Shabboth afternoons saw men and women meeting separately but exchanging much the same kinds of information. Those Oldtimer women who stayed at home learned about the factory world: about wages and timeclocks, reasonable and unreasonable expectations, relations between workers and bosses, which strategies to use to gain small victories such as a choice machine near the window, and, most important for some of the housewives, information about the availability of piecework to be done in the home. The men exchanged anecdotes about customers and suppliers, traded information regarding what they could expect to charge for a particular construction job or a piece of jewelry, and which blocks to avoid on which days because a particular policeman was a noted graft taker and would shake down any peddler he met.

The housewives, and those husbands temporarily or permanently out of work, contributed neighborhood information: who were the honest pushcart peddlers and storekeepers, and who shortchanged their customers; or which family was recently evicted, thereby leaving an apartment free. And all the while, interspersed between talk of the neighborhood and work, were discussions and arguments on local, national, and world events, and a lot of reminiscing, storytelling, and tracing genealogies.

Shabboth afternoons were also planning and strategy sessions. Separately, the Oldtimer women and men initiated and defined many community events, such as bingo games, tea parties, dinner dances, and bazaars, to raise money for the *kanayis,* or synagogues, and for the *ezrath nashim,* the Yemenite Ladies' Aid Society, which answered cries for economic help from indigent Yemenites in Palestine/Israel, and from the Haganah and the Red Mogen David. They used Sabboth as well to coordinate private celebrations and disasters, such as weddings and wakes.

Shabboth afternoons during the 1930s and early 1940s saw the birth of the Ezrath Nashim, the *kanayis,* and the *hevroh qadhishoh,* the burial society. Membership fees were about twenty-five cents a year per family. Collectors and officers were a few individuals who volunteered their time and energies. They traveled to and from Boro Park at least twice a month to the Lower East Side, climbing five and six flights of tenement stairs, the women during the day and the men at night. These individuals served as liaisons between the two geographic segments of the American Yemenite Jewish community. They carried news back and forth and were the human links between individuals and groups in both sections of the community. They were nearly always present at every event and constituted the informational hub of the community, especially since few of the Oldtimers had telephones until the early 1940s. That core of individuals, most of them women aided by a few of the men, saw to the organizing of nearly all the events that reinforced relationships.

In traditional Yemenite Jewish society it is the women and not the men who are the organizers and the administrators who initiate and run communal and private events. In the United States the Oldtimer women kept their traditional roles and coordinated trips to Bear Mountain, Coney Island, and the Statue of Liberty, to the Roxy and to Radio City Music Hall. Without them, weddings, wakes, the weekly tea parties, the biweekly local movie and theater dates, the numerous dances, and bazaars and bingo games would never have taken place. They hired the halls, selected the bands, provided the food, saw to the printing of the tickets. They contacted the donators of goods and money and services and saw to the advertising of each event. A few of the men, those few who were instrumental in establishing and then maintaining the *kanayis* and the burial society, often helped. They picked up the donations from wholesalers and retailers, and chauffered the women when they went shopping for paper goods and for foods. They aided the women to unload the trucks, helped them set up the speakers and the tables, and assisted in cleaning up the inevitable messes.

The Oldtimers managed to live and work in an industrialized society and yet retained much of their ancient communal lifestyle. Most were acculturated rather than assimilated, and it was their few numbers that helped them to stay together in a community. "We were like a family," says one of the children, the daughter of one of the core women. "Everyone knew everyone else." But it is well known that below a certain number a community cannot last long. Unless it can grow from within or recruit from outside, it will disappear. That almost happened after World War II.

POSTSCRIPT

World War II coincided with the children's coming of age. About one-third to one-half were marrying and had begun raising families, and by 1950 most were joining the American surge to the suburbs. Equally important, nearly all of them had married non-Yemenites. Although the Lower East Side had been losing its Yemenite Jewish residents to Boro Park since before the war, Boro Park was finding itself bereft of members as well. Several Oldtimers chose to retire to Florida and a few immigrated to Israel. More and more of their children were moving out of Boro Park, their exodus coinciding with the influx of Orthodox Ashkenazim who, by the 1970s, were Boro Park's dominant population. Conflicts between the Oldtimers' children and some of their Ultra-Orthodox neighbors drove several more families, including some of the Oldtimers, out of the neighborhood.

Outgroup marriage, geographic dispersion, and the effectiveness of the American education system diluted the Yemenite Jewish community to such an extent that it was under imminent threat of extinction by the mid-1950s. The immigration of the Newcomers, Yemenite Jews from Israel, literally saved the day. Since they began arriving, beginning in 1959, they have added between four thousand and five thousand more individuals to the American Yemenite Jewish population. More important, a significant minority, those who have chosen to hold onto many traditional practices, have settled in Boro Park. It is they who have given new life to the Boro Park community. In effect, the Newcomers have picked up the baton that the

Oldtimers reluctantly surrendered. With their coming have been many changes: in language, in practices, and in attitudes—the subject for another paper.

Notes

1. As one of the Oldtimers' children, I have been doing linguistic and ethnographic fieldwork among the Greater New York Yemenites since January 1970. The immigration data in this paper derive from interviews and from photographs, passports, citizenship papers, affidavits, and sundry personal and official letters that informants have shown me.

2. According to Zayidi (a Shia Islam sect that has dominated Yemen for more than one thousand years) law, Jewish children who were unmarried when their fathers died were subject to forced conversion to Islam. The basis for that decree is that under Islam, religious affiliation is derived from the father. In Judaism, in contrast, religious membership is determined through the mother. Because of Shalom ash-Shabazi's *Hemdat haYamim* ("The Time of Trouble," ms.,n.d.) we know that the edict has existed for at least three-hundred years.

3. Avraham Yairi, "AliyatYehudei Teiman liEretz Yisroel" (The immigration of Yemen's Jews to Israel), in Yisroel Yishaỹahu and Aharon Tsadoq, eds., *Shevut Teiman* (Exile in Yemen) (Tel-Aviv:Sefer Publishers, 1944), pp. 11–36.

4. Yisroel Yishayahu, "Shivilei ha Aliyah meiTeiman liTsion" (Patterns of immigration from Yemen to Zion), in Yishayahu and Tsadoq, eds., *Exile in Yemen,* p. 41. Population figures for and regional distribution of Jews in Yemen are problematic. A countrywide storehouse for birth, census, and immigration records did not exist until the 1960s. Estimates are therefore rough and range from between forty-five thousand (Erich Brauer, *Ethnologie der Jemenitischen Juden* [Heidelberg: Kulturgeschichteliche Bibliotek, 1934], p. 61ff. and one hundred thousand Jews (Shlomo Dov Goitein, "The Social Structure of Jewish Education in Yemen," in Shlomo Deshen and Walter P. Zenner, eds., *Jewish Societies in the Middle East: Community, Culture, and Authority* [Washington, D.C.: University Press of America, 1982], pp. 211–34). Based on Brauer, Goitein, Yairi, and Yishayahu, my estimates point to between sixty-five thousand and seventy thousand Jew living in Yemen, Aden, and the Hadhramaut before World War II.

5. As only Jews and Muslims have lived in Yemen for more than fifteen hundred years, Jews were Yemen's craftspeople. This does not mean that only Jews manufactured the implements used in daily life or most of the luxuries. There were a few Muslim craftspeople and a few Jewish farmers and shopkeepers, importers, and exporters, but they were the exception rather than the norm.

6. In Yemen this translated into a breakdown of 80 or so percent of its Jews living in small towns and villages, with only 20 percent occupying their own quarters in the few cities of Sanaa, Ibb, Taiz, and Sadah (Dina Dahbany-Miraglia, "An Analysis of Ethnic Identity Among Yemenite Jews in the Greater New York Area" [Ph.D. diss., Columbia University, 1983], pp. 45–46; ibid., "The Jews of Yemen," in Jane S. Gerber, ed., *The Jewish Peoples, An Ethnographic Survey* [Westport, Ct.: Greenwood Press, forthcoming]; and Goiten, "Social Structure of Jewish Education," p. 212.

7. See Yairi, "Immigration of Yemen's Jews to Israel"; Yishayahu, *Patterns of Immigration from Yemen to Zion.*

8. Dahbany-Miraglia, "Analysis of Ethnic Identity," pp. 55–57; Hayyim J. Cohen, *The Jews of the Middle East, 1860–1972* (New Brunswick, N.J.: Transaction Books, 1973), pp. 101ff.

9. Of the few Oldtimer males who married in the United States one wed to another Oldtimer, a divorcee, and two or three more married American-born Ashkenaziyat.

10. Technically, *miswoh* means "obligation," or the necessity to fulfill religious injunctions, such as the men's requirement of praying twice daily and the women's of keeping a kosher home. These and other ritual matters were taken for granted and did not attract any special attention communally. As it emerged interactionally, the term *miswoh* was most often articulated when one Yemenite helped another to find a job or an apartment, provided backup documents for the immigration authorities, and worked together to raise money for the *kanayis* (synagogues) and the ladies associations' projects.

11. HIAS, *Encyclopedia Judaica,* vol. 15 (New York: McMillan, 1967), p. 1539.

12. A *yeshiva* is a Jewish day school in which religious subjects, such as the Old Testament and its commentaries, prayers, Jewish history, and the laws governing the myriad aspects of Jewish life, are taught between 8:00 A.M. and 12:00 P.M., Mondays through Fridays and sometimes on Sunday mornings as well. The afternoons are set aside for the secular subjects of history, English, mathematics, social studies, and art. The Orthodox usually run separate institutions for females and males, whereas the Conservative and Reform *yeshivas* are almost always coed.

13. A weaver by trade, she could not sit at a loom because a few years earlier she had injured her spine when jumping from a ledge high above the women's bathing pool, located just outside Sadah proper.

14. In Yemen the most prestigious craft was jewelry manufacture, the majority of which was in silver. Unlike pottery and weaving, jewelry making was almost entirely engaged in by males. Only one Oldtimer female and two of the Oldtimers' daughters learned to set stones and to use the torch. Several of the male children who began their working careers in the building trades and as painters switched to jewelry manufacture as soon as they were able.

15. A Talmud Torah is a part-time Hebrew school that is run between one and six days a week, two to three hours a day. Hebrew is taught and Jewish religious texts and prayer books are studied. These schools were established to provide a Jewish education for those children whose parents could not afford to send them to all-day *yeshivas.*

16. Dahbany-Miraglia, "Analysis of Ethnic Identity," pp. 142ff.

17. Conrad M. Arensberg, "The Community as Object and as Sample," *American Anthropologist* 63 (1961):248–50. As an object the American Yemenite Jewish community fulfills most of Arensberg's criteria. The most important of these are territoriality, cultural and economic interdependence, the requisite number of members, and, of course, some degree of continuity through time.

18. These foods include *jaaleh,* roasted legumes and nuts, *kubaneh,* a raised Shabboth bread that is baked overnight, *hilbeh,* crushed fenugreek seeds mixed with Chinese parsley, *zahuq,* a condiment made of various hot crushed peppers and spices, and *araqi,* a brandy distilled from raisins.

Good Works, Good Times

The Syrian Ladies' Aid Society of Boston, 1917–1932

EVELYN SHAKIR

During the late nineteenth century an Englishman studying social institutions in the United States concluded that the "most American thing in all America is the American women's club."[1] He was bearing witness to the dramatic proliferation of voluntary female organizations—whether cultural, charitable, or devoted to political and social reform—that began after the Civil War and continued into the first decades of the twentieth century.

By World War I, women from the Near East were becoming a part of that movement, banding together in clubs and ladies' aid societies that provided them (and later their daughters) with companionship and a new sense of purpose—the same satisfactions offered by mainstream women's clubs. But the ethnic women's club served other purposes as well. To the immigrant woman, it was an island of familiarity in an alien world. Composed of women who shared her heritage, the club confirmed and helped perpetuate traditional values a woman held dear. At the same time, it provided a safe environment in which she could break new ground both in her sense of herself and in her relationship to family and community. The Syrian Ladies' Aid Society of Boston is a good case in point.

When I was growing up, it seemed to me that, in my house at least, the Syrian Ladies' Aid Society of Boston ranked in importance somewhere ahead of the church and only slightly behind the family itself. As a child, I took its privileged position for granted; as an adult, I began to wonder how it had come about. To answer that question, I started delving into the early history of the Ladies' Aid. I have read—or really my mother has read to me—the minutes (in Arabic) of the club's first fifteen years. I have also consulted such documents as the annual reports and day books of Denison House,[2] which was the local settlement house, and the monthly reports of the International Institute of Boston,[3] and I have interviewed several women who belonged to the club in those early years. What I have heard and read not only helps me understand why the club inspired such devotion in its members; it also constitutes valuable data on the experience of Syrian-Lebanese women in America.

The early history of the Ladies' Aid can be divided into three periods: 1917 to 1920, when the club was preoccupied with establishing itself and defining its character and mission; 1921 to 1928, when it was consolidating its position within the community; and 1920 to 1932, when, though the club continued to flourish, it also found itself at the center of controversy.

Originally called the Society for the Relief of Syria and Lebanon, the club came into being in response to the desperate conditions of the people whom the immigrants had left behind and to whom World War I had brought hunger, terror, and disease. "On Syrians and Armenians in our district," reads the Denison House report of 1915, the "burden of wartime sorrow has borne most heavily. Word has reached them again and again of tyranny and persecution, of famine and massacre, and they have been impotent to help."[4] By April 1917 the *New York Times* was reporting that the Turkish government in Damascus had commandeered all livestock in Palestine and Syria, and all grain including even that which was to be used for seed. "Fully 50% of the population," the paper said, "are dying by starvation."

That year a group of women from Saint George's Orthodox Church decided they must try to help. Rejecting the arguments of those who claimed that relief supplies would never reach their destination—"that is only an alibi given by the hard-hearted who do not want to contribute one cent"[5]—twenty-seven immigrant women, most of them from Mount Lebanon, and ranging in age from twenty to about fifty, met on November 13, 1917, to elect officers and plan strategy. Two weeks later, they launched a door-to-door membership drive, calling on people from Damascus and Beirut as well as from Mount Lebanon, on Melkites and Maronites as well as on Orthodox. Dues were deliberately set low—five cents a week—so that no one would have an excuse to refuse, and within a week, the club could boast more than 250 members.

To raise more money, the women placed collection boxes in neighborhood stores, asked merchants to contribute a small percentage on each sale, raffled off their own needlework, and held their first annual *hafli.*[6] While the war lasted, they sent what aid they could via American relief committees and the International Red Cross; after the Armistice, they were able to forward one thousand dollars directly to the Near East, to be divided evenly among the major religious sects.

Members of the Syrian Ladies' Aid Society of Boston preparing to march in the Armistice Day Parade of 1925. Behind them on the accompanying float are their children in traditional Arab dress. Photo courtesy of Evelyn Shakir.

But as boatloads of relief supplies steamed into Beirut and as those survivors who could escaped their devastated homes, the clubwomen reached a crucial decision: henceforth they would devote most of their efforts to helping needy Syrian and Lebanese people in the greater Boston area rather than abroad. Thus it happened that in the following July the club was officially incorporated as the Syrian Ladies' Aid Society of Boston.

By that time the club had already given its first half-ton of coal to a needy family and was providng milk to two families with small children; was contributing ten dollars a month toward the support of an elderly couple, and another ten dollars a month to a family ineligible for public aid; and had spent five dollars on eyeglasses for a young girl. Even with the minutes in hand, it is difficult to be sure how much money the club was spending at any given time or how many people it was helping since the names of those receiving aid were never revealed at meetings, much less recorded in minutes. They were known only to the President and the Aid Committee, whose members tended to hold office for several years at a stretch.

Even so, certain cases do stand out. In March 1920, for instance, a little Syrian girl was found wandering alone in Boston. The club members decided to care for her while advertising for her parents in local Syrian newspapers. Two months later, they located the girl's stepmother, who admitted to having deliberately abandoned her. Justice was meted out in the courts, a good home was found for the girl, and the whole story was reported in *Al-Hoda*[7] in such terms as to shed glory on the Ladies' Aid and to bolster its credibility.

By the end of that year, when the club threw its first New Year's Eve party, its fledging period was over. A major emblem of its readiness to soar was its removal, earlier in the year, to new quarters. Since its inception, the club had been meeting in rooms belonging to the women's society of Saint George's Orthodox Church. Now on May 25, 1920, it moved to its own flat, just one street away, and set about furnishing it with the same delight, the minutes suggest, that a young wife might take in decking out her first home. One member donated curtains, another prints for the wall, another an American flag, another a broom. Several chipped in to buy an elegant mirror; the club's name painted in elaborate calligraphy was framed and hung. When all was ready, the ladies held an open house at which the guests toasted their hostesses with rosewater-flavored lemonade. Club and community were now ready for phase two.

From 1921 to 1928 the club gave financial aid to increasing numbers of people not only in Boston but throughout Massachusetts. Most families seem to have received, in addition to holiday gifts, somewhere between twenty and forty dollars a month, not enough in itself perhaps to support a family, but not an insignificant amount either at a time when the average monthly salary for a wage earner was only about one hundred dollars.

Again, out of all the anonymous and often indistinguishable recipients of aid flitting in and out of the minutes, one occasionally emerges in enough detail to engage the imagination and reveal the club in action. In November 1928, for instance, Kahlil Gibran's younger sister, Marianna, who was then treasurer of the club and a member of its Aid Committee, visited an old man, sick and poor, who had been called to her attention. She found him so ill, in fact, that she sent for a doctor who immediately had the man admitted to Boston City Hospital. The members agreed that at least one of them would visit him every day. A week later he was better and wanted to leave the hospital, but since he had no one at home to care for him, the club sent a delegation to convince him to stay where he was. Soon Marianna reported that the man had left the hospital anyway, was home, but had no money even for food. Though apparently annoyed, the club voted to contribute to his support. Next he decided he wanted to go back to the old country, where he had family to care for him, so Marianna went to City Hall and to the State House, hoping one or the other might help pay for his passage. Just a week after that, when the club's president and Marianna's cousin Skeeyee went to check on the old man, they found him dead. The club sent the sad news to his nephew in another state; three days after

Christmas, word came back that the club could do what it wanted with the body—the family didn't care. In its final act for the destitute old man, the Ladies' Aid paid for his burial.

Meanwhile, the club had not turned its back on the Near East. In 1921 it sponsored a *sahra*[8] to benefit Palestinian orphans, and four years later, when fighting broke out again in Syria, the club sent another one thousand dollars to help alleviate the plight of a new set of refugees. Faced with such drains on its treasury, the Ladies' Aid held repeated membership drives—"Join in March and you won't have to pay the initiation fee"—and staged one fundraising event after another. Soon any Syrian in Boston who wanted to could enjoy a full social life just by attending Ladies' Aid functions. The demands on an active member were staggering. For most of this period, meetings were held from three to six times a month. Almost every week, one or two members hosted a *sahra* to which the community was invited; almost every month the club gave a supper—twice a year, dressed in Asian costume, they gave more elaborate meals for the "American" community. The club staged at least one major play a year, gave annual Halloween and New Year's Eve parties, and held an annual picnic, an annual bazaar, and an annual grand *hafli* with musicians brought in from New York, local folk poets, and prominent speakers such as Abraham Rihbany and Kahlil Gibran. In their spare time, the members held rummage sales, gave whist parties, marched in parades, and built at least one float. At Christmas and Easter they visited all Syrians for miles around who were hospitalized; for several years, they called on everyone in the community who had gotten married or suffered a death in the family. And every month, a cadre of faithful workers climbed up and down tenement stairs to collect dues. Little wonder that by 1925 a report of the International Institute of Boston identified the Ladies' Aid Society, four-hundred members strong, as the "most active organization in the city's Syrian community."[9]

The last period I have studied, 1929 to 1932, was an eventful and sometimes painful time in the history of the Ladies' Aid. It began happily enough with the purchase in 1929 of the famous "44 West Newton," a South End townhouse that would be the club's home and the community's central meeting place for the next thirty years. But even as the ladies were negotiating to buy their house, the stock market crashed, and by 1931 the club was besieged as never before with requests for aid. Earlier clients had been the very old or the very young, the sick, the widowed, the handicapped. Now a steady stream of requests came in from healthy husbands and fathers who had lost their jobs. In response to the new emergency, the club began to act, in a small way at least, as an employment agency, and to subsidize the families of the unemployed.

At the same time, the club was, unfortunately, having financial difficulties of its own. At the beginning of its career, it had invested its money with a respected local businessman, a Syrian, who acted as banker to many immigrants. In 1930 his business failed and he himself died, leaving the club with only a promissory note from his wife. Then in 1932 a bank in which the club had deposited another sum of money also failed.

Given those reversals and the hard times generally, it is not surprising perhaps that rumors of wrongdoing by the club began to circulate in the community. Charges were leveled that money collected in the name of charity had gone instead to line the members' own pockets. But the priests whom the club invited to examine its books could find no evidence of misappropriation of funds. The minutes, too, seem to indicate that doubts about the club's probity were absurd. The members were, if anything, overscrupulous about the uses to which they put their income. And far from dipping into the funds intended for charity, they often supplemented them either with cash or goods. In 1919, for instance, the club's treasury helped pay for an old man's passage to Syria, but the members spent their own money to make sure he went off in style. One donated underwear, another socks, another handkerchiefs, another food and cigarettes for the voyage. One woman bought him a suitcase, and another woman and her husband drove him to Providence, Rhode Island, to catch his boat. (As for mortgage payments and other house expenses, they seem from the start to have been paid out of a separate fund.)

Despite the troubles it brought, 1932 did not mark the beginning of the end for the Ladies' Aid. On the contrary, the club held on and prospered. Certainly it outworked and outlasted all the men's clubs in the community. Its history, then, lends support to scholar Maxine Seller's contention that Syrian-Lebanese women's clubs in America "had a virtual monopoly of social and charitable services within their communities."[10] In that respect, says Seller, Syrian-Lebanese women resembled Polish, Finnish, and Jewish women, rather than—as might seem more likely—women from southern Italy, Greece, and Asia.[11]

The social activism of Near Eastern women coincided with and may, in part, be attributable to their economic activism. Their success as peddlers is well known, but they were also mill hands and stitchers and often worked side by side with their men in groceries, dry goods stores, and confectionary shops. Working outside of the home, something most of them could not have done in the old country, must have helped make even the shyest girl more self-reliant and self-assured, and thus better prepared, say, to plan a *hafli*—that is, to negotiate with entertainers, rent a hall, order programs, arrange for publicity, sell tickets door-to-door; to preside at a meeting, march in a parade, or—if she were literate and especially daring—give a speech; to investigate appeals for aid, allocate monies, and keep books; to accompany immigrants with little or no English to doctors' offices or to courtrooms, and cooperate with various public and private agencies outside of the ethnic community. A woman who could earn enough to bring her parents from the old country or to put her brother through school might certainly believe that she could carry out those other tasks as well.

As it turns out, of the twenty-five women who were most active in the club's first year or so, 60 percent and possibly more were unmarried, most in their twenties, some in their thirties, working either as stitchers or, in a couple of cases, as peddlers. The rest of the twenty-five were married, mostly unemployed, and older—usually in their forties—in other words, without small children to care for. The continued prominence in the club of a corps of matrons, most of whom had probably never worked outside the home, suggests a tradition of strong and assertive women reaching back to the Lebanese village, a tradition that may help explain why some women emigrated in the first place (especially those who came alone) and why, once in America, so many became self-supporting.

But whether twenty or fifty, single or married, wage earners or home-makers, the women of the Ladies' Aid just by organizing and addressing the public, were departing from the ways of their female forebears and thus engaging in potentially unwomanly behavior. They could not have run this risk without community support, and that they seem to have gained almost immediately. One sour note occurred when a committee of men from Saint John of Damascus Church insisted that the club solicit neither funds nor members from their parish, but the incident was an isolated unpleasantness. Had the women banded togther for some other purpose, their reception might have been cooler, but in 1917 the need in Syria was so urgent that it justified even female boldness. If, as one member stood to tell the others, the women would only uncover their faces—she was speaking figuratively, of course—put aside their diffidence and work hard, they would surely succeed. Her speech was warmly applauded.

Then, too, it helped that charity was a traditional female virtue and thus a legitimate sphere for female action. The church could not object. "Charity," a visiting bishop told members, "is the most beautiful jewelry a woman can wear." Such reassurance was welcome, but a residue of anxiety still surfaced whenever the club attempted anything new or particularly exciting, like their first big *hafli*.

We were so nervous [a charter member recounted], we were afraid some men might come, bring bottles, listen to music, and get drunk. And if they did, what could we do about it! And people would say "A ladies' club! And they have such goings-on!" No, we were worried. But all went very well, very well. We made a lot of money.

My mother told me about the first club-sponsored play she appeared in.

Once I took the part of a man in a play. Elias [her brother] used to be out on the road selling for several weeks at a time. While he was away, I accepted this role. But then I began to worry. Probably it was shameful and I oughtn't to do it. But still I was going to

> *rehearsals. When Elias came back I had this thing on my mind. I said to him, "You know what?" He said "What?" I said, "I'm going to wear men's clothing and be on stage with everyone looking at me." I thought he'd say, "No, how could you agree to do such a thing?" But he said, "Ah, it's all right. It's all right. As long as you make money for the club."*[12]

The worthy end justified unorthodox, even unmaidenly, behavior. Assertion, activism, and public self-display that under other circumstances might have been suspect now had the sanction of the community, including—and this was important—the men in the community. The young actress—my mother—was worried, after all, about her brother's reaction, not her mother's.

From the beginning, in fact, a small group of men took a keen interest in the club's proceedings. According to the bylaws, men (like children) could be dues-paying honorary members, who might attend meetings if they wished but could not vote or hold major office. At the first meeting, one member's husband was elected club adviser, and for the next two years or so he and another man, who used to direct the club's plays, attended almost every meeting. Throughout the first fifteen years, men helped host the club's New Year's Eve parties, often emceed the *haflis,* and sometimes presented skits at one or the other. At Christmas and Easter they drove the Visiting Committee to hospitals throughout eastern Massachusetts, and when a major decision was to be made, such as whether to purchase a house, the club formally called upon its male members for advice. Two of the four people charged with finding an appropriate house were men, and once it was purchased men volunteered their time to refinish the floors and repair the windows.

The women's reliance on and at least verbal deference to male judgment was, of course, perfectly in keeping with their cultural training. But it was also the best possible method of assuring their own success. By involving the men in the club's activities, the women gave them a stake in its welfare, forestalled potential hostility (for instance, from men who wanted their wives at home), and secured a number of industrious workers and, when need be, of loyal defenders. At the same time, the men's support—even their share of the limelight—helped legitimize the club both in the eyes of the community and, as I have already suggested, in the women's own eyes.

In seeking to understand, then, the club's strong hold on the affections of its members, one should not overlook the exciting and relatively guilt-free opportunities it afforded them for exercising their powers and developing their talents, for leading rather than following, for being public as well as private people. But neither, I think, should one overlook the ways in which the club incorporated the traditional claims of church, family, and village.

As for the first, it was not just that club meetings began and ended with prayer. It was that in serving the needy, the members felt that they were doing God's own work, that they were putting the social gospel into action. Only in those terms can one understand the piety the club inspired. As for the second, hackneyed as it may sound, the club was a sort of family. The make-up of the group, with its mix of older married women and younger unwed girls, suggests as much, as does the fact that the club president was, by design, always a married woman. It was, too, a pleasantly liberated family since men were largely excluded from the day-to-day workings of the club, and even the two men who at first were not excluded seem to have been gentle and unintimidating figures. Moreover, the benevolent matriarchy looked out for its own. In 1923, when one young member who had no family became engaged, the women of the club held a wedding *sahra* for her. And the following year, when an older member suffered a stroke, the others assumed responsibility for the medical bills that her brother refused to pay. Finally, the club was family simply because so many of its members—and more as time went on—were actually related by blood or marriage.

For that reason, too, the club was reminiscent of the villages, with their extended kinship networks, that the immigrants had left behind. Also, in club as in village, certain families predominated as did certain religious sects—most of the members were Orthodox or Melkite, a few were Maronite. Then, too, the female cooperation and companionship epitomized by the club can be seen as an extension of village custom that brought women together to harvest silkworms, launder clothes, or crochet trousseaus.

Finally, if one were to judge the women of the Ladies' Aid only by the minutes of their meetings, one would have to conclude that they were a sober lot. But conversations with early members make clear that they were high spirited as well as high minded, as full of fun as of zeal. Many of them were quite young, after all, and came to the club after a long day bent over a sewing machine in a noisy, dingy factory. They came to be wise and good but also to laugh. At their *sahras,* they sang, danced, played silly parlor games, and teased their men friends. One woman specialized in comic imitations of her brother's macho dance style. When they got together to bake sweets for a supper, the noise of the younger ones sometimes had to be shushed by the older ones, who, like wise mothers, would give them gum to chew so that they would be less tempted to eat the club's profits away.[13]

After listening to their stories, I understand better why one member told me that she rushed home from work on Thursdays and gulped down her supper because she couldn't wait to get to 44 West Newton,[14] and why another woman said, "We looked forward to a meeting as if it were a wedding."[15] As the well-known social worker Vida Scudder wrote of another female institution, Denison House, "There was a sense of refreshing adventure during those pioneer years. . . . The activities of the House were full of joy."[16]

The Boston club is still in existence today, though in 1962 its name was changed to the Lebanese-Syrian Ladies' Aid Society. Since the 1960s the club's membership has dwindled and the range of its activities has been significantly curtailed. But the club continues to provide aid, not so much to individuals and families as to local hospitals and social agencies, to national organizations (like the heart and cancer funds), to victims of disaster around the world, and to those who have been maimed, orphaned, or made homeless by war in the Near East. As for the local Syrian-Lebanese community, the club's efforts on its behalf now center on young people and on the elderly. Each year the Ladies' Aid confers modest college scholarships on young women of Arab descent. And it will soon make the largest single contribution in its history to help build a home for the elderly in the heart of the Syrian-Lebanese community in West Roxbury (Boston), Massachusetts. That gift seems a fitting gesture since its immediate beneficiaries will include those early immigrant women and their daughters who invested their youth, vigor, and idealism in promoting the work of the club and the welfare of its constituency. Now, half a century later, it brings added satisfaction to recall that the good they did for others gladdened their own hearts, enriched their lives, and dignified the status of women within their community.

Notes

1. Inez Haynes Irwin, *Angels and Amazons: A Hundred Years of American Women* (Garden City, N.Y.: Doubleday, 1934), p. 207.

2. Denison House was established in 1892 by a group of college-educated women of privileged background who felt they must justify their existence by helping the poor and disadvantaged. The first head of the house was Emily Greene Balch (1867–1961), who in 1946 won the Nobel Peace Prize.

3. Like international institutes in other American cities, the Boston organization began as a branch of the YWCA; in 1924 it became autonomous. Still in existence today, the Institute continues its mission of helping immigrants and refugees in the greater Boston area.

4. Denison House report, 1915, p. 14.

5. Minutes of November 13, 1917 (unpublished).

6. A large social gathering, usually including music and dance.

7. A daily Arabic newspaper published in New York City.

8. Literally "evening." A party, usually on a smaller scale than a *hafli.*

9. Annual Report, Immigration History Research Archives, University of Minnesota.

10. Maxine Seller, "Beyond the Stereotype: A New Look at the Immigrant Woman, 1880–1924," *Journal of Ethnic Studies* 3 (1975):65.

11. Ibid., *Immigrant Women* (Philadelphia: Temple University Press, 1981), p. 159.

12. Interview with Hannah Sabbagh Shakir, West Roxbury, Massachusetts.

13. Interviews with Mary Shalhoub Saad, May 12, 1983, West Roxbury, Massachusetts.

14. Interview with Saada Najam Hadad, May 17, 1983, Marshfield, Massachusetts.

15. Interview with Najeebie Naddaff Khoury, September 1977, West Roxbury, Massachusetts.

16. "Early Days at Denison House," 1937, Records of Denison House, Schlesinger Library, Radcliffe College. Scudder (1861–1954), a professor of English at Wellesley College, was the moving force behind Denison House for the first twenty years of its existence.

PART THREE

INDIVIDUALS

Philip Khuri Hitti (1886–1978)

An Homage

BAYLY WINDER

PHILIP K. HITTI: THE PUBLIC PERSON

Scholar

A public figure and professional, Professor Hitti, "the Shaykh" to most of his colleagues and students, is best known as a scholar and author and, for his generation in America, as the major interpreter of the Near East, its history, and its civilization to the West. His writings are voluminous and hardly need to be detailed here.[1] It may be worthwhile, however, to set forth the significant phases of Professor Hitti's work and to mention the major works he produced in each phase. In the first phase, which lasted some twenty years, from his graduate student days in the late teens to the publication of the first edition of *History of the Arabs* in 1937, during which time the young scholar was trying to establish himself, Hitti concentrated on the traditional Orientalist disciplines of translating and editing texts and producing monographic-type analyses. Major works from that phase include:

> *The Origins of the Islamic State, Being a Translation from the Arabic with Annotations, Geographic and Historic Notes of the Kitab Futuh al-Buldan of al-Imam abu-l Abbas Ahmad ibn-Jabir al-Baladhuri,* vol. 1, *Studies in History, Economics and Public Law,* lxvii: 163. Ph.D. dissertation, Columbia University, 1916.
>
> (Editor) *Mukhtasar Kitab al-Farq bayn al-Firaq* (English title page, *Al-Baghdadi's Characteristics of Muslim Sects*), by Abd al-Qahir ibn-Tahir abi-Mansur al-Baghdadi,abridged by Abd al-Razzaq ibn Razq Allah ibn-abi-Bakr ibn-Khalaf al-Ras ani. Cairo: Matba at al-Hilal, 1924.

(Editor) *Nazm al-Iqyan fi Ayan al-Ayan* (English title page, *As-Suyuti's Who's Who in the Fifteenth Century*), by Jalāl al-Din Abd al-Rahman ibn abi Bakr al-Suyuti. New York: Syrian-American Press, 1927.

The Origins of the Druze People and Religion, with Extracts from Their Sacred Writings. Columbia University Oriental Studies, xxviii. New York: Columbia University Press, 1928.

An Arab-Syrian Gentleman and Warrior in the Period of the Crusades: Memoirs of Usāmah ibn-Munqidh (Kitab al-Itibar). Records of Civilization, Sources and Studies. New York: Columbia University Press, 1929.

(Editor) *Kitab al-Itibar* (English title page, *Usamah's Memoirs Entitled Kitab al-Itibar*), by Usamah ibn Munqidh. *Princeton Oriental Texts,* I. Princeton: Princeton University Press, 1930.

(In collaboration with Nabih Amin Faris and Butrus Abd al-Malik) *Descriptive Catalog of the Garrett Collection of Arabic Manuscripts in the Princeton University Library. Princeton Oriental Texts,* v. Princeton: Princeton University Press, 1938.

(In collaboration with Mohamed E. Moghadem and Yahya Armajani) *Descriptive Catalog of the Garrett Collection of Persian, Turkish and Indic Manuscripts Including Some Miniatures in the Princeton University Library. Princeton Oriental Texts,* vi. Princeton: Princeton University Press, 1939.

For the twenty-year period from the mid-thirties to the mid-fifties, Hitti concentrated on the three major works of historical synthesis that established him as a magisterial writer and interpreter of Near Eastern history and civilization with appeal and reach beyond the professional coterie of Near Eastern specialists. These works introduced the intelligent mid-twentieth-century reader to Near Eastern culture; they were at once authoritatively based in contemporary monographic scholarship, replete with *apparatus criticus* for the specialist, yet interesting and readable. The works in question are:

History of the Arabs. London: Macmillan, 1937.

History of Syria, Including Lebanon and Palestine. London: Macmillan, 1951.

Lebanon in History from the Earliest Times to the Present. London: Macmillan, 1957.

It might be noted that each of these works has also appeared in an abridged version and each has been translated into various foreign languages. *History of the Arabs,* in its tenth edition as of 1987, clearly constitutes a classic.

The third period, a kind of silver age, followed Professor Hitti's retirement from Princeton in 1954 and the publication of *Lebanon in History* and again lasted some twenty years, from the mid-fifties to the mid-seventies. His later works were to a certain extent a reworking of his earlier studies, an examination of the material from new perspectives and with fresh insights, but not a breaking of new ground. Major works in this group include:

The Near East in History: A 5,000 Year Story. Princeton: D. Van Nostrand Company, 1961.

Makers of Arab History. New York: St. Martin's Press, 1968.

Islam: A Way of Life. Minneapolis, University of Minnesota Press, 1970.

Capital Cities of Arab Islam. Minneapolis: University of Minnesota Press, 1973.

Nor indeed did Philip Hitti's energy for writing and scholarship ever flag. Even as his eyesight dimmed and his health failed in the 1970s, he nevertheless produced three manuscripts that remain unpublished. One is on Arab women; the second is titled *Decisive Battles in Arab History;* the third is a personal memoir.

Teacher

Professor Hitti was invited to Princeton in part because a course, Oriental Civilization, had become a "gut" course under his predecessor. Enrollment had grown to over two hundred out of a total undergraduate enrollment of perhaps eighteen hundred. Hitti delighted to report that in his second year at Princeton, undergraduate interest in Oriental civilization had declined so rapidly that registration in the course was down to some thirty odd!

Hitti was a dedicated and superb teacher, and he loved teaching. His lectures were well organized, full of enthusiasm and sparkling wit. But as a teacher, Hitti was also demanding and rigorous. Shoddy work was not tolerated. Over nearly fifty years, he taught literally thousands of students—at the American University of Beirut, at Princeton and Harvard universities, and at the University of Minnesota. To this day my wife and I meet people who were touched by him in undergraduate courses on ancient Near Eastern civilization.[2] Arab history, Islamic religion, and the like. A smaller number concentrated in Near Eastern studies and went on to become specialized professionals in education, diplomacy, or other fields.

The best way to gauge a teacher's effectiveness and quality at the graduate level is to see what his students have become. Hitti's students are more or less a catalog of U.S.-trained Arabists and Islamists of his time. The following names, which do not represent a complete list, might be noted: Constantine Zurayq, Nabih Amin Faris, Edward Jurji, George Miles, Jibrail Jabbur, Harold Glidden, Yahya Armajani, Butrus Abd al-Malik, Roderick Davison, W. Cantwell Smith, Harry Hazard, Ernest Dawn, Oleg Grabar, John Joseph, George F. Hourani, Caesar Farah, Richard Mitchell, Nicholas Heer, Herbert Bodman, James Kritzeck, and Francis Peters. In the totally innovative pre–World War II summer seminars that Hitti created at Princeton, he touched people as different as A. I. Katsch and Richard Ettinghausen, and one cannot omit from the lists scholars such as Norman Itzkowitz, Stanford Shaw, and Martin Dickson, who were drawn to Princeton by the Hitti magnet but subsequently branched off into Turkish or Iranian specializations. In short, the generation of American Arabists and Islamists now aged fifty-five to seventy-five were also all trained by Hitti. Through their students his teaching goes forward. It may be appropriate to remark, incidentally, that Hitti considered and proudly and publicly proclaimed himself to be an Orientalist. Latter-day critics of that tradition may perhaps consider that as a man of the Near East he had been co-opted by an exploitative tradition aimed at maintaining the dependency of, inter alia, the Near East. Such a view is unjustified in light of Professor Hitti's powerful defense of Near Eastern peoples, especially Arabs and Muslims, in fora of every sort. In any case, to him Orientalism meant scholarship—as objective, accurate, and sensitive as a person of a particular time and place could make it.

Perhaps the best summary of Philip Hitti as scholar and teacher is the citation read by the official orator on the occasion (April 27, 1957) of his induction as a Fellow of the Mediaeval Academy of America:

> *Philip K. Hitti, Professor Emeritus of Semitic Literature at Princeton University, builder of a great department of Oriental Studies, interpreter of the East to the West. More than any other man, he had made American mediaevalists conscious of the depth and extent of Arab influence on Europe. His* History of the Arabs *is still the standard work in the field; his translation of Usamah has introduced generation after generation of students to Arab culture. We gladly welcome him as a Fellow of the Mediaeval Academy.*

Institution Builder

As the Mediaeval Academy orator suggested, the most important institutions that Hitti built were the Department of Near Eastern Studies[3] and the interdepartmental Program in Near Eastern Studies at Princeton University. Since the university landscape is now dotted with such units, it is easy to overlook the pioneering quality that Hitti, initially in the face of some indifference, possessed. Princeton was for a number of post–World War II years the only place where a student could receive coordinated and systematic training on either the mediaeval Islamic or the modern Near East. That the department and library collections continue, thirty-five years after his retirement, to maintain a leading, if no longer a dominant, position among the newer departments indicates that the building is on a firm foundation.

Another more particular principle that Hitti insisted on in building the

Princeton program is one that was by no means clear three and four decades ago. In the older Orientalist tradition one scholar was supposed to cover all disciplines connected with his area of study, including its languages, religions, history, literatures, socioeconomic conditions, politics, and anthropology. At Princeton, Hitti insisted, the future would be different. Scholars of the Near East would be situated in their proper disciplinary departments. For example, a political scientist specializing on the Near East would have first and foremost to be a political scientist subject to peer review by political scientists and, in addition, acquire the linguistic skills (he insisted on the centrality of language competence at all levels) and historical knowledge that would enable the individual to teach and publish in a sound way about Near Eastern politics. Such specialization is commonplace today, but was unusual when the first two social scientists hired at Princeton (the late Morroe Berger in sociology[4] and Dankwart A. Rustow in politics) were given a year after their appointments as assistant professors to go to the Near East and furbish or refurbish their earlier limited knowledge of the languages and establish firsthand contact with the area.

A passing reference has been made to the Near Eastern collections in Firestone Library at Princeton. But it should be emphasized that the early building of that magnificent collection was another central element in Hitti's design. The acquisition of the Garrett manuscript collection, one of the major collections of Arabic and other Near Eastern manuscripts in the world, was a direct result of Professor Hitti's persuasive efforts (and of Robert Garrett's generosity).

It is not feasible to describe briefly Philip Hitti's numerous other roles in institutional development, but the following incomplete list of roles played at different times will at least give an impression:

- Long-time trustee of the American University of Beirut and chairman of trustees' committee on academic affairs from which vantage point he was a skillful protagonist of the liberal arts orientation of that university.
- Secretary of the association of North American alumni of the American University of Beirut.
- Chairman, Advisory Council of Syrian and Lebanese American Federation of the Eastern States.
- Chairman, American Council of Learned Society's Committee on Near Eastern Studies.
- President, Americans for Middle East Relief (AMER), now known as American Near East Relief Association (ANERA).
- Charter Member, American Friends of the Middle East (AFME), now known as America-Mideast Educational and Technical Services (Amideast).
- Director, American Oriental Society, and chairman of its membership committee.
- Trustee, Lebanon College, Sūq al-Gharb, Lebanon.
- General editor, Princeton Oriental Series.

Man of Affairs

It should be obvious from all the above that Philip Hitti was not a cloistered, ivory-tower anchorite. He was involved in the world of affairs, whether governmental or business, without allowing himself to become beholden to anything except his own deeply held ethical and moral values and his university obligations. As the best known and most articulate Arab-American of his generation, Hitti played an important role in Arab American affairs. He was an adviser to the Iraqi and other Arab delegations at the San Francisco Conference (1945), which established the United Nations. He testified on the Palestine problem before the Committee on Foreign Affairs of the House of Representatives in 1944 and before the Anglo-American Commission of Inquiry on Palestine in 1945, and also carried on a local debate with Albert Einstein, published in *The Princeton Herald,* over Zionist and Arab claims to Palestine. In addition, he and Mrs. Hitti played host in Princeton to almost every important visitor to the United States from the Near East in the post–World War II period up until about 1960. Visitors included three kings of Saudi Arabia, the regent of Iraq, the president of Turkey, and the shah of Iran, not to mention numerous foreign and other ministers and ambassadors almost without number.

On the business side Hitti was a consultant to the Mergenthaler Linotype Company on Arabic typography, to the Atlantic Refining Company (now Atlantic Richfield Company [ARCO]) on Syria, and to the Arabian American Oil Company (ARAMCO) on Saudi Arabia. In this last capacity he played a signal role of cultural mediation between King Abd al-Aziz and the president of ARAMCO in the late 1940s and early 1950s.

Finally, assuming that other people's problems constitute a part of the world of affairs, one must note that Professor Hitti displayed tireless cheerful patience and intelligent effort on behalf of the affairs of truly staggering numbers of relatives, former students, friends, bare acquaintances, Lebanese, Lebanese and Syrian Americans, and Arabs and Muslims from all over. They came to him for advice or solutions to their myriad problems precisely because he never turned anyone away and managed to help a significantly high proportion of them. For all of the above, Professor Hitti received many decorations, medals, and citations from institutions and governments in the Arab world—more, one would suspect, than did any other single individual.

Interest in Arab/Syrian/Lebanese Immigrant Affairs

Professor Hitti would have been delighted by the new interest of the University of Minnesota and other organizations in the history and affairs of his community, because the Arabic-speaking community in this country was close to his heart. At the beginning of his career, that interest engaged much of the time he devoted to writing, as illustrated in his bibliography. The following list contains only those publications that constitute separate books or small monographs:

Antūniyūs al-Bish alānī: Awwal Muhājir Sūrī ilā al-Ālam al-Jadīd. New York: al-Matba ah al-Sūrīyah al-Amayrikīyah, 1916.

Educational Guide for Syrian Students in the United States. New York: Syrian-American Press, 1921.

Al-Sūrīyūn fi al-Walāyat al-Muttahidah al-Amayrikīyah. Cairo: Matba'at al-Muqtataf, 1922.

Amrīkā fi Nazar Sharqī—aw Thamānī Sanawāt fī al-Walāyaāt al-Muttahidah. Cairo: Idārat al-Hilāl, 1924.

The Syrians in America. New York: George H. Doran, 1924.

Sūrīyah wa-al-Sūrīyūn min Nāfidhat al-Ta" rīkh. New York: Syrian American Press, 1926. (Reprinted from *al-Ālam al-Jadīd.*)

In addition to those separate publications, he wrote no less than nineteen articles on the Near Eastern American community, including the brief article "Djaliyah" in the *Encyclopedia of Islam* (new edition).

A few other points may be noted. Professor Hitti was the only Arab-American whose name was inscribed in 1940 at the New York World's Fair among those of various communities "who have made notable contributions to the living, ever-growing democracy" of the United States. He worked with many committees and organizations of the Syro-Lebanese immigrant communities and founded with Habib Katibah and Joseph Ferris the Institute of Arab-American Affairs in New York. The institute lived for only a few years, but in light of its numerous "successor states" today, it must also be noted as the result of another pioneering effort by Hitti. Once more it should be mentioned that nearly every award, scroll, certificate, and the like that lay in the power of the immigrant communities to bestow flowed to this man. The desk set from which I now write is inscribed, "Presented to Prof. Phillip [*sic*] Hitti, Phoenicians of New Kensington, Pa., 1937."

One may conclude this section with the following words delivered by Charles Malik, then ambassador of Lebanon to the United States, at a retirement dinner held in New York in 1954 for Professor Hitti:

No man has been more active in or more understanding of the affairs of the Americans of Lebanese or Syrian origin than Professor Hitti . . . and no one is more respected or beloved by those who call themselves Syrians or Lebanese than he.

The Syrian and Lebanese emigration during the last one hundred years to all the corners of the earth, and in particular to the two Americas, is a tremendous tale yet untold in its completeness. There is here a depth of significance not only of an economic or political or religious or even individual order, but of the most ultimate human pathos.

Because there wasn't enough love or responsibility in their homelands these men and women dispersed and struggled; they roamed the seven seas, not because they had a message nor were they under some dominant national impulse, but in search of a living; they suffered in ways and forms they themselves did not understand and perhaps could not even comprehend; nevertheless they made a distinct, if modest, contribution wherever they went; they retained the deepest love and attachment to their original homes, not only sentimentally, but in real acts of genuine sacrifice; their suffering is far from ended; and now the second or third generation merges indissolubly into the new social and economic pattern—all this constitutes a profound, if yet uninterpreted, saga of search, suffering and heroism. The inner truth of this entire phenomenon—I do not mean its statistical truth or the tales of adventure and success with which it is punctuated, but its inmost spiritual significance as seen and apprehended by the eyes of the eternal—the inner truth of this whole phenomenon is still to be worked out. And there we bow our heads in deepest respect for and wonder at this strange modern inter-cultural and inter-demographic movement with which Professor Hitti, in one sector of his activity, is identified.[5]

PHILIP K. HITTI: THE PRIVATE MAN

It is not easy to write coolly about someone whom you admired, respected, and loved as I did the Hakim, but I shall try to say something of the private person I knew. Philip Hitti was a family man in the deepest, most reverent, and best sense of that term. His mother and father, his two sisters, his wife and his daughter, his five brothers, and far from least his second Ruh Qalbuh, his grandson—not to mention the extended family, which we knew privately as the *qabilah,* the tribe—were, together with his academic work, at the center of his life. He gave love to them all, but naturally, never soppily, and all reciprocated. He had the highest respect for women. A particular extension of his devotion to family was his love of small children, who reciprocated to an uncanny degree. In many cases they were a reasonable nuisance to the rest of us, but Professor Hitti suffered them gladly. Another kind of loyalty is exemplified by that which he felt for Columbia University, grantor of his doctorate and publisher of his first important books. He wore Columbia's light blue hood with evident pride at ceremonials in the orange and black environment of New Jersey. And in his last years, when Columbia was in evident financial need and Professor Hitti was faced with daunting medical expenses, he frequently made out modest checks to the order of Columbia University.

Hitti was a simple, humble, and kind man of absolute integrity. He certainly could distinguish quality from mediocrity. He was proud when he was recognized, but he never pushed himself forward or asked for things for himself. He had a sparkling sense of humor—never coarse—which could convulse large audiences or in conversation cause him near laughing seizures if he had not heard "that one" before. A smile was usually luffing around his mouth.

Philip Hitti was also a *mens sana in corpore sano* person. An avid tennis player until he was sixty, he continued to canoe until he was perhaps seventy-five, and always he walked for long distances. For organized American team sports he had little use, however, and the football "hype" each autumn was to him something childish, incomprehensible, and irrational that simply had to be endured with resignation, like another peculiar American affliction from which he suffered—poison ivy. He never drank spirits and would only take a single glass of wine when the doctor, for a year or two, ordered it. In addition, he drank no coffee and little tea. At an advanced age he once observed that "you have to have some intelligence to stay alive." He used his in caring for his body.

Professor Hitti had two great patriotic love affairs: with the United States and with Lebanon. He was in a sense stereotypical of the deeply committed immigrant. For him it turned out that the streets of America were paved with gold after all—the gold of freedom, liberty, and democracy. He had felt some slights or discrimination in America, but the opportunity and the living democracy were what counted. He served his new country in two world wars and in the second did not disdain supervision of a wartime publication outside of his field, namely *Tarikh al-Shab al-Amriki* (the history of the American people; by Farahat Ziyadah [Farhat J. Ziadeh] and Ibrahim Furayji. [Princeton: Princeton University Press, 1946])—a work subsidized by the United States government and designed to present, for the first time, an accurate history of the United States to the Arabic-reading public. Not that he could not discern weaknesses in America and its society. He found salaries for superstar athletes and other stars a travesty, and he deplored single-issue politics and much of the tawdriness of American life. But once, perhaps in 1948, when I asked whether he was seriously considering running for the presidency of newly independent Lebanon—a possibility being talked about in various Lebanese political circles—he looked at me incredulously and wondered if I really thought he would "be a dirty politician when I could be a professor in an American University like Princeton." Whatever inner pangs he may have experienced, he gave no thought of turning back.

And yet Lebanon continued to be the other pole of national or ethnic identification. The nearly annual summer trips after his retirement, during which he stayed with his sister and her husband in his native village, Shimlan, gave Professor Hitti a chance not only to keep up with current political and intellectual trends, but also to recharge his Lebanese and Arab batteries. He was always glad to come home—to America—but meanwhile the absolutely incomparable grapes and figs of Shimlan and the assertion that Lebanon was really a country in which one could live (*Lubnan bilad tuskan*) symbolized his deep and abiding love for the country that had nurtured him and instilled in him a set of values that, in turn, had enabled him to develop himself fully in the United States.

Hitti's feeling toward the two countries was distilled in his connection with two universities: Princeton, which was the context for his full development; and the American University of Beirut, whose most illustrious alumni and loyal trustee he was. That both universities bestowed honorary degrees on Philip Hitti was perhaps the most satisfying and appropriate honor that this teacher-scholar could have received.

Hitti was brought up in the Maronite tradition. Liturgy was in Syriac; the village priest was the chief academician. Church attendance was an absolute obligation for all the people of the village—as natural as the sunset or cockcrow. As a mature man Hitti was not a churchgoer, was sympathetic to many ideals of Protestantism, and had a gentle anticlerical bias. His study of the Semitic origins of Christianity did not dispose him to literal acceptance of dogma. He wrote as follows:

> *No extraordinary event in Christ's life—virgin birth, astral association, miracle performance, cruxification, descent to the underworld, exaltation to heaven—lacks its parallel in earlier Near Eastern religious experience. Hardly a teaching of his was not anticipated by Hebrew prophets or early Semitic teachers. But nowhere can one find such a concentration of noble thoughts and such emphasis on lofty ideas, and at no time can one discover a character who so completely practised what he taught.*[6]

As recent American history has revealed, roots do run deep, and Hitti's request had long been that his final service be according to the Maronite rite with a Maronite priest, and that the liturgy be in Syriac.

The description of Professor Hitti in these pages is best closed with his own words about himself. In them the reader will find more of Philip Khuri Hitti than any other person is likely to convey:

> *As I listened to the recital . . . of the few achievements generously attributed to me, I could not help but think of the cloud of witnesses, the host of men and women, Eastern and Western, young and old, who should share credit for whatever has been accomplished and without whom the measure of success attained would have been impossible. First of all comes the picture of those two Lebanese parents—simple, unsophisticated villagers. One of them, the mother, could not read or write and knew no foreign language. Oh, yes, but she spoke a language understood by all, the universal language of love. With good will toward all, that saintly mother cheerfully went about her daily task from dawn till late at night, caring for six living boys and two girls, and saving from the pittance of an income of her husband to send her son to a neighboring American high school, when no one from that village had been through that school before. The eldest son of the family contributed his share. A carpenter's apprentice, he shouldered every morning the tools of his trade, stopped at the next village to add to his load the tools of the master and proceeded to Alayh, Bhamdoun or Sawfar to construct the red-tiled roof of the summer home of a rich Beiruti, trudging back home in the evening or sleeping on the fragrant boards polished by his plane.*
>
> *A broken arm at the age of eight introduced me to the American institutions of learning. It was a compound fracture which the shepherds of the village and the vicinity failed to cure. Gangrene set in. A young graduate of the school of medicine at the American University of Beirut passed by and advised immediate removal to the city.*

There Dr. Post performed two operations which not only saved the limb but also my life. My weakened physical condition confirmed my family in its conviction that I should earn my living by intellectual rather than manual pursuits.

The village elementary school differed from the image of any school that word might invoke in your minds. It had no walls, but had a roof. The roof consisted of the overhanging, shady branches of a venerable oak tree, that is still standing.[7] *The benches were of stone. The faculty consisted of a black-frocked stern monk who not only believed in the adage "spare the rod" but practiced a revised version of it: "Let go the rod and you spoil the child." From the position of the shade cast by the tree he could tell noontime. When a student could read the Psalms in Arabic and Syriac there was nothing more for him to do but graduate.*

Likewise the American high school in neighboring Suq al-Gharb was a high school by courtesy. Its resemblance to any high school with which you are familiar is purely incidental. But there as a teen-age student I came under the influence of a young teacher, the daughter of the principal, who had just returned from a period of study in Northfield Seminary, in Massachusetts. It was she who took me by the hand, guiding me along the rocky, tortuous path of knowledge that has proved to be pleasantly endless. It was she who aroused in me the desire for knowledge, the thirst for research that has never been quenched, the quest for that elusive something called truth, the chasing for which has been like the chasing of a mirage in the Syrian Desert, or better still the chasing of a rainbow. This was the teacher who introduced me to the niceties of the French language, the intricacies of the English, and when she wrote on my exercise book "Je suis fière de vous!", "I am proud of you!" no Nobel prize winner, no candidate for membership in the Academie Française could have been more encouraged or gratified.

No, she was not a pretty girl, but she possessed a mind as sharp as a razor and a character as shining with nobility as the armor of a medieval knight.

The principal of the school himself was a puritanical, conservative theologian, more Calvinistic than Calvin. A stern disciplinarian, he once whipped us because, feeling lonesome one Sunday, we went home without his permission. In a sermon he maintained that even the stones on the Day of Judgment would bear witness against the evil-doer.

One summer day I came to his office. I had finished the school the year before and on his advice acted as teacher in a neighboring Druze village with the expectation of saving, in collaboration with my family, five French pounds, which would see me through the freshman class of Beirut. The entire University fees were then eighteen pounds for board, lodging and tuition. As a fourteen-year-old teacher, I had received one pound a month salary, with no maintenance, and now I told the principal of the school that I had only been able to save four pounds. This was a critical moment in my life. Mr. Hardin paused, then without a word put his hand in the pocket of his trousers, pulled out a gold pound and piled it on top of the four I had saved. If he had not, . . . well that is one of those "ifs" in history which no one can answer.

The scene changes. As a young man I was now a teacher at the American University of Beirut. One bright August day President Howard Bliss met me in that tiny picturesque village, Shimlan, my birthplace and his summer resort, and reported that I was designated to represent the University at a conference of the World's Student Christian Federation to be held in the summer of 1913 at Lake Mohonk, New York. I was told that I could spend a year of graduate study in America, with the understanding that my monthly salary of three pounds would be continued, that some compensation for maintenance would be made and that the Federation would pay traveling expenses. I could not believe my ears. Only one member of the Arabic-speaking faculty of the University had had one year of graduate work in the United States. The only difficulty lay in that I was then helping my brothers, one older and two younger, to receive their university education.

Happily all three continued; the older spent his life as a teacher mainly in Suq al-Gharb school, one of the younger two is now a practicing physician in Beirut and the other, an engineer. . . .

My first adventure in the streets of New York found me with a letter of introduction from Howard Bliss to Cleveland H. Dodge. The envelope read "99 John Street", but there was no "99" between "98" and "100". No problem in higher mathematics had ever so baffled my "green head" until a passer-by directed me to the other side of the street.

As a graduate student at Columbia it was necessary for me to supplement my modest income with work as custodian of the periodical room at the University library and as clerk in the registrar's office. One day a young lady from Waterbury, Connecticut, came with a mutual friend to register for the summer school. This was my introduction to the one who became my partner in life. Her unbounded confidence in me and high expectation sustained me throughout the many years of hard labor at Columbia, at my Alma Mater and finally at Princeton. At Princeton in 1935, when we planned to launch a summer program in Arabic and Islamic studies, an old professor at the University said that I could not get a two-cent stamp from the President for such a project. But the President at the first interview promised $2,500 to match the sum offered by the American Council of Learned Societies for that purpose. . . .

To you, fellow alumni, and fellow countrymen, whether here or abroad, I owe much of my inspiration. To our Arabic newspapers which always and generously gave space to what I had to say or write and which without exception commented on my retirement from the chairmanship of the Princeton department as the beginning of a new career, I owe unfailing encouragement and a debt of gratitude.

The words of the last verses of the "Chambered Nautilus" by Oliver Wendell Holmes come to mind. Little did I realize when they were penned on my notebook by my teacher in the Lebanese village of Suq al-Gharb that some day I might have even a remote association with Harvard, where the poet was a professor.

Build thee more stately mansions, O my soul,
As the swift seasons roll!
Leave thy low-vaulted past!
Let each new temple, nobler than the last,
Shut thee from heaven with a dome more vast,
Till thou at length art free,
Leaving thine outgrown shell by life's unresting sea![8]

Notes

1. For an incomplete listing of Hitti's published works, ssee James Kritzeck and R. Bayly Winder, eds., *The World of Islam: Studies in Honour of Philip K. Hitti* (London: Macmillan, 1960), pp. 10–37.

2. It may be appropriate to mention here that Hitti was basically trained (under Richard Gottheil) as a Semitist. When he first went to Princeton, he taught Hebrew, Aramaic, and cuneiform. Only gradually did interest in his native Arabic become the focus of his activities.

3. The department was first called the Department of Oriental Languages and Literatures and subsequently the Department of Oriental Studies before acquiring its present name.

4. See, incidentally, his "Americans from the Arab World," in Kritzeck and Winder, op. cit., pp. 351–72.

5. Charles Malik and Philip K. Hitti, *Swift Seasons Roll* (New York: American Friends of the Middle East, [1955]), pp. 2–3.

6. *History of Syria,* op. cit., p. 329.

7. One can only hope that it may have survived the recent carnage; apparently, the village itself is mostly destroyed.

8. Malik and Hitti, op. cit., pp. 10–14.

The Symbolic Quest of Kahlil Gibran

The Arab as Artist in America

JEAN GIBRAN AND KAHLIL GIBRAN

Kahlil Gibran's life, like his aphorisms in *The Prophet* and *Jesus The Son of Man,* was touched with irony. Now, more than one hundred years after his birth in 1883 near the fabled Cedars of Lebanon, this poet-painter remains the most respected of all the Arab intellectuals who immigrated to "al-New York," wrote, and published at the turn of the century. Gibran anecdotes are zealously shared by his countrymen, who delight in remembering him either as an adolescent struggling in Boston's South End, where his family first settled in 1895, or as a mature artist in his Greenwich Village studio. For first, second, and now third generations, Gibran has symbolized the preservation and transmission of their Arabic background and language. He is their cultural hero.

Since his death in 1933, Gibran's books have enjoyed increasing sales and translations. Unique in the history of American poetry is *The Prophet,* unchanged and continuously in print since its 1923 appearance. Reasons for its continued popularity have eluded scholars. Gibran was not the first Arab-American to publish in English. By 1911, Doubleday had brought out Ameen Rihani's *Book of the Khalid,* which Gibran had illustrated. Seven years later *The Madman,* Gibran's first English book, appeared under Alfred Knopf's imprint. While acknowledging Gibran as a major influence on the mood and style of Arabic writers, critics did not extol the mechanics of his Arabic technique. The scholarship of Mikhail Naimy, Gibran's friend and biographer, surpassed Gibran's mostly self-taught colloquial approach. An examination of his manuscripts written soon after his return in 1902 from the Beirut college al-Hikmah confirms Gibran's struggle with spelling and grammar even as he began contributing to the New York Arabic-language newspapers *Mirat al-Gharb* (Mirror of the West) and *al-Mohajer* (The Emigrant).

Together with tracing the two worlds of Gibran's Arab and American colleagues, biographers have had to address other dualities in his life. A synthesis of his complex surfaces should include the sequence of his Arabic and English works, his development as a graphic artist and painter, his evolution from Maronite Catholicism to the "Gibranism" that he once described as "meaning freedom in all things,"[1] and his nationalist concern for Lebanon's independence during World War I, which was in contrast to the pacifism of his American colleagues.

Gibran often articulated that duality to Mary Haskell, the Boston headmistress whose journals recorded his emotional and intellectual growth from their first meeting in 1904. He complained of "being in two worlds. Were I in Syria, my poetry would ensure notice to my pictures, were I an English poet, it would ensure them English notice. But I am between the two and the waiting is heavy."[2] That outburst occurred in 1912, when he already had spent two years studying art in Paris, had exhibited drawings in several one-person shows, had published four books, including *al-Arwah al-Mutamarridah* (Spirits Rebellious) and *al-Ajnihah'l Mutakassirah* (Broken Wings), and was writing articles for the Arab newspapers.

Gibran's powerful charisma needs acknowledgment if one is to understand his growth within a context from which he admittedly felt estranged. As early as 1898, just after Gibran had returned to the Beirut university, the poet Josephine Preston Peabody summarized how the fifteen-year-old prodigy had impressed his Boston sponsors: "The boy was made to be one of the prophets. This is true. His drawings say it clearlier [*sic*] than anything else could. There is no avoiding that young personality. You are filled with recognition and radiant delight."[3]

Similar descriptions continued to corroborate that aura. "I hope I shall always remember the simple and shadowy beauty which no picture will ever convey," wrote his friend and mentor Mary Haskell in 1908. "The boy [is] still tender in the man. . . . There is a rapt spiritual quality about him when he is released in mind."[4]

A decade later Americans were becoming fascinated by the author of *The Madman*, and a New York reporter tried to portray the maturing poet:

> *Gibran is Broadway or Copley Square or The Strand or the Avenue de L'Opera—a correctly dressed cosmopolitan of the Western World. . . . His dark brows and moustache and somewhat curly hair above a good forehead, the clear brown eyes [are] thoughtful but never abstracted in expression. . . . It is not a lack of individuality with him but on the contrary, an unusual common sense and sympathy which transcend differences and enable him to understand so well each environment in which he finds himself.*[5]

While Gibran's specialness attracted many admirers, his reticence about personal origins mystified friends and associates. Embroidering his past, he would allude to his birth in India or describe a charmed childhood spent in luxurious surroundings. Throughout his life he meticulously avoided references to the humiliating circumstances that drove his mother, Kamila Rahme Gibran, and her four children to the United States. His father's involvement in a local tax-collecting scandal forced that arrogant and willful man to stay in the mountain town of Bisharri. Separation from his parent weighed heavily on the boy. Gibran's own rebellious nature and subsequent disdain for the unjust institutions of his native country often are linked with the events of his family's emigration.

They came to Boston at a propitious time. If his arrival had been delayed another year, the young artist might not have witnessed the social and literary climate that encouraged his rapid immersion into the Boston world of arts and letters.

When Gibran showed his sketchbook at the Denison House, then a recently opened settlement center, his drawings so impressed the art teacher that she alerted a social worker. The woman in turn contacted Fred Holland Day, photographer and partner in the short-lived publishing firm of Copeland and Day. Jessie Beale's intervention into the life of the fourteen-year-old immigrant precipitated Gibran's meeting the colorful personality most instrumental in forming his precocious entrance to Brahmin Boston.

At the zenith of his creative powers in 1896, Day helped Gibran become a book designer and simultaneously nurtured his Arabic language and culture. The adolescent's passion for the Middle East was evident in his remarkable cover illustrating *Omar Khayyám, the Tentmaker.* That its respected author-critic Nathan Haskell Dole and its publisher L. C. Page had selected the immigrant's drawing of a brooding Omar, more Arab than Persian in dress and demeanor, testified to Gibran's early talent. It is difficult to determine whether Gibran's pride in his heritage strengthened his resolve to write in Arabic and English, or whether his Brahmin mentors were responsible for his retention of his native language as he learned another. Whatever the reason, Gibran's patrons always challenged him to develop two languages. For, as Mary Haskell once explained, dependence on one language was like "having a double Psyche to transmit and giving but one."[6]

Considering his early involvement in the arts, Gibran's youthful experiences greatly differed from those of his New York Arab contemporaries. His life in the South End "city wilderness" did parallel conditions of immigrant Arabs living in crowded slums. Kamila Gibran first supported her family by peddling laces throughout Boston suburbs. The family then opened a small dry goods store, but sickness and disease prevented the business from flourishing.

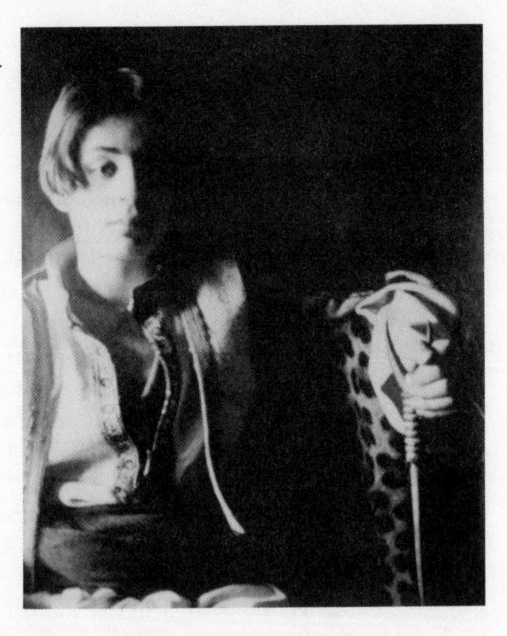

Kahlil Gibran as a young man in Boston. Photo by noted photographer Fred Holland Day, courtesy of Jean and Kahlil Gibran.

When Gibran was studying classical Arabic in Beirut, he learned that his youngest sister, Sultana, was stricken with tuberculosis. He returned to Boston soon after her death in 1902 and faced the suffering and agonizing deaths of his half brother, Peter, and his mother, Kamila. After the tragedy, Gibran and his surviving sister, Marianna, tried to run the business. His determination to write about conditions in his native land forced him to relinquish shopkeeping and to concentrate on drawing and writing.

The combination of personality, talent, early recognition, and resilience in the face of tragedy allowed Gibran to survive and flourish in a sometimes alien environment. He was eventually able to fuse the best of his two worlds and produce the exquisitely illustrated and authored volumes that inspired both his Arab and American audiences.

If one message determines how historians view Gibran's art, it is the sentence reproduced on the back of countless *Prophet* copies. Most critics depend heavily on the blurb: "His drawings and paintings have been exhibited in the great capitals of the world and compared by Auguste Rodin to the work of William Blake."[7] That uncredited remark had been attributed to a New York reporter, Henry de Beaufort, who wrote about Gibran between December 1912 and January 1913. During that time Gibran mentioned the article to Mary Haskell, and admitted that de Beaufort was capable of misleading, misquoting, and misunderstanding.[8] Despite an arduous review of New York journals, the precise location of that article was never found.

Kamila Gibran with her two daughters, Marianna and Sultana. Photo by noted photographer, Fred Holland Day, courtesy of Jean and Kahlil Gibran.

By disposing of that oft-quoted inaccuracy, one can begin to sort out some specific trends to which Gibran belonged and which associate him with the International Movement of Symbolist Art. The tendency to link Gibran in nonspecific terms with any artistic school, depending on the writer's perspective, can be found in Alice Raphael's early essays on his art. She first wrote about Gibran in the magazine *Seven Arts,* and then again in her introduction to his *Twenty Drawings.* In the first of these she vaguely alluded to his combining the best tradition of two cultures: "It is at the dividing line of east and west of Symbolism and Representation that the work of Kahlil Gibran presents itself."[9] Again, other contemporary appraisers used meaningless geographical generalizations that compared, for example, his work to the automatic Saracen art or to Persian miniatures, or assigned his drawings to the "poetical and imaginative temperament of his race."[10]

Interestingly enough, some of the most serious Arab critics focused on Gibran's Parisian period from 1908 to 1910 while ignoring his aesthetic roots. The overlooking of Gibran's earliest and most specific origins is attributable in part to the temporary eclipse of the fin-de-siècle personalities, artists, and writers to whom Gibran had been exposed.

With the discovery at the Norwood [Massachusetts] Historical Society of the Jesse Beale letters to Fred Holland Day, Gibran's entrance to the center of Boston's literary and artistic society was documented at last. The

Day papers led the journey one step closer to another significant influence, while Josephine Preston Peabody's journals and letters, now at Harvard's Houghton Library, revealed details of Gibran's formative period.

The first letter that linked Gibran to Fred Holland Day mentioned the main branch of the Boston Public Library and the sculptor Frederick Mac Monnies's *Bacchante.*[11] That was the statue that the young boy had drawn and that merited attention from his art teacher at the Denison House.

It is important to note how critical an influence the newly painted murals were in that splendid new showplace of culture—the Boston Public Library. It was there that Gibran first encountered major Symbolist painters. Just consider the young immigrant's amazed recognition of John Singer Sargent's mural *Astarte Syriaca.* Gibran saw the painting in 1896, soon after Sargent installed the allegorical panel depicting that Middle Eastern goddess. She was a new concept of woman and a favorite theme of Symbolist painters.

The young Gibran would choose the first of two kinds of women often depicted in Symbolist art. The earth mother, personification of purity and selfless maternity, as opposed to the second archetype, Salome, the femme fatale and lustful destroyer. Throughout his career Gibran's stories and illustrations reflected his involvement with the "great Astarte goddess of love and beauty."[12]

Together with his youthful discovery of Sargent's *Astarte,* the library's Puvis de Chavannes murals revealed another major Symbolist influence. Gibran's admiration of Puvis's visionary art continued. Long after Gibran's youthful initiation, he would be transfixed by the Saint Geneviève murals at the Pantheon in Paris.

But Gibran's baptism in Symbolist art and literature was deeper than the mere admiration of a spectator. His participation and firsthand experience during his apprenticeship at Fred Holland Day's publishing house made him part of the fin-de-siècle scene in Boston.

If any turn-of-the-century figure epitomized the revolt against the material world and held the tenets of spiritual unorthodoxy in a quest for visionary refreshment, it was Fred Holland Day. His adventures as a bibliophile and ardent collector of Keats and his fine contribution to American bookmaking had been brilliantly described in several scholarly theses. Nowhere was there an exposition of Day's triple role as publisher, photographer, and philanthropist. His importance in Gibran's career has not previously been recognized.

Gibran's coming of age coincided with the height of Day's Boston activity. All the contributing factors of the Symbolist movement—the fascination with exotic ages and cultures, the medieval conceits of the architect Ralph Adams Cram, the Catholic predilection of the poet Louise Imogen Guiney, the obsession with the neoplatonic Belgian writer Maurice

Maeterlinck—reflected the latter-day Transcendentalists' avid acceptance of the young immigrant. And so Gibran, with his exposure to the excellent literature published by Copeland and Day, witnessed the events adjunct to Bohemian Boston. The Mass commemorating the death of the recently converted Aubrey Beardsley, Day's notorious staging of his major photographic series *The Last Words of Christ,* and the exhibit of Day's Kelmscott Press collection at the Copley Square Library were all part of Gibran's early repertoire between 1895 and 1898. All this was exotic, yes, but the practical experience of working in a publishing house illustrating poems and creating cover designs initiated him into the art world.

Symbolists were idealists. They nurtured the found, the primitive. Certainly the poet Josephine Preston Peabody was the radiant embodiment of poet as muse. Recognizing the young Gibran as a natural, "Posy" Peabody cultivated his naive talent and rejoiced in the purity and clarity of his unsophisticated expression. His several drawings of her, now at Harvard Library, invariably incorporate the winged symbolism they both shared. Wings and spirits were important obsessions; they adorned her first book, about which Gibran wrote to her from Lebanon in 1899. Upon his return to Boston in 1902 her journal was studded with references praising her "Syrian Genius."[13] Ironically, because of Josephine's secret symbol—her special sign for Gibran, a stylized monogram of Arabic script standing for the initialls GKG—remained unidentified in both her formal journals and her day-to-day diary. Josephine's popular following diminished after her death in 1922. Her influence on the young Gibran and the link between them was overlooked. Her personal identification with the winged figure as shown in her play *Wings,* and later reflected in his Arabic narrative *Broken Wings,* was almost forgotten.

The 1904 fire at the Harcourt Studios on Irvington Street was the greatest obfuscator of Gibran's early period. Gibran lost all of his portfolio, which had been exhibited at Wellesley College and at Day's studio, as did Boston's leading artists, including William Paxton, Edmund Tarbell, and Joseph Decamp.

It is difficult for any prodigy to mature. Gibran's predicament was doubly hard. He became increasingly remote following the deaths of his sister, brother, and mother. If we analyze the Symbolist doctrine—its preoccupation with death and resurrection, with dreams and visionary escape—we can recognize Gibran's obsession with those themes. Indeed, their tenets became a natural extension of his own experience.

In 1909 at the Parisian Académie Julian, the nurturing place for many French Symbolists, Gibran began his formal painting education. He could easily have directed his studies toward Impressionist painting, the Pseudo-Neo-Renaissance, or even Salon painting. His true predilection, though, was to continue in the vein of his Boston influence through his exposure to

Gustave Moreau, Odilon Redon, and Puvis de Chavannes. Especially influential were the *nabis* (meaning "Prophets" in Arabic) and who included the painters Maurice Denis, Pierre Bonnard, and Jean Vuillard. Those artists, disillusioned with the prevailing vividness of experiments in science and social reform, took refuge in the mystery of dreams and legends. They clothed themselves with the poetic and vaporous shades of an art born of awe and wonder.

For Gibran, the Symbolists' disenchantment with the materialistic age and their interest in Eastern thought must have been irresistably magnetic. He wrote to Mary Haskell discussing his own concept of art. He explained he was trying to find himself "through nature" and then characterized his pursuit of the ideal as "to give a good expression to a beautiful idea or a high thought."[14] Gibran's two major inspirations in Paris were Pierre Marcel Béronneau, an artist known for his dreamlike paintings of Salome and a disciple of Gustave Moreau; and second, Eugène Carrière, whose figures, wrapped in a sort of yellowish fog, inhabited the visual atmosphere. That all-enveloping mist became characteristic of Gibran's paintings.

The Arabic critic Khalil Hawi speaks of the "crystal" or "mist" in Gibran's poems. "They represent two states of one and the same thing—definite, particular existence and its dissolution into universal life."[15] Gibran's lines from *The Garden of the Prophet*—"O Mist, my sister, white breath not yet/held in a mould,/ I return to you, a breath white and voice-/less,/A word not yet uttered"[16]—describe that ephemeral reality.

Gibran's use of parallel symbols in illustration and poetry continued to develop. He used them carefully—they became his second language. Large existences holding small figures translated into the greater self, pools, and seas were the absolute, the roots of trees represented man, their blossoms, God. His art strove to give visual expression to spiritual concerns, to create poetic impressions through suggestion rather than by factual statement.

In New York from 1910 to 1931, Gibran matured both as a visual artist and as an Arabic and English poet. His preoccupations and associations again were predictable. His friendship with Claude Bragdon and Arthur B. Davies supported his previous Symbolist leanings. Certainly his recognition by Albert Pinkham Ryder deserves special mention. During Gibran's 1914 exhibit at the Montross Gallery, the critic Henry McBride asked Ryder, who was standing before one of Gibran's paintings from his "Centaur" series, how Ryder liked the exhibit. Ryder responded positively: "He seems to mean it—that's the important thing."[17]

Probably the most representative American Symbolist is Ryder's *Temple of the Mind.* It is obvious that Gibran recalled that title when he named his own portrait series "The Temple of Art," in which Gibran had drawn Auguste Rodin, Claude Debussy, William Butler Yeats, Harvard president Charles Eliot, Abdul Baha, Carl Jung, and Sarah Bernhardt as well as imaginary portraits of Arabic poets and philosophers. His friendship with Ryder led to Gibran's drawing the older artist's portrait and writing a poetic tribute to Ryder, his first published work in English.

Almost simultaneously with the publication in 1918 of *The Madman*, his first book in English, and *al-Mawakib* (The Procession), Gibran stopped painting in oils and concentrated on watercolor and pencil drawing. His drawing triggered a return to his earliest commitment, the art of the book. True to Symbolist doctrine, he was involved as an artist, writer, and designer. The unity of his message, mirroring text and pictorial medium, became his final preoccupation.

Much of Gibran's innovative calligraphy appeared in *as-Sayeh* (The Traveler) and in *Al-Funoon* (The Arts), Arabic New World journals that benefited from his fresh approach in designing covers, titles, and illustrations. Gibran took pleasure in rendering the stylized signatures and colophons for his Arabic literary group Arrabitah (The Pen Bond). One member, William Catzeflis, remembered Gibran's influence on the New York Arabs: "Arrabitah, with Gibran in the lead, threw a bombshell by saying, 'if the meaning or beauty of a thought requires the breaking of a rule, break it . . . if there is no known word to express your idea, borrow or invent one . . . if syntax stands in the way of a needed or useful expression, away with syntax.' "[18] Arrabitah's motto, which Gibran placed on an open book inscribed in a circle, was from the Prophet Muhammad: "How wonderful the treasures beneath God's throne which only poets' tongues can unlock." That particular junction of word and picture could have summarized the poet's life.

The unprecedented success of *The Prophet* is not an unexplainable mystery or an accident. Gibran's long association with early twentieth-century idealists, his exposure to one of America's great bookmakers, his affiliation with many prominent figures in Symbolist art, and his duality of cultural and linguistic background combined to fill a need for millions of readers. Gibran's attraction for today's generation endures. Those youths who reject the materialistic era and share concern with those same mysteries and exotic hallucinogenic fantasies, the visionaries who wear beads and dally in Eastern religions, reenact conditions concurrent with the inception of Symbolism.

Such a rebirth gives rise to a permanent Symbolist recurrence, thus perpetuating Gibran's appeal. In October 1979, Charles Eldredge, then director of the Spencer Museum of Art at the University of Kansas, formed the first major exhibit of American Symbolists and included Gibran.[19] That recognition firmly established Gibran's art in the International Symbolist Movement.

There is a real need for further scholarly research into Gibran's pictorial ties to the Symbolist school. A fine catalogue raisonné should be assembled. It would be a task that would involve investigating the major holdings in Boston, Chapel Hill, Savannah's Telfair Academy, and Lebanon, as well as in scattered museums and collections around the world.

In the fast track of the contemporary art world, where practically anyone can become a superstar overnight, it is difficult to absorb the inferences and lyric allusions of Gibran's symbols without exposure to his poetry on which they are based. Although Gibran's writing has been widely accepted, his pictorial art has been misinterpreted by scholars who have tended to lump him with the Salon or point to an all-too-simplistic relationship to Blake. Now that Gibran's earliest influences have been revealed, his ties to the Symbolists become apparent.

By combining pictorial and poetic Symbolism, Gibran did succeed in what he once summarized as the major theme of his work—"The whole Prophet is saying just one thing—you are far greater than you know and all is well."[20]

Notes

1. Kahlil Gibran to Witter Bynner, 14 April 1925. The Josephine Preston Peabody Papers, Houghton Library, Harvard University (hereafter cited as Peabody Papers).

2. Mary Haskell, MS journal, vol. 40, events of 7 September 1912 entered under 6 August 1912. Minis Family papers, Haskell-Gibran Series, University of North Carolina, Chapel Hill (hereafter cited as Minis Family Papers).

3. Josephine Preston Peabody Journal, 8 December 1898, Peabody Papers.

4. Mary Haskell, miscellaneous folder, visit on 5 May 1908, recorded on 10 May 1908. Minis Family Papers.

5. Josephine Gollomb, "An Arabian Poet in New York," *N.Y. Evening Post,* 29 March 1919, book sec. 1, p. 10.

6. Mary Haskell to Kahlil Gibran, 6 February 1912, Minis Family Papers.

7. Kahlil Gibran, *The Prophet* (New York: Knopf, 1923).

8. Kahlil Gibran to Mary Haskell, 26 January 1913. Minis Family Papers.

9. Alice Raphael (Eckstein), "The Art of Kahlil Gibran," *Seven Arts* (March 1917), pp. 531–34.

10. F. W. Coburn, "Syriac Suggestions," *Boston Sunday Herald,* 22 April 1917, p.5.

11. Jessie Beale to Fred Holland Day, 25 November, 1896. Archives of Fred Holland Day, Norwood Historical Society, Massachusetts (hereafter cited as Day Archives).

12. Kahlil Gibran, *Nymphs of the Valley* (New York: Knopf, 1948), p. 28.

13. Josephine Preston Peabody Journal, 13 and 22 December 1902. Peabody Papers.

14. Kahlil Gibran to Mary Haskell, 14 March and 23 June 1909. Minis Family Papers.

15. Khalil S. Hawi, *Kahlil Gibran: His Background, Character and Works* (Beirut: Arab Institute for Research and Publishing, 1972), p. 267.

16. Kahlil Gibran, *The Garden of the Prophet* (New York: Alfred Knopf, 1933), p. 64.

17. Henry McBride, *N.Y. Sun,* 1 April 1917, sec. 5, p. 12.

18. William Catzeflis introduction to George Kheirallah, *The Life of Khalil Gibran and His Procession* (New York: Arab-American Press, 1947).

19. Charles C. Eldredge, *American Imagination and Symbolist Painting* (New York: Grey Art Gallery and Study Center, New York University), pp. 149–50.

20. Mary Haskell, MS journal, vol. 62, 30 May 1922. Minis Family Papers.

Additional References

Coburn, F. W. "Syriac Suggestions." *Boston Sunday Herald,* April 22, 1917, p. 5.

Eldredge, Charles C. *American Imagination and Symbolist Painting.* New York: Grey Art Gallery and Study Center, New York University, 1979.

Gibran, Jean, and Kahlil Gibran. *Kahlil Gibran: His Life and World.* Boston: New York Graphic Society, 1974; reprinted, New York: Avenel Books, 1981.

Gibran, Kahlil. *Lazarus and His Beloved,* ed. Jean and Kahlil Gibran. Greenwich, Conn.: New York Graphic Society, 1973.

———. *The Prophet.* New York: Alfred Knopf, 1923. With introduction by Alice Raphael (Eckstein).

———. *Twenty Drawings.* New York: Alfred Knopf, 1919; reprinted, 1974.

Gollomb, Joseph. "An Arabian Poet in New York." *N.Y. Evening Post,* March 29, 1919, book section, pp. 1, 10.

Dole, Nathan Haskell. *Omar Khayyám, The Tentmaker.* Boston: L. C. Page, 1898.

Hawi, Khalil S. *Kahlil Gibran: His Background, Character and Works.* Beirut: Arab Institute for Research and Publishing, 1926.

Hilu, Virginia, ed. *Beloved Prophet: The Love Letters of Kahlil Gibran and Mary Haskell and Her Private Journal.* New York: Knopf, 1972.

Hirsch, Richard Teller. *Eugène Carrière, 1849–1906: Seer of the Real.* Allentown: Allentown Art Museum, 1969.

Kheirallah, George. *The Life of Khalil Gibran and His Procession.* New York: Arab American Press, 1947. With an introduction by William Catzeflis.

Kraus, Joe Walker. *Messrs. Copeland and Day, 69 Cornhill, Boston, 1893–1899.* Philadelphia: George S. MacManus, 1979.

McBride, Henry. *N.Y. Sun,* April 1, 1917. Sec. 5, p. 12.

Naimy, Mikhail. *Kahlil Gibran: A Biography of His Life and Work.* New York: Philosophical Library, 1950; reprint ed., Beirut: Khayats, 1965.

Parrish, Stephen Maxfield. "Currents of the Nineties in Boston: Fred Holland Day, Louise Imogen Guiney and their Circle." Doctoral diss., Harvard University, 1954.

Raphael, Alice Eckstein. "The Art of Kahlil Gibran." *The Seven Arts* 1 (March 1917):531–34.

Young, Barbara. *A Study of Kahlil Gibran: This Man From Lebanon.* New York: Syrian American Press, 1931.

———. *This Man from Lebanon: A Study of Khalil Gibran.* New York: Alfred Knopf, 1945.

"There's a Wire Brush at My Bones"

GREGORY ORFALEA

Father's mother was called "the Rock," as in Gibraltar. When I was a kid and visited her Wilshire district home with the gabled roof on Mansfield—a street lined with tall palms and scarred-for-life sycamores—I figured Gibraltar was somewhere hidden in her garden, or the shed. I once asked her directly about the so-called rock she was supposed to be like. She shooed me off and crowed, "If I was a rock you wouldn't be here." Then she asked if I would like some coffee with milk in it. The parents scowled and she cackled like the Wicked Witch of the West. For all I know she might have been a witch. She had a tattoo of a small blue cross about the size of a dime on the underside of her left wrist. It straddled two tendons there; near the cross were two blue dots. "That's because I went to a doctor who cut a boil off me," she said. She was proud of that marked wrist, and would hold it up to the light, like someone who had survived a suicide attempt.

"Nazera! Nazera!" she would sing and dance around and around, crying out her name before the gathered family as if she were a last dinosaur from an extinct world, and all better take note and savor the steps of her feet, for worse times were ahead. We would clap for her. Her long gray hair, still long at her age of eighty-eight, swayed behind her. And the daughter who took care of her and suffered the brunt of her lifelong campaign against the meek, would shriek. Aunt Vernice did not talk, speak, answer, retort, utter, remark, or partake of any other commonplace verb. She shrieked and sang over the telephone, "Noooo, Roooose! Mom is at it again. Reeeeally!" Her mother took down the gray crowning glory and as it sashayed, a frazzled storm cloud, Aunt Vernice squealed like a filly. Nazera never did this in front of strangers. With them, she was demure.

But with the family, after a meal of grape leaves, *kibbe,* and vats of sour *leban,* she would wrap herself in a shawl she crocheted in all the colors of the rainbow and go happily into her own world. She used to give me a little clawlike iron bell that resembled the gold bell at Communion and ask that I ring it. I did. "Oh, that's nice!" she smiled. "I got that bell from a beggar in Cleveland for two vials of holy water."

And how did she get the holy water? "I blessed it myself."

Grandmother Nazera was, in her time, a grape picker, moppet, huckster, peddler, and self-styled prophetess. She never claimed she was a saint. I make that claim, humbly, now that her motley of colors has drained off onto the dusty streets of the world and they have sold her home to a young couple who want to "restore" it. More than any home that my own family had, Nazera's represents childhood to me, and no tinkering with awnings, mending of moldings, or unstripping to the original wood can restore that quality.

Actually, no house could hold her, though the Mansfield one came close to doing so. No church could either—she was raised a Melkite, married an Orthodox, and brought up the children as Roman Catholic because, in her words, "Sonny boy, that was the closest steeple in Cleveland." If it had been the Elks Club we might all have been raised Elks.

By American standards, she was not a beauty, though at times her knowing eyes and smile bloomed; if not a rose on her cheeks, certainly it was a hybiscus. A photo of her sticks out in my mind. It was one of many brown photos hidden in an ebony endtable that was never the end of anything, but always, so it seemed, in the center of her living room. In that special browned picture stands Grandfather, a tall, charming chap if there ever was one, with a noble, high forehead and gold fob chain hanging down from his vest. The young and short Nazera looks like she has just swallowed an olive pit. Black hair is tight on her head; her jowls are caved and her black eyes point the finger. The photographer must have taken a few belts after snapping that one. A more unlikely duo could not have touched this earth. They lived together for fifty-five years, enduring world wars, cancers, strokes, colostomies, Parkinson's disease, and other accoutrements of age. They were unsuited; they had six children, the last being my father.

But I am getting ahead of my story. I should say something about where she was born, though it wasn't long before she wrote that place off. It is a land that has not seen peace for five thousand years: Lebanon. She cracked into the world in a mountain village near the eastern Mediterranean, a village with an air so pure that asthmatics pilgrimage to it from around the globe, between various civil wars, bloodlettings, confrontations between giants and giants, giants and pigmies, and pigmies and pigmies. The village is a stronghold of Melkite and Orthodox Christians, many of a hermetic bent, and it is called Zahleh.

Nazera Jabaly Orfalea, ca. 1910. She had immigrated to the United States from Zahleh, Lebanon, in 1894. Photo courtesy of Jeannette Graham.

A jumpy, cold stream—the Bardowni River—rushes down the center of the village. Fifty years after Nazera had last seen it, she could still remember its sound. "It goes chlchgllchgl," she said. When I visited Lebanon in 1972 she gave me specific instructions as to where her house was, what window to look out, and what tree I would find along the Bardowni just out the window. When our group found the house, now inhabited by a Muslim couple, we were allowed upstairs, where one naked lightbulb hung from a bilious green ceiling. I looked out the designated window to find, sure enough, the ripe poplar and the rushing stream she had mentioned. Legions of poplars hobnobbed it down the river. She once said, "A broad leaf catches more rain."

She spent her earliest years helping her father in his vineyard on the outskirts of Zahleh, and visiting her own grandmother on donkeyback. She never tired of telling the story about how her grandmother would know when she was coming by the donkey ears bobbing above the stone wall. "*Mittle hamar,*" Nazera would call, and wiggle her own ears "like a jackass" on into her ninth decade.

The vineyard cost her a toe. One day, hopping on top of the limestone wall that bounded the vines while her father and the workers picked the fruit, she slipped. She smashed her toe on a rock when she fell to the ground. A deformed, blackened, ingrown nail on the wrecked toe announced her scrappiness to the world through open-toe slippers many years later. To Grandmother, walls clearly were not meant for contemplation. And toes? They were made to dance and to break!

She escaped death before she was seven, the year she and her father left for America. Three Druze approached her father at the vineyard one day as he was piling clusters of grapes in a basket, wiping his forehead from sweat. They wanted to buy some grapes, they said. But they gave Barakat Jabaly too large a coin. With a knowing look, he called to little Nazera, "Go to get change!" She sought out the cave where they slept during harvest and kept their wherewithal, but couldn't find the secret cache of gold. On her return, Barakat tried to cover her mouth before she blurted it, but it was too late. The words "gold" and "cave" were out.

That night they awoke in the cave to sounds of rustling. "Don't make any noise," Barakat whispered. "Get on my back." Quickly, with stealth, he crawled with his daughter out of the cave right under the thieves' noses. "We left them dinner," Nazera smiled.

"The Druze," Grandma told me, "were thieves from day one." According to her, if you left so much as a wine jug in your vineyard, they'd sweep it up. A loner offshoot of Islam, the Druze managed to elicit her strongest venom. But to be fair, Grandma had plenty saved up for the Jews, the Arabs, the bankers, presidents Nixon and McKinley, the door-to-door Fuller Brush salesmen, and Lucille next door with the white hair who was cold and had bars on her windows.

Grandmother's assignation of guilt over the cave incident may have been induced by stories of the Druze massacres of 1860, twenty-six years before her birth. The period of the 1880s was one of relative calm in Zahle, and robbery and arson could just as easily have been carried out by Bedouins or by vagrants of any religious stripe. As I grew, of course, the Druze metamorphozed in my mind from lit fuse to human being when, as a teenager, I snapped my fingers to the rock and roll tunes of L.A.'s top disc jockey, a Druze named Casey Kasem.

Grandma's sister, Rose, had been a kind of Lebanese mail-order bride for one Boutros Hamrah in the United States. In 1893, when Nazera was seven years old, she and her father and her two brothers sailed from Beirut to New York to link up with Rose. Now émigrés, the children were also motherless.

When Nazera was an infant Zahara Sahadi Jabaly had suddenly deserted her children and husband and fled to Brazil. In her twenties she died there of yellow fever. It now seems that that uncharacteristic abandonment by an Arab mother at a harrowing time must have thrown Nazera's life permanently off kilter. But they had no time to think about that on the cold Atlantic; like everyone else in steerage, they were sick to their stomachs.

Fresh off the boat, or F.O.B., she was prodded by immigration officials on Ellis Island: "Where are you from?" "Syria." "Syria? Where is that? Is that in Africa?" On the streets of New York people had no more notion of Syria or Lebanon than the dark side of the moon. She was called nigger, dago, chink. Racist or not, none hit the mark. She was a no-race, a scratch of the head. Immigration records showed her as among the first thousand Arab women to enter the United States.

Soon, Nazera was an orphan. Her father—remarried briefly—died young. Shortly thereafter, her sister took off to Connecticut, notched ten children and as many miscarriages. One brother, George, hopped a merchant marine ship to China and the Boxer Rebellion; the eldest Jabaly sibling, Joseph, was run over and killed in New York City by a horse-drawn American Express wagon. By the turn of the century, Nazera was alone with the Statue of Liberty.

Nazera went to school for a few months in the city, then skipped it. Add that to a few months in Lebanon and you get a life with less than a year of formal education. "Honey," she proclaimed in a voice born for bold print, "I went to the world school." And so she did. She hooked up with a couple of other Arab immigrant girls—among them one Sadie Dibs—hung a peddler's tray from her neck stuffed with beads, cheap necklaces, toilet water, and yes, vials of holy water, and the group was off making the circuit of the five boroughs of New York.

Imagine those olive-complected ragamuffins swinging down the brownstone street in their faded cotton dresses singing, "Holy Wahtaar!" The rails of Grand Central Station pinched, the ferry boat to Staten Island tooted to their laughter! It wasn't long before Nazera and her cronies expanded business. They added new items such as cigarettes, snuff, and exotic perfumes (probably squeezed from oranges). Next they struck out from New York City. It was no longer big enough for them—they had to conquer Philadelphia, Baltimore, Washington, D.C., Pittsburgh, Cleveland, then on to New England—to New Haven, Providence, Boston. Nazera's gang implanted the East with notions wild and various.

Sadie Dibs was the leader's favorite. Nazera fancied herself like Sadie—green eyed, coy, with long olive limbs. Nazera was the little colonel at five-feet even. The two walked down the street draping their arms around each other the way true friends do—not holding the shoulder but laying the arm loosely around the friend's neck letting the wrist hang free, all the while hoisting the long trays of notions that folded and became a satchel. Once a construction worker on Washington Street spied the duo and let down his hook, snaring Nazera's tray by the handle. Up in the air it went! But it fell amid the jeers of the Irish workmen, scattering her notions on the pavement. The stiffest blow came when Sadie went off and married the first man she met on their big circuit, a snuff manufacturer in Boston. Nazera never offered snuff from her tray again.

Nazera carried her hurt around for a few years; old members of the group dropped off, new ones came on. Then in Cleveland she met my future Grandfather.

Aref was a Syrian making more money than were all the other Arabs in Cleveland put together. The owner of a few dry goods stores that specialized in linen, Aref dressed impeccably—a three-piece suit, a gold fob watch, a silk shirt, and a moustache trimmed with painstaking precision. His skin was powder white. His eyes had a distant, wounded, boyish look about them and he was tall, about six feet. His lips were full and he faithfully smoked Camels; three fingers of his right hand were stained caramel for life. The gent was a man about town. He had fifty women after him just waiting to siphon his pockets. Beautiful women, petticoated, swirl-hair types, smitten by his gentility and mood of inner detachment. So he fell for a peddler.

If there ever was a chase in a love affair, this was it. Nazera, who should have fallen down on her knees after Aref and begged his acceptance, flaunted her lack of interest in him, rejected his overtures for lunch, demands for dinner, and telegrams for midnight rendezvous. She bragged of the interest a handsome salesman named Schwartz was taking in her.

If Aref had been given to drink he would have begun drinking, but he wasn't, so he didn't. Most Arabs are not keen on alcohol and find other ways to express their disenchantment with the world, such as popping blood vessels from shouting, developing ulcers, or working themselves into an early grave. After one year of chasing her through every depot, lounge, marketplace, and café in the East, Aref was worn out. Abruptly, without so much as a "Forgive me," Nazera did an about-face and returned one of his agonized letters with a note. Aref must have smashed the note into a thousand creases. An answer! An actual reply from this jade of the alleys!

They were married in Cleveland and settled there.

Nazera drove a four-door Chandler, and later one of the most expensive Packards of the era, a touring car complete with jump seat large enough to transport the six children who came in rapid succession—four daughters, then two sons. It was a loud, peppery brood and mischief was constant. The eldest boy, George, once plucked a goldfish from a bowl and fried it. He said he was hungry. My father, the youngest, wanted to skate, so he let the hose run all day in the backyard until the water froze, creating his own personal rink. Another time, George tied Father to his bicycle face down and prone, like some sort of human sled, and dragged him for two blocks, dislodging his nose and breaking it in too many places to count. Father alluded to that incident to describe the abnormally long yet unusually straight nose of his. "I had it planed down by the sidewalk," he said.

Aref Junior as a teenager once fell asleep in a movie theater; his date left him there sleeping peacefully. He slept on while the janitors did their work. He slept through the closing of the doors and ticket booths. He was still snoring at 4 A.M. when Nazera broke down the doors with a crowbar.

How did such an independent, hot-headed woman churn out a large family in so short a time? Above anything else in the world she loved her family, was in fact idolatrous of it and extremely protective, the way one is with a possession one hasn't counted on having. But her anger was bone shattering; she could lock a child in a closet for an hour or two. She used her hand liberally and would shout till the veins in her neck bulged. She had the righteousness of Allah, Jehovah, and God combined. In some ways her love was a cage from which only my Father escaped.

It came to explode about the time her husband was losing everything in the depression. One by one his prosperous dry goods stores were boarded up. Still he continued to dress to the hilt and make the rounds of the fine restaurants in Cleveland. In such a place Nazera found him one noon with another woman. Dumbstruck, she went straight home, gathered up the six children, took them down to the restaurant where Grandfather was just finishing desert, and shoved them in front of him and the strange woman. "This is the kind of man your father is!" she screeched. And left them there with Aref holding the spoon.

Illicit or not, who could say? Her husband was a mild man. I never in my life heard him raise his voice, save one day over Nazera's bickering about her wayward daughter's reading habits, the way Adele would stretch for hours on a lavender divan reading pulp novels after her second divorce. "Leave her alone!" Aref shouted in such a way the whole family turned their heads and the chandelier swayed. He shook by nature. He had Parkinson's disease most of his adult life.

Nazera's temper wasn't all of it. Aref had to put up with his wife's brother, George Jabaly. I can best characterize that tight-fisted, loud individual by noting that his ears literally smoked with hair. As a child I couldn't help spying on him behind his chair and seeing the thick ear hair. As he ranted about the Boxer Rebellion—"Tamahooda! Tamahooda!" was the call on the ships as they unfurled their sails in Shanghai—I felt sure he would blow his stack. His ears were two hairy fuses! One day it happened. He simply shook his head and rested it on Nazera's shoulder, the victim of a massive coronary.

When Nazera and George got together they could scorch the entire planet with their judgments. This is to suggest that if Nazera's husband was cheating, he probably did it to preserve his hearing.

Judgments—Grandma had plenty of them. When I was no longer a child she said she would love to parcel out a few for my benefit. I would turn on the tape recorder. She didn't like that and asked if it was on. I said no and she continued: "I came here in 1893. I struggled; nothing came easy.

I fought for what I have. But when all is said and done, the country is run by the Yahood. They have the papers, the radios, *yi,* they have everything! Now they want to grab the Jordan River, the Golan Heights, grab this and that. I think they are grabbers, young man! The Arabs? They are not much better. In fact, they are worse. They don't grab; they got nothing *to* grab. They don't own a thing of value so they act like dogs. [This was before oil bestowed its mixed blessing on the Gulf states.] Farouk? *Yi!* He sleeps on the pillow and his people eat flies. Nasser—he shouts into the microphone like a hyena and when it comes time to fight, the Yahood clobber him. Honey, I am an American. I am no foreigner. I speak better English than an Englishman. And my taxes go to the Yahood and my sons go to America. I gave my sons to this country for the war." They had, in fact, survived—George, the Burma campaign, and Aref Junior one of the few alive from the mangled 551st Parachute Battalion of the 82d Airborne during the brutal Battle of the Bulge. His feet were almost amputated after freezing in the Belgian winter; he heard about the German surrender from a hospital bed at Fort Meade.

Despite Nazera's caustic opinions, she welcomed anyone from any race or group into her living room and admired those who could assert their ideas with some semblance of proof. "If people want to visit me they can come to my home," she said. "If they want to see furniture, they can go to Barker Brothers."

After the war and the discovery of "the woman," one by one the family headed out West. Adele and Nazera were the last to come, in the Packard. Driving was Nazera's sport, her "sovereignty" as the Wife of Bath would put it. Husband Aref left the driving to her. He never learned to operate an automobile, never had a driver's license. In her eighties Nazera was still twisting the large wheel of an old Pontiac, the car she bestowed to me on my sixteenth birthday.

Los Angeles more than any other American city owes its character and growth to an America flushed with victory over Germany and Japan. Before World War II, L.A. was a secret of the movie rich and a curiosity stop for the Dust Bowl poor. After the war, the sprawl and feisty largess of the victor gravitated West.

It appears that many civilizations at their peak have worshiped the sun—the ancient Egyptians did, and so did the Aztecs. And so did the Americans with their need to be free gunned, like a car circling a new-built Mecca in the sun. Voilà, the cold, concrete network of freeways that makes us hot blooded, and the custom-made pools set like opals in the city's suburbs. Voilà, the post-War movies' spouting of heroes in Europe and Japan, and the orgasmic growth of a Hollywood culture that snapped neon lights down all boulevards at the city's heart at the same time that Disney created the stainless park of fantasy. Los Angeles. Elbow-room in the sun. It spawned a hydra-head of tolerance and intolerance unlike any metropolis in the country, and drew a squat peddler like Nazera to a house with a gabled roof. Soon she built a dollhouse in the backyard and planted near it a pomegranate tree. I call that house the House of Dreams.

Aref Senior had gone out West a year ahead of Nazera. When she arrived, they had a cool reunion in Los Angeles, but the coolness faded. The word "cool" did not exist for Grandmother. She had a way of injecting life into a stone; if the stone broke from feeling, too bad. A stone was better broken than cold.

Her lean years were her fruit trees' fattest. She set to planting lemon, orange, peach, and apricot, and hooked me by the halter as I—her first grandchild—ran around, green as the fig she would take hold of. I saw her wrist's cross; I saw the swollen fig. "You were born in August," she smiled. "You came when the figs were ripe." And then she touched the clear syrup at the lip of the fig. "See? The *asil* comes off. Tell me if there is a taste like that on the earth." In the foggy winters I walked around her haphazard orchard, bewildered. "Gram," I asked. "Where is the fig tree?" And she pointed to a gnarled, gray, lifeless thing. "But it is ugly, Gram." "No," she frowned. "It is waiting to be beautiful."

In dead center of the backyard stood another plain tree with small, sharp leaves. Its fruit came slowly and every other year, scarcely. But when it came—ah! The pomegranate tree was the sacred center, and October the sacred month. All the family drew toward it for the plucking. Nazera would set out deck chairs on the grass, hoist the laundry pole off the line, and go about knocking down the highest pomegranates first. My father held the bag and chased her and the red, throbbing rain of juice. Everyone laughed and clapped and, injecting their nails into the hard rind of the fruit, squirted purple juice on their faces. We ate pomegranates all afternoon; her four daughters—all past middle age and childless—would suck the fruit till they were sick.

The time came to cart the remaining pomegranates in large sacks to the basement. In an off year, only a small bag of the fruit remained, so we didn't have to go into the dungeon. One such year was the year Nazera died.

The dollhouse. When I was a boy, tigers, elephants, and dolls lived in there—the blue ceiling was so high! When I was about thirteen the ceiling was dangerously close to my head and I would while away afternoons alone, lying on the dollhouse floor, my head touching one wall, my feet the other, and dream of girls larger than dolls. One day the dollhouse contained only trunks of old letters. I could neither stand nor lie down inside. The place only received my head. And when I removed it and shut the blue door that now barely reached the height of my heart when I stood, I knew I was a man, and never opened it again.

The grape arbor that fringed the entry to the dollhouse was always in use. Nazera was a superb cook, and however rough and proclaiming her voice, no one ever sounded the word "delicious" the way she did. She spent days making grape leaves, picking them off the vine, blanching them, grinding the lamb by hand, pressing chunks with her wrist, wetting the blue tattoo cross and dots. She had a running argument with her daughter, Vernice, about the "wrap."

"Vernice, your wrap is too loose. The lamb spills out."

"No, Mom. Pleeeese!"

"I'm telling you this because you must learn."

"But, Mom, I'm sixty years old!"

"It is never too late to learn the correct wrap. You must tuck the ends in. You must cover the holes eaten by the snails. If you get a leaf with a hole, plan ahead!"

Like most Arab women, Nazera did not hear refusals for food. She offered more than anyone could eat; she even offered portions of the main meal after the dessert was finished. Only Father's bark would stop her brandishing the *kibbe,* the mint salad, the round bread, the chickpea dip, the *bethanjan,* the peas, the chicken. She worshiped Father. Her heart quickened at the sound of his motorcycle on her driveway.

After dinner I would leave the adults chattering about the Middle East and, with a *ghrabi* cookie in hand, go stand on top of the floor heater in the hall between bedrooms. Staring down through the grate, I saw a blue flame twitching. It was my feeling when young that the entire house sat on fire—blue fire—of which that small flame was just the tip. I stood and took Communion—that is, gave myself the hoop of butter and dough that would stick to the roof of my mouth like Communion—and all the while the gas heater pressed hot air up my legs to my face. Aunts, uncles, cousins, or Nazera herself, cracking the wood floor with their heavy shoes as they passed me on their way to the toilet or to take a nap after dinner, knew never to get me off that floor heater. "It's hiiiis spot," sighed Aunt Vernice. "He won't budge from that grate." Once I asked Nazera if I could sleep on it overnight, but she said, "No, you'll be fried to a crisp."

In the late hours Nazera's dining room table that had steamed with food and coffee—the widest table in my memory—became a stage and a casino. On that table I first felt an arousal for my cousin Bonnie, George's daughter. On that table Aunt Adele threatened to leave—leave the table, Los Angeles, the United States, the Northern Hemisphere, and finally step right off the globe because no one understood her, no one realized what it was like to be flattened for six years by a three-hundred-pound importer. There Aunt Bette (who had discarded her original name, Nazera) sat with the smoke easing lazily out of her nostrils and heard her husband Jerry's jokes get dirtier by the year. There Aunt Jeannette slapped her hand down on the table so hard from laughing that it woke her husband Orville from his snooze. Around that table first rang the word "Hell"; there I first heard the phrases "Heaven's to Betsy," "I'll coldcock you," "Pass it on," "*Immie,* you're the greatest," and "Goddamn your country." Marathon poker games found Father sinking below the tablecloth, pulling out his seventh card at stud; it gave him nothing, but he would jump up as if he had the game won, and smack down his cards. He never had a poker face. Grandma would say, "Here's the bitch," and lay down three queens and take all the money. She was good at poker and knew it.

The table warped at the first of Uncle George's theories on race war, broke out in knots when Aunt Bette referred to her own nose as "bulbous." The aunts, having no children of their own, loved us children of the last child to excess. And I, never once thinking this was abnormal, grew up believing it must be natural to have so many people love you.

It was the House of Dreams. It was also the Abode of Sorrow, where curses spilled on the oriental rugs like too-hot coffee. It was where Uncle George spouted infinite schemes to "get rich quick"—make Syrian bread to be sold in plastic bags; sell pickled turnip with a pair of handwoven socks; contrive a scheme for dual membership in a country club and a mausoleum ("You move from one putting green to the other"). Through all of this sat Mother, spotless and kind, uncomplicated and bewildered at such Americanized Arabs, since she came from a poorer, more traditional Arab family.

In Los Angeles all took turns bailing out of one form or another of the clothing industry. All accused Father—who reached the pinnacle of his profession on the West Coast—of working like a slave. He lost his shirt, too, or rather, dresses.

Eight years before it would end, Nazera contracted cancer of the rectum. They removed the organ, as well as a large portion of her intestines. From then on she excreted through a small hole on the side of her belly. The bathroom at the Mansfield house began to take on the odors of alcohol and urine; her contraption for siphoning waste was laid discreetly behind the toilet bowl.

Gut hole or not, for a while she was her indefatigable self. She attended meetings of the Altar and Rosary Society of Saint Anne's Melkite Church, as well as meetings of the Hamasne Club, a group of ancient women from Hama and Homs, Syria, the latter her husband's hometown, who bored her to death. Though she herself was from Zahleh, she put in some time for her husband at the Syrian club, particularly after he died of a stroke shortly before the onset of her own cancer. He had been paralyzed for three years. I remember visiting him one day and watching him struggle to speak. His neck muscles grew taut and his jaw opened but nothing came out. His head fell back on the pillow. That quiet, gentle man died without having the last say. I wonder what he would have said. Perhaps, "Nazera, stop shouting at Adele." Or, "Nazera, why didn't you marry Schwartz? Nazera, go climb in the drainpipes and give the world some peace. Nazera, I love you, stupid as I am."

One last touch of glory remained.

On a warm spring night Nazera bundled up her cancers to witness the fiftieth wedding anniversary of my mother's parents at the lush Huntington Sheraton in Pasadena. There were more than five hundred people in attendance; the simple folk had done well. At the end of the dinner an *oud* was plucked and a *tabla* patted. Then one little member of the crowd stood up in the smoke-filled room.

She stood in a trance and let her eighty-eight-year-old feet take her out to the dance floor, and began to lead one foot ahead of the other, turning her hands slowly as an Arab woman does when dancing, turning and kneading the air, turning around slowly, always letting the front foot guide and draw the foot behind like a magnet, keeping the head still and kneading the air gently as if everything we breathe were dough.

The crowd was stunned when they saw Nazera's solo. They knew she was the oldest woman in the banquet room. For a few seconds it was just Nazera and the *oud* and the *tabla.* Then the people began to clap—sharp claps to the slow glide of the ancient woman and the ancient eggplant-shaped *oud.* They were riding her and she knew it. Or at least I think she did. As the claps grew louder, enough to tremble the chandeliers above, Nazera stopped dancing. She walked with her arms still up and hands kneading to one side of the dance floor, then the other, and her eyes went further in trance. She was not there. She was somewhere with a beat only she could hear, for her legs had given out, and she was no longer gliding. She was plummeting sideways. Maybe that caused everyone to clap louder, holding their breath. Her eyes seemed to grow white, as if they were snowing. Her smile became the timeless, terrible expression of the Sphinx. No one dared to stop clapping, for no matter what her legs were doing her hands were still up. Finally Father retrieved her. Grandfather Awad on the other side of the family went over and kissed her even though she smiled so strangely it seemed she would bite his belt. He was crying. Her eyes were sleeting.

It was given to me to feed her that last summer when I came to visit. I could barely hold the spoon. How could one feed the Rock? Who was I to hold out food to a woman who had once laughed at the hole in her stomach and said, "I talk so much they've given me another mouth." Now she sat silent. In her trance Nazera scorned me. The bit of applesauce stuck to her bottom lip.

Still I led her to her small porch out front, nothing like the giant L-shaped porch of mother's parents, but Nazera always was one to make do with the minimal. As far as she was concerned, it was the length of the boardwalk in Atlantic City. Her trimmed hedge was the hedge of a king. And those tall palms on Mansfield, swishing and swaying in the breeze, were tall men like Aref, and they were not in Los Angeles. They were in Syria walking on the road from Homs to Zahleh, where her husband should have met her—tall shadows like the ones she followed across the Atlantic for a better life, the shadows she followed each day from toilet to kitchen to porch seeking a life free from scorn and fire and finding herself still under a hot sun and staring at tall, slippery shadows that contained on top—if you strained yourself enough you'd develop lesions—a sweet, brown fruit with a hard, thin nut.

In her eighty-seventh and eighty-eighth years, donning a crocheted cap, she took to writing a journal and was faithful to it. Here is one of the entries:

> February 6, 1973. *it is windy Lucle was Here Vernice called chicken for supper and baked potato I had my lunch I enjoyed it and thank God for his grace Im little better my leg is not better but I am able to bare it no other way grin and bare it Im grateful it is time 12 am Now a new paragraph I tryed to lydown but cant find rest it is best to sit up and suffer I dont think this will ever get better this will be the end of me I called Vernice she is very discourage busissin is lousey I dont know what is happening to our country so much change in government peoll dont know what to look for the weather is cloudy time 325pm Im waiting for Mick douglas Show.*

Invariably she started an entry with a praise to the light, and somewhere down the line mentioned her pain. She never knew, or admitted, just what it was that was doing her in. She had had cobalt treatments and they were supposed to be successful. She never said the word "cancer." The entries dwindled. One of the last said, "There's a wire brush at my bones."

Even as she screamed on her deathbed she never said what she had; the screams raised her back, turned her face red, her withered breasts green, her legs purple, her kneecaps black. She screamed, "Color! Color!" and she got her wish. Father's mouth opened wider as if it would rip at the edges, but no sound came out—until with a final huff, her body fell back, and he collapsed at the foot of her bed, crying hoarsely. Vernice covered his shoulders with Nazera's shawl of many colors and all left him there, alone.

Select Bibliography

Abraham, Sameer, and Nabeel Abraham, eds. *Arabs in the New World: Studies on Arab-American Communities.* Detroit: Wayne State University Center for Urban Studies, 1983.

The Arab Immigrants. Special issue of *ARAMCO World Magazine.* 37:5, September–October, 1986.

Aswad, Barbara C., ed. *Arabic Speaking Communities in American Cities.* New York: Center for Migration Studies, 1974.

Elkholy, Abdo. *The Arab Moslems in the United States: Religion and Assimilation.* New Haven: College and University Press, 1966.

Hagopian, Elaine and Ann Paden, eds. *The Arab Americans: Studies in Assimilation.* Wilmette, Ill.: Medina University Press, 1969.

Hitti, Philip. *The Syrians in America.* New York: George Doran, 1924.

Hooglund, Eric, ed. *Taking Root: Arab-American Community Studies.* Washington: American-Arab Anti-Discrimination Committee, 1985.

Katibah, Habib Ibrahim, and Farhat Ziadeh. *Arab-Speaking Americans.* New York: Institute of Arab American Affairs, 1946.

Kayal, Philip, and Joseph Kayal. *The Syrian-Lebanese in America: A Study in Religion and Assimilation.* Boston: Twayne Publishers, 1975.

Macron, Mary Haddad. *Arab-Americans and Their Communities of Cleveland.* Cleveland: Cleveland Ethnic Heritage Studies, Cleveland State University, 1979.

Mehdi, Beverlee Turner, ed. and comp. *The Arabs in America, 1492–1977: A Chronology and Fact Book.* Dobbs Ferry, N.Y.: Oceana Publications, 1978.

Naff, Alixa. *Becoming American: The Early Arab Immigrant Experience.* Carbondale, Il.: Southern Illinois University Press, 1985.

Nasser, Eugene Paul. *Wind of the Land.* Belmont, Ma.: Association of Arab-American University Graduates, 1979.

Orfalea, Gregory. *U.S.–Arab Relations: The Literary Dimension.* Washington, D.C.: National Council on U.S.-Arab Relations and Arab American Cultural Foundation, 1984.

Rizk, Salom. *Syrian Yankee.* Garden City, N.Y.: Doubleday, 1943.

Sengstock, Mary C. *Chaldean-Americans: Changing Conceptions of Ethnic Identity.* New York: Center for Migration Studies, 1982.

Wakin, Edward. *The Lebanese and Syrians in America.* Chicago: Claretian Publishers, 1974.